Race, Research, and Reason

RACE, RESEARCH, and REASON:

SOCIAL WORK PERSPECTIVES

*Report of the Institute on Research Toward Improving
Race Relations, held at Airlie House, Warrenton,
Virginia, August 13–16, 1967*

Roger R. Miller, Editor

*Director of Research
Smith College School for Social Work
Northampton, Massachusetts*

NATIONAL ASSOCIATION OF SOCIAL WORKERS
2 Park Avenue, New York, N.Y. 10016

Grateful acknowledgment is made to the Lois and Samuel
Silberman Fund, Inc., for a grant that made possible the
institute and publication of this volume.

Preface

In August 1967, in the wake of a series of riots that had exploded in ghettos across America, the National Association of Social Workers held an Institute on Research Toward Improving Race Relations. Dramatically signaling the emergence of a new phase in Negro-white relations, the riots exerted an unanticipated but powerful influence on the conference deliberations. The broadly based Negro violence and destructiveness—and the resultant white backlash—provided a glimpse of a future that seemed simultaneously possible yet unimaginable. And it was difficult to escape the implication contained in these events of a wholesale failure on the part of the white community, the Establishment, and the social work profession to understand, to care, and to act.

The institute was conducted in an atmosphere of urgency and uncertainty. The rules of the game had apparently changed so that established positions no longer afforded the illusion that lawless social forces had been comprehended and mastered. Familiar appraisals of the past, present, and future in race relations seemed to require an open and searching re-examination.

In response to a state of near crisis, the participants used the conference as an occasion for the study of some fundamental issues. What is the nature of the race relations problem and what conceptual tools best serve to bring it into focus? What adjustments are indicated for the mission, the organization, or the delivery of social services, consequent to the state of race relations? In what way can research activity aid in charting an appropriate course for the field?

In emphasis, the deliberations departed somewhat from the program originally planned. Papers had been commissioned on three related topics: the nature of the problem; perspectives on practice, program, and change; and issues and opportunities for the study of race relations.

5

This organization was, of course, achieved prior to the riots. It had been anticipated that the first two areas of concentration, conceived as an opportunity to identify gaps and redundancies in research activity, would provide a necessary foundation for the major concern of the conference—research. Attention was, in fact, given to research strategy and tactics, and a number of topics meriting study were identified; the deliberations were, however, centered chiefly on preresearch concerns. By tacit agreement, attempts to elaborate research plans were deferred in favor of some reconnaissance work. Priority was given to a re-examination of the nature of the problem and the place of social work with regard to that problem.

Although the discussion departed in emphasis from that foreseen by the planning committee, the content and format devised for the meeting proved to be aptly suited to the tasks undertaken there. Twelve papers were considered during the meetings. Other than an opening address by Dr. Inabel B. Lindsay, no formal presentations were made. Authors introduced and elaborated on their written work, made available to the participants earlier, and the subsequent discussions followed the interests of the group.

The race relations institute, one of a series designed to facilitate and strengthen social work research, was initiated by the Steering Committee of the Council on Social Work Research of the National Association of Social Workers and implemented by a Planning Committee comprised of Harris K. Goldstein, Lawrence K. Northwood, and Joseph Golden. The Planning Committee, with able staff assistance from Mrs. Marjorie J. Herzig, planned and arranged the program. A debt of gratitude is owed to these individuals, as well as the Lois and Samuel Silberman Fund, Inc., which extended financial support for the institute and the publication of the proceedings.

The participants were an interdisciplinary, biracial group of social scientists—chiefly from sociology but including the disciplines of political science, anthropology, psychology, and education—and social workers with research interests in a variety of professional areas. Nathan E. Cohen, through a statesman-like conduct of the chairmanship, helped to make this diversity a strength.

Symbolic of the cultural discontinuity present in contemporary America, the meetings were held at a magnificent country estate, Airlie House, Warrenton, Virginia, now generously made available as a study center by the Airlie Foundation. In its publicity, pride is expressed in the architectural preservation of the traditional atmosphere of early Virginia. In this pastoral retreat, recalling a bygone era, an acutely contemporary and peculiarly urban problem of America was studied.

ROGER R. MILLER

Northampton, Massachusetts
November 1968

Contents

Introduction

Presented in this monograph are ten papers, grouped according to the three themes of the Institute on Research Toward Improving Race Relations. Following each set of papers is an account of the discussion bearing on that theme. Excerpts from two papers not reproduced here are also included in the discussion sections. Because the participants were articulate—indeed, eloquent—some direct quotations drawn from the transcript of the proceedings are used.

Nature of the Problem

Collectively, the three papers presented in Part I afford a survey of perspectives on problems related to race. Common to them is a pursuit of frames of reference capable of clarifying the dynamic character of Negro-white transactions. Dr. Inabel B. Lindsay's opening address draws attention to the history of self-help by Negroes and the achievements fostered by Negro-white collaboration. It is a curiosity of the conference that little attention was subsequently given to historical matters. Perhaps the history of this country is too painful to bear inspection and, at least in gross terms, too well known to require it. The general avoidance of historical themes may also have resulted from a sense that a break with the past has occurred. It was observed that history offers at best an unreliable guide to the future. Dr. Lindsay's presentation, however, offers a sample of an ingredient otherwise largely absent from the conference.

From a thoughtful analysis of the dilemmas posed by the concepts of race and minority status, Herman H. Long suggests the strategic advantage of adopting and emphasizing a racial definition of the problem. And from his observation of the stability in the status of the Negro during

9

two decades of progressive desegregation, he questions the relevance of an integration model to our society. A case is made instead for concern with the response dimension of Negro life, some aspects of which are analyzed in this paper. Long's deceptively subtle, low-key presentation both requires and merits careful review.

In the third paper, Hylan Lewis discusses the political implications of changing ideas organized around the concepts of race, class, and culture, including myths created or supported by research. A review of some studies of the Negro family, Negro characteristics, and Negro subcultural groupings is used to support a recommendation for formulations of the problem that accommodate the effects of extra-individual forces, especially sociopolitical processes. Lewis' forceful presentation thus extends the range of analyses reviewed in the initial section of the monograph.

During the discussion generated in part by the three opening papers, the conference participants attempted to sort out the place of race, class, and minority status concepts for describing Negro-white relationships.[1] Also addressed was the scope and nature of change in these relationships, in the course of which attention was given to Negro community, leadership, and identity; the sources and dynamics of power; and the place of conflict in organizational life.

Perspectives on Practice, Program, and Change

In the four papers contained in Part II, facets of the social work field are held up for examination in the context of race. Collectively these papers suggest an answer to the question: "Where do we stand on race

---

[1] Provided as resource material to the participants was Nathan E. Cohen's report of "The Los Angeles Riot Study," published under that title in *Social Work*, Vol. 12, No. 4 (October 1967), pp. 14–21.

relations?" The answer is not a happy one. The picture of social work's response to the problems of race is painfully reminiscent of an early response to poverty—the distribution of Christmas baskets. Even this suggestion of harmless, if ineffective, effort may overstate the case, however; failures of commission as well as omission appear on the record.

The analysis by Andrew Billingsley and Jeanne Giovannoni of the scope of interracial adoptions, the most racially specific practice considered, highlights the current unwillingness of the white community to accept Negroes into intimate relationships and reveals the slowness of the welfare establishment to devise suitable provisions for the substitute care of Negro children. In the joint paper by Joseph W. Eaton and Neil Gilbert, concepts intended to facilitate the identification of exclusionary practices are introduced. The point is made that statistical differences in the participation of Negroes and whites in service programs would benefit from interpretation against the concept of diagnostic differentiation as distinguished from discrimination. It is further argued that policies of preferential treatment must be distinguished from discrimination in reverse. The reader may wish to consider whether Charles T. O'Reilly's survey of discriminatory practices in social welfare, presented next, would have benefited from the introduction of the conceptual refinements suggested by Eaton and Gilbert. O'Reilly's data point to some past and current evidences of denial of services to Negroes because of their race, underrepresentation of Negroes in the composition of boards among welfare agencies generally, and a history of aversion to the examination of race as a factor in staffing and in the specification of service populations.

The problems identified by Jerome Cohen, in the final paper of Part II, are more subtle but probably more pervasive than the raw discrimination for which O'Reilly searched. The network of forces inherent in our society that militate against the Negro's electing an institutionalized resource for help, against his finding a resource appropriate to his needs, and against his using help are identified in Cohen's sophisticated analysis. Practitioners will be especially interested in the barriers to service identified here. Reviewed are research findings concerning the Negro's distrust of the Establishment, the structural arrangements governing practice, and especially the complexities attending the formation of a cross-racial treatment relationship.

The discussion sparked by these papers ranged from concern with the here-and-now arrangements for care of Negro children to problems of policy and the place of social work in promoting social change. The participants struggled to find terms to capture the nature of the exclusionary practices common to liberal elements in our society and mirrored in social work practice. Attempts were made to supplement and extend the Eaton-Gilbert formulation and to trace out some of the programmatic implications of these ideas. From practice, the discussion returned to policy issues: How can social work achieve a better articulation with the movement of the Negro community? How can social work prepare for what lies ahead?

Issues and Opportunities

What's in your bag? This question, put to the participants early in the meeting, called attention to the individual biases and conceptual habits with which the content of the meeting was approached. Some answers to the question emerged in the analyses of the problem and in the appraisal of the social work response to the problem. But as the focus of the meeting shifted to research matters, personal preferences and predis-

positions became more evident. In each bag were individual conceptions about the potentialities and risks of research, stylistic preferences, and beliefs about the place of research activity in social work and in relation to the subject of race.

In the first of three papers included in this section, St. Clair Drake offers an impressive review of research on intergroup relations from World War II to the present. Made conveniently available here are the results of a series of studies directed at the reduction of intergroup conflict through action chiefly at the neighborhood level. The products of these intraneighborhood conflict-avoiding efforts present an interesting contrast to the results of some subsequent neighborhood-community conflict-evoking activities. The reader may be especially interested in the implications drawn from this body of experience for the practice of social work at the neighborhood level.

Elizabeth Herzog and Cecelia E. Sudia, in a review of research on the one-parent family, demonstrate the potentiality of a tangential rather than a direct approach to the study of race. The target here includes, but is specifically not limited to, a Negro problem. The data and the history of their use provide the basis for some recommendations about research strategy in a politically sensitive area.

In the final paper, Lawrence K. Northwood and Robert Reed advance ideas about a general strategy for social work research related to race. Suggested are the goals of (1) establishing realities and dispelling myths in areas that have action consequences for social work, (2) identifying incipient and developing problems in order to prepare appropriate countermeasures, and (3) evaluating the consequences of service efforts in areas affording alternative courses for action. Suggested too are a number of avenues for inquiry and specific focal points for research.

In the discussion stirred by these papers,

ideas about research as a vehicle for promoting change were examined in conjunction with the attempt to define the place of
research in social work. In addition to extending the catalog of attractive research
targets, the discussion addressed some strategic and tactical problems of social work
research.   What should not be studied?
When has enough research been done? The
reader may wish to compare his own ideas
about these questions with the thoughts
expressed in Part III of the monograph.

Part I

Nature of the Problem

One Hundred Years of Race Relations

INABEL B. LINDSAY

Conflict in intergroup relations has recently become so dramatic, pervasive, and destructive as to overshadow other characteristics of Negro-white relationships. Symptomatic as the recent urban riots are of a collective American failure to find adequate solutions for a common problem, it would nonetheless be grievous if these outbursts were allowed to obscure the record of solid achievement deriving from the sustained work of many interested citizens. It may be useful, therefore, to review some of the collaborative and self-help efforts that have preceded, have accompanied, and may outlive the current turbulence.

Inabel B. Lindsay, DSW, is Social Services Adviser to Assistant Secretary for Individual and Family Services, U.S. Department of Health, Education, and Welfare, Washington, D.C. This paper was the Howard University Centennial Address, presented at Airlie House, Warrenton, Virginia, August 1967.

History of Howard University

One strand in the fabric comprising Negro-white relations is visible in the history of Howard University. Expressed by its very founding and throughout its first century of service is a collaborative commitment to the pursuit of a more viable democracy. Self-help supported by the wider comunity has enabled the university to make some noteworthy strides toward this goal.

In 1867, at a prayer meeting at the First Congregational Church in Washington, D.C., a small group of community leaders responded to the appeal of Union Army General Oliver Otis Howard to become involved actively in meeting a crucial need of the time—the provision of educational resources to train leaders, mainly Negroes, to cope intelligently with the problems that arose in the aftermath of the Civil War.

15

General Howard and his colleagues determined to found a university that would be a university *in fact* as well as *in name*. They agreed that "in view of the pressing demand of the southern field," only high-quality education at the college level would meet the need. Since they were not wealthy men, they were faced immediately with the problem of financing their dream if it were to become a reality. The operations of the Freedmen's Bureau were being terminated piecemeal and General Howard (who had been commissioner of the bureau) recalled an unspent balance from some activities that had previously been terminated. He therefore proposed to his colleagues that an appeal be made to Congress to allocate these funds for the establishment of the university. His suggestion met warm approval from his fellow dreamers; Congress responded favorably and the dream became a reality.

The tradition of federal grants in partial support of Howard University was thus established. This support, although implemented each year, did not carry a guarantee of continuity, however, until 1928. In that year Congressman Louis C. Cramton of Michigan proposed a resolution putting the commitment on a permanent basis. Affirmative action by the Congress paved the way for the stable growth and development of the university.

The little band of seven founders of Howard University, in addition to a commitment to meeting community need with intelligence and competence, were dedicated to a realization of democracy. Some who became trustees of the university enrolled their own children there. Thus, there were four young white women, daughters of members of the Board of Trustees, in the first graduating class.

Consonant with the philosophy of its founders was Howard's early and continuing response to identified community and minority group needs. In 1870, barely three years after the chartering of the university, the American Missionary Association, in co-operation with the Freedmen's Bureau, started Lincoln Mission on the site of what is now Lincoln Congregational Church in Washington. This little mission, designed with the idea of developing the potentialities of ex-slaves for participation in the economic and social affairs of the nation's capital, was an early prototype of a modern social settlement. Its staff was composed largely, if not entirely, of Howard faculty and students. It provided a laboratory for practice for students that would be roughly comparable to social work field practice of the present day. Initially the students were assigned from the Department of Commerce. Subsequently, the District of Columbia Board of Education absorbed the educational activities of the mission while the Congregational Church took over the religious functions.[1]

During the severe depression later in the 1870's, a group of citizens known only as the "Hill Group" and including many with affiliations at Howard bound themselves together to supply the material needs of disadvantaged fellow citizens at the "foot of the hill." The Hill Group bought quantities of food, fuel, and clothing and collected funds for rent. They dispensed these to the needy in accordance with crudely designed eligibility criteria.[2]

The Howard University School of Social work was itself established in response to needs of a minority group. With the onset of federal programs to help meet the critical needs of large numbers of the population during the mid-1930's, local welfare pro-

---

[1] Walter Dyson, *Howard University, Capstone of Negro Education, A History: 1867–1940* (Washington, D.C.: Graduate School, Howard University, 1941), p. 425.

[2] Inabel B. Lindsay, "The Participation of Negroes in the Establishment of Welfare Services: 1865–1900," pp. 157–158. Unpublished doctoral dissertation, University of Pittsburgh School of Social Work, 1952.

grams were expanded or developed. Negro college graduates were among those staffing these programs, in many instances for the first time and certainly for the first time in any substantial numbers. The Negro workers employed in the new District of Columbia public welfare program were barred because of race from the only existing local facility for professional training. Since most were Howard liberal arts graduates, they turned to their alma mater for help. The university responded and a program of graduate courses in social work was established in the Department of Sociology in 1935, under the leadership of the late Dr. E. Franklin Frazier. With this small beginning, a full-fledged autonomous School of Social Work was established a decade later.

In the early 1940's the university again responded with positive action to another community need. This time the infant School of Social Work was the chosen instrument. A group of thirteen young women had organized themselves into a voluntary service unit identified as the "Baker's Dozen," to provide leisure-time activities for teen-agers. Their program proved so popular that the Baker's Dozen soon outgrew the limited space provided by established settlement houses and the local Negro branch of the YMCA. These dauntless young women then raised enough money to make a down payment on two adjoining old houses in the most socially pathological section of the city, where they opened their own Teen Center. At this point they recognized their need for professional help and turned to Howard University, from which most of them had graduated. They were referred to the School of Social Work by the university's president. The school provided the necessary assistance and a new and unique social service was born. It continues, in somewhat changed form, to the present.

The concern of the university with social policy and social services has continued to this day. Organized and co-ordinated efforts to support and give leadership to community services were reflected in the university's active involvement in the University Neighborhood Councils in their beginnings in the late 1950's. It also gave leadership and financial support in the development of the neighborhood services project of a group of churches in a disadvantaged neighborhood. These churches were deeply concerned with juvenile delinquency, unemployment, poor housing, and the multitude of problems evident in their community. Since the early 1960's, the university has also devoted faculty and student time and energy to the structuring of multifaceted research and services to youth. These varied activities are now co-ordinated under a single division known as the Center for Community Studies.

Parallels of the Howard experience can be seen in other predominantly Negro institutions of higher learning. Schools such as Fisk University, Lincoln University, Talladega College, Atlanta University, and Tuskegee Institute—to mention only a few —have seemed to feel a compelling sense of responsibility for exploring and offering help toward what were frequently described as "problems of race betterment."

Beginning in the last decade of the nineteenth century, Atlanta University held a number of conferences on racial problems, usually under the leadership of Dr. W. E. B. Dubois. These conferences not only identified the severe handicaps and problems induced by prejudice and discrimination, but also suggested some approaches to coping with them. Emphasized was the need for co-ordination and collaboration among the many small independent efforts under Negro sponsorship. In addition, Dr. Dubois endorsed the building of co-operative relations between Negroes and whites. Tuskegee Institute, under the leadership of Dr. Monroe N. Work, established a valuable resource for scholars concerned with documenting the denial of constitutional rights and the abridgment of human freedom for

Negroes in his *Negro Yearbook*.[3] Fisk University's annual race relations institutes under the leadership of Dr. Charles S. Johnson afforded analyses of problems and insights into remedial efforts that were of inestimable help to those hopeful of the realization of democracy. All these and many others were and are illustrative of the universities' long and continuing concern with the improvement of the condition of the Negro and of race relations in the United States.

The Negro Urban In-migrant

The social forces to which the universities, no less than other institutions, have attempted to find accommodation have been powerful and corrosive. Complex and interrelated factors such as industrialization, urbanization, and rapidly advancing technology have encouraged the concentration of populations in urban centers or metropolitan areas. Such social phenomena as the flight to the suburbs, dispersion of industry and commerce, decay of the inner city, and a reduced tax base for support of essential services in the inner city are too well known to need discussion here. The special in-migrant status of the Negro may, however, deserve comment.

Since the Civil War the movement of populations has reflected the hopes and ambitions of Negro Americans to share the benefits and responsibilities of American democracy. A distinguished journalist-economist characterizes the new period as follows:

The immigrants still pour in—not from County Cork, or Bavaria, or Sicily, or Galicia, but from Jackson, Mississippi, and Memphis, Tennessee, and a host of towns and hamlets with names like Sunflower, Rolling Fork, and Dyersburg. No single European ethnic group ever increased as rapidly, or accounted for

as large a proportion of the big cities' population as the current wave of newcomers. The new immigrants, however, are distinguished from the older residents neither by religion nor by national origin; they are Protestant, for the most part, and can boast of an American ancestry much older than that of the established city dweller. Their sole distinguishing feature is color: the newcomers are black.[4]

In the aftermath of the Civil War, when Negroes followed the general population trend to the cities, they found little opportunity for employment in the mills and factories other than in the most menial jobs rejected by the whites. The new southern army of laborers, continuing the tradition of the Confederacy, expressed the feeling that cities were for whites. The unaccustomed income derived by the poor whites from factory jobs, however, made it possible for them to hire servants. Thus domestic service was added to the menial factory jobs as a source of subsistence for Negroes in the cities.[5]

The steady plod of Negroes toward the cities was quickened to a veritable flood in 1879. This mass migration, which was so great as to arouse the South to action in an attempt to save its labor supply, was the culmination of several forces. The elimination of the Freedmen's Bureau and the withdrawal of federal troops left the freedmen at the mercy of the white South, which the Negroes still feared and distrusted. Then, too, they hoped, although futilely, to share the more lucrative and happier position occupied by workers in the cities. Another influence was the spectacular high-pressure advertising of the railroad companies, intended to lure workers, both Negro and white, to construction jobs.[6]

---

[3] The *Negro Yearbook* was published at irregular intervals by Tuskegee Institute, Tuskegee, Ala., during the 1920's, 1930's, and continuing into the 1940's.

[4] Charles E. Silberman, *Crisis in Black and White* (New York: Vintage Books, 1964), pp. 19–20.

[5] Arthur M. Schlesinger, *Political and Social Growth of the United States 1933–1952*, Vol. II (rev. ed.; New York: Macmillan Co., 1953), pp. 277–278.

[6] Lindsay, *op. cit.*, p. 18.

Community Response

The impersonality of life in crowded cities in contrast to the neighborliness of rural communities forced the creation of social structures to handle the many problems that arose. Already such reform movements as the temperance and women's suffrage movements were receiving considerable attention. With industrialization and the consequent urbanization of the population, it followed logically that housing reform, charity organization, relief and prevention of pauperism, and care of children should also engage attention. Public provision for dependent, defective, and delinquent groups in America had been made in varying degrees of adequacy since colonial days, but the early programs were largely local and undifferentiated in nature. It was not until the growing industrialization brought in its wake the urban community that the state as a unit of government undertook some measure of supervision and control of welfare services.

Specific major private welfare services did not become established on the broad national scale now taken for granted until the beginning of the twentieth century. There were, however, notable social movements inaugurated during the latter half of the nineteenth century. Attempts were made to bring order and system to the administration of relief to the poor, the settlement movement was initiated, and specialized services to children were begun.

The migration of Negroes to the large cities in both the North and the South continued and accelerated in the twentieth century. However, the bright hopes for the attainment of full equality continued to be blocked as the problems attendant on urbanization pressed more heavily on Negroes. The spirit of self-help begun in the aftermath of the Civil War grew more rapidly and organizations primarily under the leadership of Negroes began to emerge. Many of these had their beginnings in the last quarter of the nineteenth century under church leadership and later with active promotion by Negro women's clubs. Most of these were small and insignificant in comparison with the broader social movements that characterized the times. However, they did show a commitment to and a concern for the welfare of the race by Negroes themselves.

The hordes of travelers from South to North and from rural to urban centers and the appalling lack of preparation for urban living motivated committees, usually of Negro women, to organize to protect and guide the newcomers to the cities. So-called "working girls' homes" were organized much after the pattern of the YWCA. Women's committees—occasionally with the help of some men—frequently met the boats and trains coming from the Deep South. These committees might be considered a prototype of the Travelers Aid Society and Immigrant Aid Association of a later day.

Out of deep concern for the social and economic well-being of the new migrants, committees, frequently including liberal whites as well as Negroes, were formed to investigate social and economic conditions and to propose ways of meeting them. Out of such late nineteenth- and early twentieth-century efforts grew two early movements on behalf of Negroes: the National Association for the Advancement of Colored People in 1909 and the National Urban League in 1910. The primary objective of the NAACP was to open up channels for the achievement of equality through legislation; the Urban League focused its attention and efforts on the achievement of economic opportunity through jobs, education, housing, and other social services.

Self-help movements proliferated in the early twentieth century.[7] Among these

---

[7] Ira de A. Reid, "The American Negro," in Joseph B. Gittler, ed., *Understanding Minority Groups* (New York: John Wiley & Sons, 1956), pp. 76–82.

"the Tuskegee idea"—self-help primarily through vocational education—foreshadowed some of the philosophy advocated currently in recommendations to build up the ghettos and make them adequate for living, forgetting about integration until a strong, separate Negro community is achieved.[8] The race relations movement, on the other hand, with its beginnings of interracial co-operation to solve racial problems, laid a foundation for other present-day activities. The Negro women's movement reflects again the preoccupation with the improvement and strengthening of welfare services, especially for children and handicapped groups. The "Legal Crusade" obviously continues into the present and has been accelerated in the past decade by Supreme Court decisions.

When the United States entered World War I with great hope and idealism, this spirit permeated even to the underprivileged Negroes. Negroes added to the slogan "to make the world safe for democracy" the words "and the U.S. safe for Negroes." Many of the issues of this and other periods have a familiar ring. There was talk of discrimination, deprivation of freedom of speech, urban congestion, slum housing, insecurity of employment, unemployment, and the like.[9] Although there was increased attention to the needs of special groups and pressure to develop programs to give people some security with respect to specific conditions, few of these special efforts, except for those of the National Urban League, gave particular attention to the needs of Negroes.[10]

---

[8] Frances Fox Piven and Richard A. Cloward, "The Case Against Urban Desegregation," *Social Work*, Vol. 12, No. 1 (January 1967), pp. 12–21.

[9] Clarke A. Chambers, *Seedtime of Reform: American Social Service and Social Action 1918–1933* (Minneapolis: University of Minnesota Press, 1963), p. xi.

[10] *Ibid.*, p. 53.

America's Other Minorities

Other minority groups are also set apart from the mainstream of American life, primarily by the factor of skin color. Although the Negro minority constitutes about 92 percent of those reported by the U.S. Census as nonwhite, the needs of other nonwhite minorities in the United States are of increasing significance and concern as the nation strives to achieve its ideal of democracy.

The oldest group of Americans—in fact, the only native-born Americans—the Indians, are beset by many of the same social problems encountered by Negroes. The treaties negotiated by the United States in annexing the lands of this Indian minority were more often than not disregarded. An early policy of segregation, expressed in the establishment of Indian reservations, served to insulate Indians from American culture. In recent decades, efforts have been made to promote the integration of the Indian into our twentieth-century industrial world. The move from the reservation to the city has not been easy, however. Sources of support familiar to the Indians—mainly those of an agricultural and tribal society—have not been adapted to city life. Many Indians have been found to lack the educational preparation that would equip them to compete in an industrial society. Although normal services to Indian in-migrants have been provided (with some reluctance in many cases), their arrival in the city has frequently been an occasion for frustration and despair on both sides. Even with the extension of special services, such as those offered by the Bureau of Indian Affairs, life in the city has been hazardous. The transitional problems experienced by many Indians have become painfully familiar to social workers in many urban areas.

Another large group of "new Americans" or foreigners temporarily residing on our shores are the Mexicans in the Southwest and Northwest. Drawn in on the ebb tide of the nation's expanding economy during World War II, when domestic manpower was scarce, the Mexicans were soon stranded by the country's altered needs. As war-related activities diminished and as the United States moved into a period of depression, opportunities for these immigrants evaporated. Mexicans came to be seen as presenting unwelcome competition to native American labor, a view that accentuated prejudice and discrimination based on color. Like the Indians, the Mexicans' encounter with urban life eroded the customary supports and controls for behavior, accelerating social breakdown for these new arrivals.

A third group frequently set apart by color in the United States, in spite of their full citizenship, is the Puerto Ricans. Motivated primarily by economic need, the Puerto Ricans came to the mainland searching for higher incomes and a better way of life. The currents of the job market on the mainland are reflected in the numbers of yearly arrivals in the United States. In many urban communities, especially along the eastern seaboard and increasingly in Chicago and other midwestern cities, the numbers have reached substantial proportions. One author comments:

The Puerto Rican, in spite of his American citizenship, is a "stranger in a strange land." English is a foreign tongue to about half of the migrants. Many customs are different and his attitudes often diverge widely from the norms of the host society.[11]

There are many problems of adjustment to the mainland induced by the conflict of what is called the "American culture" and the Puerto Rican's indoctrination to his original Spanish culture. Since many of the Puerto Rican migrants come from rural or small-town areas on the island, they are unprepared for the hustle and bustle of the teeming metropolitan centers to which they

gravitate. Finding employment is especially difficult for the Puerto Rican male because of language barriers, unfamiliarity with work habits and patterns, and the use of technology.

Puerto Ricans present a wide spectrum of skin color as do American Negroes, and the Puerto Rican migrant whose skin color is dark often faces a problem stemming from color discrimination on the mainland.

While discrimination exists in Puerto Rico, it is limited largely to the inherited attitudes of upper class standards. Puerto Ricans seldom judge a person's ability by the color of his skin. But when they move to New York, from an environment in which Spaniards and Negroes have lived for several hundred years without serious race conflict, they suddenly discover an atmosphere charged with the feeling that a white skin means innate superiority.[12]

Unmet Needs: Challenge for Social Work

As self-help efforts have expanded and as recent efforts to force social change have taken new and sometimes violent forms, race relations have become a national concern. In the late 1960's it becomes increasingly apparent to many observers that in spite of civil rights progress, a number of problems have scarcely been touched.

Residential segregation is still the rule, resulting in a de facto segregation of schools. Negro unemployment rates are two or three times higher than those for whites in a period when general employment is at an all-time high. Moods of Black Nationalism are prevalent in Negro communities arising as counter-currents to the drive for integration.[13]

If the social work profession has been

---

[11] Clarence Senior, "The Puerto Rican in the United States," in Gittler, ed., *op. cit.*, p. 114.

[12] *Ibid.*, p. 116.

[13] St. Clair Drake, *Race Relations in a Time of Rapid Social Change* (New York: National Federation of Settlements and Neighborhood Centers, 1966), p. 4.

less surprised than other elements of society
by the persistence of serious social problems and by the psychological responses of
Negroes to their status, it seems to have
shared with the wider community some
uncertainty and confusion about how to
relate to these problems.

There was an increasing tendency to redefine
the problem of the Negro as one facet of the
problems of the poor and [the belief] that
emphasis should perhaps be shifted to an indirect assault upon Negro disabilities rather
than a frontal assault. At the same time the
controversial Moynihan Report opened up a
discussion as to whether all gains might not
be lost and further gains be made impossible
unless something were done to strengthen the
Negro family.[14]

Conflicting Philosophies

The struggle through which social settlements have gone and are going in the
effort to resolve some of the problems affecting race relations illustrates how complex
are the challenges faced by social work.
The search of the National Federation of
Settlements and its member groups for
guidelines and solutions to the problems
of intergroup conflict is not new to this
segment of social agencies. They have had
long familiarity with prejudice against
ethnic rather than racial minorities since
they early attacked the problem of injustice
toward immigrants. Since then the bur-
geoning of Negro populations and their
concentration in the city, especially in the
ghettos and slum areas, have brought the
problem sharply into focus.

Since its beginnings in the mid-nineteenth century, the settlement philosophy
has emphasized the need to help in the
achievement of democracy. It has also
emphasized the right to self-determination
of the clientele served. From Drake's study
there now emerges evidence of conflict between these two philosophies.[15] The majority of the neighborhood centers and

settlements participating in this study expressed commitment to integration as an
ideal—a goal to be achieved. On the other
hand, they felt strongly that groups of
clients using their facilities should have
autonomy in formation of natural groupings and development of program emphases. There was also some disagreement
as to whether the settlement houses should
push those groups that preferred to remain
segregated toward a goal of integration, if
the overriding determination is to support
a democratic ideology and to achieve genuine integration of all segments of the population. Thus the issue posed is not only
for this group of social agencies, but for
others as well, to identify the best means of
achieving the goal. Action-oriented research is needed to help in solving the
problem.

It has been comparatively easy to identify the underlying frustration and hope-
lessness that have motivated youths to engage in destructive and violent behavior.
It has not been equally as easy to identify the possible satisfactions that accrue
from such behavior. A staff member of
one of the neighborhood houses, in a report submitted for Dr. Drake's study,
commented that

these teenage, rebellion-motivated youngsters
who engaged in the undesirable behavior . . .
were looking for a fast way of becoming local
heroes. Such behavior was reinforced when
they received adult sanction.[16]

Another troubling aspect of present-day
ferment as depicted in the spreading big-
city riots is the loss of any semblance of
control by the Negroes in leadership roles,
previously respected and receiving positive
response. A complaint heard with increasing frequency is the breakdown of communication between stable middle-class Negroes and those who are in open revolt.
What are the effective channels of communication and how may they be developed?
How can the alienated youths, who pre-

---

[14] *Ibid.*
[15] *Ibid.*

[16] *Ibid.*, p. 89.

sumably are supplying the leadership in the current wave of antisocial activities, be motivated? What satisfaction can be substituted? How can militant approaches be channeled into constructive ends?

Other issues of considerable urgency in view of the perilous situation in which the country finds itself and to which social work research may contribute understanding and paths to solution include an analysis of the components and sources of Black Nationalism. Social work research can help to analyze the types of service systems needed. What can be effective in mobilizing change? Can traditional services be maintained? What efforts are essential to introduce new service systems more adequate to meet and cope with the unrest of the times? Even though some of the approaches proposed may be controversial, as long as these include the objective of impartial evaluation they can make a contribution. An aspect of the need to modify existing service systems can be met through research efforts to analyze what methods work and how to determine the speed with which social movement— social change—is propelled forward.

Finally, increasing approval is being given to a philosophy of building up segregated neighborhoods and services and reducing the amount of energy and effort put into achieving integration. The appeal to separation as compared with integration is put forward eloquently by Piven and Cloward.[17] On the other hand, Whitney Young, proponent of the "domestic Marshall Plan" (for preferential treatment) argues that the only way to achieve the goal of equal opportunity is through collaboration. He further emphasizes the need to create a spirit leading to new self-respect and determination.[18]

As social work matures and takes its full share of responsibility in the achievement of a democratic society, progress can be vastly accelerated by effective research and the implementation of such research. The profession has an urgent job to do, which can be aided vastly by the active intervention and involvement of all its members.

---

[17] *Op. cit.*
[18] Whitney M. Young, Jr., "The Case for Urban Integration," *Social Work*, Vol. 12, No. 3 (July 1967), pp. 12–17.

The Negro
As a Minority Community

HERMAN H. LONG

The task of this paper is to assess the present status of the Negro as a minority community, identify significant changes and trends with respect to that status, and indicate some perspectives from systematic study of the Negro that may be useful for social work research and practice. Comparison with other racial, ethnic, and religious minorities will be made only incidentally, for a systematic effort in this respect would seem to require a somewhat different and special undertaking.

Alternatives to the
Negro's Uniqueness

A preliminary word is in order in regard to the context within which the Negro experience in America might profitably be viewed, if one is to avoid the trap of thinking it to be a special and entirely unique

Herman H. Long, Ph.D., is President, Talladega College, Talladega, Alabama.

case. While the Negro is undoubtedly the classical instance of gross and categorical group exclusion on the American scene, both historically and in terms of the size of the victimized population, to give singular emphasis to the "special" qualities of the case can—and too frequently does— lead to a kind of strategic dead end. One is led unwittingly, on the one hand, to a form of social romanticism that, no matter how well it dramatizes the reality, is limited programmatically. The effect, on the other hand, is like getting lost in the woods— of being surrounded, in other words, by a veritable thicket of colorful data and unable to find a useful path of generalization and viable social policy. Social work may be getting deeper in the woods, inasmuch as events have literally outdistanced both our knowledge and the profession's "late and little" efforts toward helpful social intervention. It is not that we have failed to produce a substantial body of fairly systematic knowledge about the Negro—

far from it—but, rather, that much of it no longer tells us what our next steps ought to be. Knowledge, like many other things, has a time and place, and a great deal of what has been known largely speaks to an age, not long past, when for most Americans the Negro was just being discovered as an important social reality in the national community.

Minority Conception

If the alternatives of romanticism and uniqueness are to be avoided, assuming that it is desirable to do so, we are then faced with the question of context. To *what* does the experience of the Negro in America relate beyond itself and what are the elements that connect it with the universal human experience? This may be the basic question, for it poses considerations that are significant for social and institutional policy on the one hand, and for human values on the other. The late Louis Wirth framed the major thrust of his contributions in this area in terms of the dichotomy of "dominant" and "minority" groups, and because the author has long felt that this was a useful and broadly oriented conception, the title of this paper, "The Negro As a Minority Community," seemed especially appropriate.[1] It is a singularly clear designation; all mystery and theoretical elaboration are gone; the minority is the group that is the object of systematic discrimination, the group without power, driven to cohesiveness and group self-consciousness by these influences. Negroes, Jews, and a wide variety of groups identified by language, nationality, and culture fall within the category and share commonality, with the exception of differences by the groups as to their major or-

ientation toward possible goals of assimilation and separatism. The basic factor in all cases is political, since by the nature of the circumstances, the minority is seeking by various efforts to acquire power and the means to change the qualifying history of the case. In this perspective, the Negro in America is a minority, not because he is Negro and all the qualities that may infer, but because he constitutes a community without power and remains the object of systematic exploitation.

Racial Conceptions As a Social Product

This would be enough of a context except for the fact that race and color have been associated with Negro status and response, as well as with the attitudes and valuations in regard to the Negro that are in essence race-bound. One is led, therefore, to a consideration of the Negro community as a so-called racial group and hence to a context of what has been called race relations. By and large this term has come to be applied almost exclusively to the relationships between Negroes and whites, or it might be better to say the attitudes and beliefs that are substituted for such relationships. This in turn has caused a major preoccupation with the qualities and characteristics of the Negro as a so-called racial group, even to the extreme of a search for "Negro essence." To put the matter this way suggests that what has been largely involved is an indulgence in mystery, for the very delineation of a given characteristic only enhances the racial category. A great deal of what has taken place would thereby seem to be circuitous. But the point here is that the limited preoccupation with the Negro per se has robbed the term race relations of its generality and relevance to issues of public policy. This is quite the opposite from what was intended by Robert E. Park, doubtless the most systematic and consis-

---

[1] *See* the compilation of Wirth's essays contained in Wirth, *Community Life and Social Policy* (Chicago: University of Chicago Press, 1956).

tent race relations theorist among American sociologists, who conceived of race relations as a unifying concept.[2]

Race relations are essentially a by-product of "race consciousness," and race consciousness, in turn, enters into the determination of status, position, and opportunity in which "differences" are perceived as being biologically determined. And because of the biological presumptions that are the key factor in the racial concept, individuals and groups designated as having subordinate status are forever denied full inclusion into human society. Park saw this as a quality involved in the relations between all sorts of ethnic and genetic groups, and by making race relations universal he sought thereby to objectify racial problems and make them amenable to policy resolution. He did not, of course, seek to give validity to the biological component, but rather to emphasize its crucial place in the belief system encompassed by the racial ideology. Robert Redfield, one of Park's closest associates, has described the underlying purpose of Park's race relations conception as an attempt to unify:

Park wanted us to understand that the relations between Negroes and whites do not constitute a type-form in the natural history of ethnic relations but are rather to be seen as an instance of a most variable class of human relationships between groups.[3]

Park therefore thought in terms of race relations—as well as all forms of ethnic relations—as undergoing a cycle of competition, conflict, accommodation, and assimilation. He did not believe that racial prejudice could be made intelligible, but looked on it as a body of sentiments supporting racial taboos and of the same general order as caste and class prejudice.

Color, or any mark of physical difference, was believed to be a symbol of moral divergence in society, but at the same time it was part of a more basic factor having to do with status and cultural difference. In a review of this and other classical formulations of race relations and the so-called Negro problem, Frazier has pointed out that they were based on assumptions

that the Negro is an inferior race because of either biological or social heredity or both; that the Negro because of his physical character cannot be assimilated; and that physical amalgamation is bad and undesirable.[4]

However useful these formulations were as an attempt to objectify the Negro problem, Frazier went on further to say that they were essentially rationalizations of the dominant public opinion and attitudes of the American people. He thus called for a more dynamic theory that would take into account the changing patterns of race relations in American life.

These were aspects of a discourse among sociologists at about the end of World War II and since that time a great deal has taken place with respect to both the status of the Negro and the character of race relations change. But whether the Negro has come to be seen as a more objective social entity or whether a more dynamic and general theory has evolved for interpretation of the "Negro problem" is highly doubtful. The terms "intergroup relations" and "human relations" have been widely used in the popular sense as efforts to broaden the context, and a notable attempt was made by the late Dr. Charles S. Johnson to provide a dynamic frame of reference.[5]

---

[2] Robert E. Park, *Race and Culture* (Glencoe, Ill.: Free Press, 1950). *See* especially his essay "The Nature of Race Relations," pp. 81–116.

[3] Robert Redfield, "Ethnic Relations, Primitive and Civilized," in *Race Relations: Problems and Theory* (Chapel Hill: University of North Carolina Press), p. 27.

[4] E. Franklin Frazier, "Sociological Theory and Race Relations," *American Sociological Review*, Vol. 12, No. 3 (June 1947), pp. 265–271.

[5] Charles S. Johnson, "Human Relations—The New Agenda." Unpublished paper presented at the Eighth Annual Race Relations Institute, Fisk University, Nashville, Tenn., 1951.

He pointed out that the "issue we call race is more clearly a complex of basic forces in American life than anything itself racial," that a revolutionary world of "new dominant forces and power stresses" had made necessary the use of the broader reference of "human relations." The salient elements of this new context, according to Johnson, were the evolution of a basic welfare concept, development of a systematic collectivism, modification of the common law by the inclusion of economic rights and liberties, and the emergence in world consciousness of an affirmative doctrine and concept of human rights. He believed, accordingly, that the task of the immediate future was one of "directing the current of conflict into channels for realizing the common aims of mankind." In this sense, he held that the conflict of race had given impetus to the unification of mankind.

But what has transpired since Johnson's statesmanlike perspective of 1951 is both a broadening of the world of race as an international phenomenon and, at the same time, an intensification of it in terms of domestic events. Although contained in the impersonal and powerful forces of economics and politics, the racial element remains in the many expressions of "race consciousness" relating to the status of the Negro and his presence as a factor in American society. Hence, to view the status of the Negro in the classical scheme of race relations is still useful, especially because it connotes a belief system in which biological dogma is a prominent element. The Negro in America is thus a minority community in the sense of being an exploited and powerless group in society, and is also a racial group in the sense that a pervading and persisting racial ideology provides justification for continuing to exclude him from the system of opportunity and status.

Implications of the Racial Perspective

To maintain a race relations reference in regard to the Negro community stands in opposition to the view which holds that if race is an invalid biological category, the best strategic departure is to separate Negroes from the racial context. By and large this has been done in varying degrees in the case of Jews, Catholics, and some of the so-called cultural minorities. But even in these cases, since much that is involved has to do with belief systems and ideologies, a question remains as to how much of the animus relating to the groups has been removed thereby. A counter-strategy—and one that is more realistic—seems a more fruitful possibility: namely, to highlight the racial and hence biological reference within which the Negro alone is viewed in America and thus to expose the point of greatest vulnerability of the system as a whole. It may be easier to deal with the irrationality which holds that an entire category of human beings is inferior because of color inheritance than to manage the rational belief that group inferiority is "proved" by lower general educational and economic status. Indeed, it is extraordinarily difficult to get across the latter factors as causal rather than the opposite.

Finally, in this regard it would certainly appear that the question of context is crucial. There may not be, in fact, a clear and consistent perspective, and what one has to deal with largely is what Hughes has aptly seen as a situation of anomaly and paradox growing out of the fact that "Negro Americans have got out of the place in which it used to be said they were all right, only to find that, in some respects, the new place is worse, or at least, less comfortable." [6] Somewhat the same perspective is provided

---

[6] Everett C. Hughes, "Anomalies and Projections," *Daedalus*, Vol. 94, No. 4 (Fall 1965), pp. 1133–1149.

by Coles in referring to the danger of talking about millions of people as a group in the context of a probing discussion of issues relating to Negro identity:

I *do* know that there is a concrete *reality* in being an American Negro; that millions of people are tied down to it; that some of them are driven mad by it; that others are frightfully torn by its prospects; that the spectacle of what its consequences have been for this nation is not yet completed; that in its grip people have fled and battled their way; and that, finally, the worst and best in mankind have emerged.[7]

Two Decades of Change

The major achievement of the last twenty years or so of accelerating change relating to the status of the Negro as a minority has been a reshaping of the public policy designed to provide access to full citizenship. Prior to World War II the rights of Negroes as citizens had remained unchanged over the long period since the Reconstruction. The murder and brutalizing of some six million Jews and the threat of world domination by Nazi power and ideology found America tragically compromised by a racial ideology of its own. Consequently, the task of building national unity and mobilizing industrial manpower and armed forces for the protection of freedom abroad became at once a task of redressing the nexus of national and institutional policy that not only kept Negroes outside the opportunity system but also supported the public expectation that they would remain there.

Political Foundations for Change

Beginning with the elimination of "lilywhite" voting primaries in the early 1940's and the presidential order for fair employ-

---

[7] Robert Coles, "It's the Same, But It's Different," *Daedalus*, Vol. 94, No. 4 (Fall 1965), pp. 1107–1132.

ment practices in the war-production industries, the redress of policy began to take definite shape, and by 1949, when the Supreme Court invalidated the enforcement of racially restrictive housing covenants by any form of state action, the most sacred domain of racial taboo was entered upon. By 1954 ultimate confrontation with the historic compromise of democratic public policy was inescapable, at least at the frontier of constitutional law, and the sweeping decisions on segregated public education left no form of state restriction on basic rights hinging on color and so-called racial origin any longer tenable.

It may be said that the foundation of the civil rights revolution of the 1960's was thus formed. What was accomplished in terms of policy allowing access to legal and political citizenship, however, only provided a base for the prosecution of rights that could be claimed only through the tortuous procedures of law and administrative process. The substance and reality of the new rights were yet to be attained. The racial system had been complete and it covered the entire institutional process through which access to jobs, education, housing, and civic participation was made possible. Consequently, forces to displace its powerful inertia were required, and these in large part have been provided by the Negro protest revolution and the acquisition of direct forms of political power. Partly through the long-term redistribution of Negro populations to the centers of electoral strength in the North and West, and partly through the economics of an enhanced purchasing power, Negroes achieved the ability to influence the outcome of national elections through a balance-of-power vote and thereby affect decisions of national policy.

Accompanying Social Reverberations

These are changes that have occurred at the level of policy in the situation affecting the Negro community, but they also involve expectations on the part of the Negro as to the immediacy and reality of rights. Change in the social component of inclusion or access has lagged, and it is here that the element of paradox is most prominent and serious. Because gains in policy and the dimension of theoretical opportunity have accelerated so rapidly and broadly, the gap between expectation by the minority community on the one hand and the reality of a continuing inaccessibility on the other has doubtlessly increased. In this sense, it is misleading to conceive of changes in the status of the Negro as a minority or in the character of race relations in terms of progress, for the effect of the change has been to expose how deep the patterns of injustice lie and how complex and slow-moving are the processes of amelioration. While residential dispersion in the geographic sense, for example, has expanded in comparison with earlier patterns of containment, Negro residential segregation has also intensified, and although job and economic gains over recent decades have been substantial—again looked at in terms of the Negro's own situation in a previous period—the disparity between Negro and white opportunity appears at the same time to be widening rather than narrowing. Moreover, while change takes place toward amelioration, racial self-consciousness also increases (in the sense of an awareness of persisting discrimination) and so does the pressure exerted by Negroes toward the extension of change to full enjoyment of rights.

In substance, the period of greatest change in the history of American race relations does not appear to have significantly altered the status of the Negro as a minority. Although a broad mobilization of governmental, legal, and voluntary organizational resources has taken place and a distinctly new kind of social process has emerged—namely, desegregation—the goal of inclusion seems to have receded rather

than accreted. And while Negro economic, educational, occupational, and general cultural status have improved, the effect for those Negroes who have benefited most from the process has been the creation of larger and larger numbers who occupy the status of "marginal men," persons whom Park described as living in more than one social world at the same time and not being fully a part of any. The projection of a segment of the Negro community into marginal status may be one of the most significant effects of the decades of enhanced change, for it is at the same time evidence of a limited kind of social mobility. It is also an expression of the fact of class differentiation within the Negro community.

Integration and Access to Opportunity

Over the years we have become accustomed to an approach to the so-called Negro problem that has concentrated largely on Negro characteristics or, rather, on a description of the status of the Negro in terms of educational, economic, and social indexes. While this remains as a dominant interest, even heightened by the many failures of the integration process to provide meaningful access to a widened scope of real opportunities in jobs and education, it has largely overlooked an important dimension of Negro life as a minority community. It has missed the dimension of Negro response, by which is meant the qualities of expectation and morale that sustain the life of the group and provide it with a dominant orientation toward itself and future possibilities. Studies of Negro leadership movements and of Negro communities, although surprisingly few in number, have been partially informative, as were the earlier efforts that concerned the phenomenon of "passing" and the functional significance of color. But to the extent that we have been informed at all, the view has been largely from the "outside" and from value premises of the dominant white society. And so we have missed a great deal of important substance and useful insight that might otherwise have been possible in looking at Negro life in its own context.

Shifting Orientation of the Negro

Pointing strongly to the validity of this is the fact that the white community has failed to anticipate by a wide margin of error, or even to understand later, the "big event" in Negro life and its corresponding effects on race relations. By this is not meant any single event, but rather the series of continuing and related events that give indication that a radical break with the past has taken place and that a new expectation and dominant orientation has emerged. In this regard the author is thinking, for example, of the "Negro Renaissance" of the 1920's; of the concerted efforts toward and direct insistence on equal rights (not integration, for this was a later quality) that came during World War II and were highlighted by the march on Washington movement; of the student sit-in movement of the early 1960's and the ensuing wave of boycotts and direct action efforts taking place under conditions of almost total mobilization of the Negro communities that became involved; and currently, of the new burst of self-initiative, essentially political in nature, couched in terms of power acquisition and black identity, shared by a conspicuous segment of the Negro communities. Each of these changes in mood and orientation had an accompanying "race riot," although violence constituted more a symptom than a cause of the change. At the same time, in almost every case, each shift in dominant orientation produced its corresponding phe-

nomenon of "the new Negro." It is a term which at least recognizes that a profound difference in substance and psychology has transpired in the response dimension of Negro life, but that otherwise informs rather poorly.

This dimension has been used by Drake and Cayton in their study of Chicago's Negro community by the description of what they call the "axes of life" around which Negro existence is sustained: staying alive, getting ahead, praising God, having fun, and advancing the race.[8] An interpretation by Johnson has described the Negro as a "man in motion," acting in response to forces both internal and external to the Negro community that have produced physical as well as psychological mobility.[9] In the same context he distinguished both centrifugal and centripetal social forces as crucial elements of Negro response and status. The former category involves a process of inclusion into community affairs, co-optation of Negro leadership, and what Johnson termed "whiteward mobility"— general upward mobility plus the drive toward personal assimilation into the majority group. The latter, on the other hand, includes increased minority group identification, enhanced awareness of the need for mass action, and a feeling of "interdependence of fate" with other Negroes. In summary, he pointed out:

The last ten years has witnessed a sharp increase in the tendency of American Negroes to become orderly and effective aggressors rather than avoiders and acceptors, particularly since their observations of successful desegregation efforts elsewhere furnished them with that valuable action ingredient of *knowing that movement is possible.*[10]

---

[8] St. Clair Drake and Horace R. Cayton, *Black Metropolis* (rev. ed.; New York: Harper & Row, 1962).

[9] Robert B. Johnson, "Changing Status of the Negro in American Life," *Journal of Intergroup Relations*, Vol. 1, No. 2 (Spring 1960), pp. 56–71.

[10] *Ibid.*, p. 73.

Shifting Identity Patterns

In addition to a variety of modes of response by the Negro at any given time, a case can be made for changes in dominant orientation that reflect discontinuities of expectation created by changes in situation. These involve responses from both Negro and "white" points of reference, but in any case a context is needed that is as much historical as it is sociological and psychological. Important generational differences are most likely involved in what has been termed the new militancy of Negro youths and their willingness to take chances outside the roles that have been traditional for their parents and grandparents. One may speak of them as being racially unsophisticated in this sense. No doubt there is a considerable element in this matter that is primarily a reaction against the past and its symbols and meanings. But there is also a strong possibility that the new role and self-expectations are the result of the absence of the deliberate inculcation of Negro "place" and appropriate behavior in the child-rearing system of reward and punishment meted out by Negro parents of the first and second generations for the sheer sake of survival. The third generation of Negro parents has probably been a kind of transition group between the old and new ways, and while systematic evidence is lacking, there are abundant clues which indicate that even telling the young child that he is "a Negro" is avoided, except for those final and desperate moments of explanation when nothing else seems adequate. Much of this may be a middle- and upper-class phenomenon, but it probably extends as far back as families of the "underclasses" who are oriented toward opportunities of middle-class life.

What may thus be taking place in the process is the production of a generation of Negro young people for whom the deeper emotional components of fear and defensiveness in their identification of being Negro are gone, but young people who otherwise have learned that they are Negro at the level of perception and from the inescapable clues and meanings surrounding their lives. If this is true, then elements of conflict are in a sense literally built-in, and it can be said that the perceptual world of the Negro has undergone a most radical transformation. To stretch the possibility a step further, it might be conjectured that they are faced with both an unreal feeling about being Negro and a quite clear Negro reality at the same time. And this has no reference to the world "out there" beyond the self, where revolutionary change in the Negro situation has taken place (for which "improvement in race relations" might serve as a euphemism) and other objective roles and expectations have arisen that vary widely and are also conflicting. It is a world in which the goal of inclusion or of integration, as one may choose to express it, seems to be receding in distance the closer it is approached through the intervening social mechanisms.

Attitude of the Majority Community

Rose has described the problem of integration as consisting primarily in the Negro's ability to "gain acceptance" as a coequal with whites.[11] There is on the white side of the ledger a similar problem of conflicting expectations as to Negro role that will be mentioned only briefly, since the reference might be distracting. Both the National Opinion Research Center survey data, garnered over a twenty-year period, and the more recent effort by Louis Harris and Associates on assignment for *Newsweek* show conspicuous gains in belief and attitude related to integration and

---

[11] Arnold Rose, "New and Emerging Negro Problems," *Journal of Intergroup Relations*, Vol. 1, No. 2 (Spring 1960), pp. 71–75.

Negro acceptance.[12] As reported by Sheatsley, only one-third of the total population favored school integration in 1942 along with 40 percent of northerners and just 2 percent of southerners.[13] By 1963 acceptance of school integration had not only become a dominant view for the population at large but the proportions had increased to 75 percent in the northern segment and 30 percent among southerners. The Harris data for 1963 show 91 percent of white majorities favoring equal voting rights for Negroes, 87 percent for the right to a fair jury trial, the same proportion for nonsegregated bus and train transportation, and 72 percent for integrated education.[14] And yet the realities involved in what transpired in the process of actual school desegregation, for example, fall far below what these trends might suggest. According to Brink and Harris, most Americans would "just as soon admit to injustices and move on to a pleasanter subject." Their description of the conflict of expectations, which follows, is most apt:

One of the incredible marks of affluent America in the 1960s was that it had the capacity to put itself into the shoes of the Negro, but at the same time continue to play the role of discriminator. Some rationalize it all, like the businessman in Seattle who said, "It would be pretty bad to be a Negro." Then as an afterthought he added, "But, after all, they aren't like white folks. I don't think it bothers most of them." A laborer on the West Coast said, "They're only a hundred years old in civilization and expect to catch up, and we been civilized for thousands of years."[15]

What all this amounts to in substance is that the integration model to which we are

currently oriented for assessing race relations and Negro status leaves a great deal wanting in the way of much-needed understanding. This is no argument against integration or even the model itself, except to suggest its limitations as a frame of reference for both race relations and Negro life. Part of the difficulty lies in the fact that integration as a goal of group effort is largely an abstract ideal and not a concrete entity, and this has led to nonproductive preoccupations. One of these is what might be called the "game of definitions," into which considerable effort has been put by way of drawing fine distinctions between desegration and integration. Another is the matter of racial quotas and so-called cutoff points of Negro concentration in order to maximize the possibilities of integration, a consideration, however, that does bear important implications for policy and program. Whether it warrants a high level of primacy or makes a significant programmatic difference, when once determined, is another matter. Still further is the related idea of integration as a kind of mathematical model, carrying the assumption of the desirability of something like an even or proportionate distribution of the Negro population across the geographic as well as institutional map. This, in turn, has evolved into assumptions about eliminating Negro institutions and preventing Negro population concentrations that carry negative overtones that are racially presumptive.

Integration As a Social Process

But looked at in terms of social process, integration becomes a useful point of reference as to the dynamics of race relations change and Negro response as well. Here the crucial question is the degree of meaningful access to opportunity and participation by the Negro minority community. However, even in this perspective the process of effective penetration appears to be

---

[12] *See* Paul B. Sheatsley, "Changing Attitudes on Race," unpublished paper presented at the Twenty-first Annual Race Relations Institute, Fisk University, Nashville, Tenn., 1964; and William Brink and Louis Harris, *Black and White* (New York: Simon & Schuster, 1967).

[13] *Op. cit.*

[14] Brink and Harris, *op. cit.*

[15] *Ibid.,* p. 126.

only at the beginning stage. Whether it is schools, jobs, housing, education, or acquisition of power, what seems to be eventuating is a gross pattern of selective admission to opportunity. Minority group individuals whose social characteristics vary most widely from the dominant white middle-class norms are largely excluded. If they are not actually excluded, access is so severely qualified and rationalized as to leave the great mass of the Negro community outside the pale of favor. Integration then comes to be regarded as a special privilege to be accorded selectively and not a right to be claimed on the basis of common citizenship and humanity. The process becomes further distorted when there emerges, as in the current day, a philosophy of cultural determinism (in the form of cultural deprivation theory) that provides an "explanation" for the continuation of inequities.

Much of this has remained below the surface in current discourse, but in the crescendo of programs aimed at educational remediation and the reclamation of the so-called "poverty group" in society the assumptions are now quite explicit and inescapable. The danger lies in the fact that we may be in process of creating a massive pathological Negro image or, even more, a special social class driven to a new kind of awareness as an outcast group by the very programs created to address their social disabilities. Although these consequences are unintended, they nevertheless reflect a syndrome characterizing low-income groups and ghetto inhabitants, with primary reference to Negroes in general. To the extent that cultural determinism is inferred, the effect is not unlike that of a new form of racial ideology.

There is also a preoccupation with "Negro apathy" and low motivation in the face of the kind of confrontation that the integration process has brought to bear. Although it is insufficient to dismiss these considerations as further expressions of either middle-class or dominant group prejudice, they nevertheless infer valuations which suggest that the Negro "ought" to measure up to the range of new opportunities now that the doors have been opened. To launch programs of reform aimed singularly at these factors may prove to be both illusive and unworthy.

Strategic Implications

This doubtless represents another case of wrong emphasis on a single element of the circular causation in which the Negro in America is caught, but it does suggest that in the effective effort to create social knowledge useful to the improvement of race relations a major—indeed *the* major —consideration is strategic. The task at hand now requires departures that are not just palliative but address themselves to the tasks both of lessening the differentials between Negro and white opportunity and, at the same time, changing the conditions that define Negro disadvantage. It is a task that Fein has described as effecting a "redistribution of the fruits of progress" rather than engaging in a battle "over the spoils of war." [16] The difficult but essential functions to be performed will require skill and balance in keeping the tactical goals on target and, even more, of providing the kind of input that will sustain the dynamics required for continued prodding of the sluggish and resisting racial system.

---

[16] Rashi Fein, "Economic and Social Profile," *Daedalus*, Vol. 94, No. 4 (Fall 1965), p. 842.

Race, Class, and Culture in the Sociopolitics of Social Welfare

HYLAN LEWIS

Even before the shocking reminder given by the riots that swept the country in 1967, it was clear to many people that the key problems of the metropolis, and therefore the nation, stem from the consequences of the increasing separation of the Negro and the poor from the white and the middle class by the coinciding lines of race and ethnicity, income, education, and residence. And there was awareness too that the problem of understanding race relations in the metropolis today is all the more difficult because the data have changed in detail and meaning more rapidly than social theory, research methods, and public and private ways of thinking and talking. A factor in the changes and in the future of race relations is the emergence of new patterns of social stratification, affecting and involving Negroes as well as whites. Class

Hylan Lewis, Ph.D., is Professor of Sociology, Brooklyn College, City University of New York, Brooklyn, New York, and Fellow, Metropolitan Applied Research Center, New York, New York.

along with race is assuming new political relevance in the metropolitan area.

The orientation and the content of this paper are strongly influenced by the shadow of the midsummer riots of 1967. First some thoughts about these disruptions and their implications for perceptions of race, class, and social welfare will be presented. The author's general preoccupation will be some features of the sociopolitics of race, class, and social welfare. There will be concern for such matters as the politicization of race relations, the semantic variable in race and class relations, the effect of certain research emphases and methods on perceptions of race and race relations, and the implication of these for social welfare concepts and policies and for public expectations.

Race, class, and culture are three interrelated ways of framing and labeling behavior; they have great popular as well as scientific usage. They impinge on and color thinking and policy about social welfare in critical ways. One of the reasons they are controversial and fraught with emotion and conflict is that many public and private decisions made in their name arbitrarily affect the chances, reputations, and treatment of whole categories of the population, especially Negroes and the poor.

The issues and stakes involved in race, class, and culture are political as well as scientific, moral as well as behavioral, semantic as well as factual, pragmatic as well as sentimental. A key task of behavioral science research in relation to social welfare should be to open people's eyes to the manner in which policy is affected by interests and tensions related to or perceived in terms of race, class, and culture.

A New Perspective

The explosive violence of Newark, Detroit, Los Angeles, and other cities has thrown a harsh and bright light on contemporary race relations, relative class positions, and outlooks. These events have signaled the return to race relations with a vengeance; they underscore the fact that the tension and struggle between Negro and white, rich and poor have become intensely political—and in ways that are at once both new and sophisticated and old and atavistic. The events dramatize the active belief of many, especially the poor and Negroes, that despite many new programs and some changes, the most important things affecting relations between Negroes and whites have changed little—the uneven distribution of power, respect, prosperity, and the many subsidies and unearned increments in education, housing, and selective income guarantees and supports enjoyed proportionately more by whites and the middle class in our expanding economy. The events have also underscored Haggstrom's description of how the attitudes that maintain and enforce a split social structure along racial and income lines perpetuate tension between rich and poor, black and white.

People isolate and segregate those they fear and pity. The stronger of the two communities has traditionally acted to alleviate the results perceived to be undesirable without changing the relationship of the two communities or ending the division into two communities. *Since persons designing and implementing such programs did not consider the consequences of the division for their aims, they were able to maintain an intention to bring the poor into their society.* [Italics added.] [1]

The recent upheavals have demonstrated also that perceptions of race and of race relations change quickly under some circumstances. They show that Negroes and the poor are defined by what they do as well as by what is done to and for them. What a small fraction of urban Negroes did during the riots caused sharp changes in perceptions of Negroes and the poor and in race relations: the violent Negro (and poor), the angry Negro (and poor), the rebel Negro (and poor), the arrogant Negro (and poor), and, for some, the animal, savage Negro lately have come to join the effective cast of the interracial drama that heretofore featured, if not starred, the inarticulate, alienated, passive, responsible, deserving, and undeserving Negro (and poor). Now, as before, what Negroes—or a significant proportion of that category—are called and how they are perceived or defined affect significantly public and private views of what people can or want to do about them and what they want to do or feel confident to do about themselves in relation to welfare, education, and local government, for example.

The Politics of Language

Deutscher observes that there is a constant and deliberate process by which people attempt magically to change phenomena by changing their names through

---

[1] Warren C. Haggstrom, "The Power of the Poor," in Louis A. Ferman, Joyce C. Kornbluh, and Alan Haber, eds., *Poverty in America* (Ann Arbor: University of Michigan Press, 1965), pp. 325–326.

the application of euphemisms or epithets.[2] Of course, any number can play the essentially political game of renaming friends, antagonists, targets, and programs. Efforts are thus made to change the system and its alignments as well as to maintain the status quo. Because language can both reflect and shape changes in attitudes, agendas, and priorities, politically conscious Negroes are changing names and inventing new slogans and epithets—black instead of Negro, Black Power, whitey, honkie, and the like—to change conceptions of themselves as well as of others, mobilize followers, keep opponents off balance, and influence the rate and schedule of change.[3] A revolution means a new language.

Revolution implies . . . the speaking of a previously unheard of language. . . . The emergence of another kind of logic, operations with other proofs. . . . Each major revolution has used another style of argument, a way of thinking which prerevolutionary men simply could not conceive or understand. . . . *Once men begin to talk according to the new syntax of a major revolution, a rupture of meaning has occurred; and the old and the new type of men appear insane to each other.* [Italics added.] [4]

Another earlier result of the Negro revolution that has been hardened and hastened by the recent violence is the resurfacing of ethnicity and race as crucial reference points in assessing the adequacy of persons and institutions and its translation into eth-

---

[2] Irwin C. Deutscher, "Notes on Language and Human Conduct," 1967, pp. 35–36. (Mimeographed.)

[3] The evocation and aggressive affirmation of blackness are partly instrumental, inasmuch as blackness sharpens the dichotomy between Negroes and whites and changes the rules of the name game for them. It represents an inversion of symbols. Skin color among Negroes runs the gamut, thus hair type and styling (*au naturel*) are as important physical signs of blackness as skin color.

[4] Alfred Meusel, "Revolution and Counter Revolution," *Encyclopaedia of the Social Sciences*, Vol. 13 (New York: Macmillian Co., 1932), p. 370.

nic and class political behavior. This has been the result of the multiplication of direct confrontations, near-misses, and sideswipes between Negroes and whites. At bottom this reflects explicit testing of whether and how soon some of the legal spoils, protections, and resources of society are ready to be democratized. Changes in the political relevance of ethnicity and race have been triggered and reinforced more by the heating up of attitudes of both Negroes and whites when Negroes pressed to share old privileges and increments of whites— many unearned—and whites, especially those in ethnic groups, resisted or resented this. There is a chance that the mainspring of the new ethnicity—a resurgence of racial feelings in this context—is based more on the coincidence in pragmatic interests of specific individuals, families, entrepreneurs, and politicians than on any sudden welling up of collective consciousness and group memories. The resurgence of consciousness of being white and a member of an ethnic group that comes with resistance to change and confrontations in education, housing, and jobs has its response in an affirmation of being black. The initial driving forces of the new white ethnicity and black consciousness were at least as pragmatic as they were sentimental. They are reflexive as well as instrumental.

The word and concept "black" are undergoing an aggressive and rapid affirmation and upgrading in partial response to ethnic and class invidiousness, especially in the areas of family, child-rearing, sex, and learning ability. These changes have important implications for welfare and educational policies, inasmuch as the aggressive demonstration of desires and demands for self, family, and children often run counter to the statistics and theory, as well as the capacity and will, of the community.

Today, ethnicity and race are not only used to identify segments of the population but also to reaffirm, refurbish, and claim heritages, some of which never existed. And they are used as critical variables along which to measure and to try to explain differences in family structures and family behavior and in the calculated and perceived competence and achievements of groups and individuals.

Contemporary Conceptions

Although race, class, and culture are demonstrably dynamic rather than static variables, undergoing accelerated modification, strenuous efforts are made to freeze these forces in order to develop the illusion of understanding and mastering them. Either in the framing and conduct of investigation in these contexts or in the selective reception accorded to the results of such studies, research is vulnerable to serious distortions deriving from social and political commitments. A review of some of the contemporary conceptions about the Negro family, culture- and class-typical behavior, and racially specific characteristics reveals the appeal of simple explanations for complex processes.

The Negro Family

A popular thought and feeling pattern goes something like this: (1) The Irish, the Jews, the Italians, the Poles, the Japanese, the Chinese, and other immigrant groups all made it or are making it in American society. (2) All these groups have had or now have stable family structures, with two parents, strong fathers, and low rates of illegitimacy. (3) The key factor for all groups that have made it and are making it in American society is the family. (4) The American Negro has not made it and is not making it in American society with the same measurable success as European and Asian immigrant groups and their descendants. (5) The American Negro characteristically does not have a stable family situation; there are large numbers of one-parent, female-headed families, illegitimacy

rates are high, and the male is frequently absent or unable to act effectively as husband and father. (6) The Negro is the only racial or ethnic group with a persistently high rate of family instability. (7) The key reason the Negro is not making it in American society and is not likely to make it in the near future is this family instability, which contributes to a "tangle of pathology."

Laying aside for the moment the merits of this simplistic, but popular, view of the interrelations among ethnicity, race, and the family on the American scene today, and holding in abeyance numerous questions about the factual basis of some of these assertions, attention will be called now to some important points that are often overlooked. First, it is never just the family alone, it is the family and its extra-family supports that count insofar as viability and child-rearing options are concerned. Especially in modern urban society, the image of the redoubtable family prevailing against or in spite of the world is romantic but unreal. Second, the fragility of families on the American scene is related primarily to structural and situational factors, not to ethnic or racial traits. Third, family capacity to cope with failure and prosperity, unemployment and employment is not ethnically grounded. In some ways, although not entirely, the problems the statistics of pathology present—much crime, vice, and illegitimacy, for example —are not so much the results of the failure of established families as they are of the inability or unwillingness of young adults, mainly male, to try to launch a viable family and maintain it through the critical first phase. In a certain wry sense, some students and critics of the Negro family are referring to a family that has never had a full chance for existence and therefore has never been tried. A part of the problem is the young family that never was, that never got going.[5]

----

[5] A version of this discussion was first presented by Hylan Lewis in "New Perceptions of

Statistical and Social Reality

Among the assumptions of much of social research and its interpretations are that there is considerable homogeneity and stability of types and norms among the disadvantaged; that the values of the poor and of Negroes are significantly different from those of the rest of the population; that certain family structures and sexual roles are characteristic of the poor, the lower class, and Negroes, and that these are indications of and productive of unstable families; and that the lower-class condition and the persistence of its characteristic pathologies are related to the imperatives of race, class, and cultural values. Material from a five-year study of low-income families conducted by the author in Washington, D.C., in the early 1960's suggests, however, that the theory and method associated with the cultural and class approach are themselves conducive to neglecting the significant variability among the poor and within classes statistically described. Homogeneity is inferred or asserted and statistical regularities may exist that are not indicative of the range and context of behavior.

The field materials . . . indicate that the low-income parents in this study group—whether they are adequate or inadequate, dependent or not dependent—tend to show greater conformity to, and convergence with, middle-class family and child-rearing standards in what they say they want (or would like to want) for their children and themselves than in their actual child-rearing behavior. This was evident in . . . such matters as parental concerns and control, self-appraisal, education, and sex and illegitimacy.

That much of a basic strain toward conformity to standard values and practices among low-income families is missed or ignored is probably due to tendencies to underestimate heterogeneity, variability, and change. Paradoxically enough, this is due in part to the effort to be scientific or to the uncritical adoption and application of selected findings or concepts. Prime examples are the use of the terms "culture" or "subculture" to describe behavior under contemporary urban conditions and of summary statistics alone to indicate social characteristics of an area. Although it may not be intended, concepts and statistics too frequently are interpreted as indicating a kind of homogeneity and a degree of regularity that are just not present.

For social welfare practice this kind of trying to say the most with the least about complex, multi-dimensional behavior is often premature and dangerous. Loose use of concepts and too great a dependency on statistics only tend to obscure and—what is worse for social welfare practice—to dehumanize.[6]

The riots uncovered something about the location and the spearheading of active discontent in the ghetto that puzzled some people at first: The most poor were not the most active. And this was despite an old social science proposition that has been around a long time: The locus of active discontent in a relatively fluid society is among those who are marginal, not the worst off. Those who have an acute sense of being blocked in movement toward commonly valued goals are the most likely to act out their frustration, bitterness, and anger. Yet much of the massive but still inadequate investments of the federal government in depressed areas and in volatile areas since the Watts riots have been toward helping the hard-core poor, with a prime goal being the dampening of ghetto tension and lessening of the chances of violence. If a primary aim of assistance and rehabilitation programs is to dampen tension—and this is not necessarily a social welfare goal—the programs appear to have sadly missed the mark, and not just because

---

the Family: New Agenda, Different Rhetoric," pp. 14–16. Paper presented at the Forty-third Annual Conference of the Child Study Association of America, New York City, March 1967. (Mimeographed.)

[6] Hylan Lewis, "Child-Rearing Practices Among Low-Income Families," in *Case Work Papers, 1961* (New York: Family Service Association of America, 1961).

of inadequate resources and money. The important point is that this was not due to any lack of knowledge about the fact that those marginal to the system are most likely to act in revolt. In looking for reasons for this miscalculation in supporting programs and distributing funds to those potentially less volatile, although no less needful, it might be useful to examine the extent to which some assumptions and false perceptions of the range and quality of poverty-related behavior in the Negro ghetto, related to the culture of poverty and to the lower-class culture, helped this miscalculation and possibly led to failure to achieve effective tension reduction when and where it was needed most.

Racially Specific Characteristics

A distinguished social scientist has suggested that the social sciences "have succeeded admirably in documenting the prevalence and persistence of white-Negro differences, and in demonstrating the social rather than biological origins of most of these differences." [7] Yet many social scientists have actually contributed to and reinforced the sense of significant cleavage between Negro and white, rich and poor, with their overriding preoccupation with differences and by the use of theories and methodologies designed to document statistically significant differences that need not be socially significant, not to mention generally valid. Many scattered surveys, both major and minor, and many analyses that use census data are concerned with discovering and documenting racial differences from assertedly "hard" data. Frequently the term hard data is used to intimidate and silence valid questions about assumptions, qualifications, and units of data. This preoccupation with race, class, subcultural, and

area differences is on the increase, and for reasons of policy and politics as much as for reasons of science. Data and findings for one or more of these different kinds of units are frequently used interchangeably or for improper inferences about the others.

There is a swing now toward reassessing the role of genetic factors or biosocial forces in social competence. This coincides with the interest in stressing cultural and structural factors as the cause of presumably stable and essentially irreversible differences in learning capacities and in social competence among Negroes and the lower classes. And, of course, all this coincides with the revival of ethnic and race consciousness and, despite euphemisms such as culturally deprived, adds to race consciousness and invidiousness.

Glass says that the variation in emphasis on genetic thinking can be attributed partially to the sociopolitical attitudes prevalent among scientists during a given period. These shifts have affected social welfare practice, policies, and legislation.

Genetic thinking in the sciences of human behavior and infrahuman behavior has ranged from extreme emphasis on genetic determinism to virtual denial of the importance of heritability. . . . Liberal attitudes are presumed to be correlated with acceptance of an environmental approach, whereas conservative attitudes are thought to be more compatible with a genetic view of behavior. . . . Contemporary social scientists no longer adhere to a simplistic environmental determinism, just as contemporary biologists no longer embrace a genetic determinism. In both fields the importance of an interaction between the organism and his environment is recognized. Neither the genetic parameter nor the environmental parameter alone can account for more than a portion of behavioral variability. [8]

Pettigrew, in a review of the literature on the Negro American personality, pointed to the narrow framework of previous research and the admixture of policy,

[7] Karl E. Taeuber, "Negro Population and Housing," p. 1. Unpublished paper, 1967. (Mimeographed.)

[8] David Glass, "Genetics and Social Behavior," *Items*, Social Science Research Council, Vol. 21, No. 1 (March 1967), p. 1.

human, and scientific considerations in psychological research on race:

. . . attention has been concentrated on such areas as intelligence which are related but not central to personality. The popularity of such research can be traced to the century long debates over racial superiority and inferiority. Up through the 1920's the vast majority of these psychological studies supported the theories of white superiority. . . . The 1930's witnessed sharp change. Though still crude in some respects, a new series of more rigorous race studies appeared that emphasized environmental factors and answered racists' claims. In this sense, there was a defensive quality to these newer studies; but less defensive, more carefully controlled research of the past two decades has replicated and confirmed the basic findings and conclusions of the 1930's.[9]

In summary, Pettigrew asks and seeks to provide answers to the question "Why isn't more known about the Negro American personality?" yet he does not indicate what should be known about this asserted phenomenon, and why. He writes in the same paragraph about "the Negro's personality" and "the Negro American personality." Without quibbling as to whether these are the same thing, there is a basic question as to whether "the Negro American personality" is a valid concept, and certainly whether it is a relatively stable reality, tied primarily to ethnicity. These are the prior questions. Further, do we actually know as much or more about "the white American personality" as "the Negro personality"? The personality traits of American Negroes can best be understood in the contexts of (1) the interaction, direct and indirect, of Negroes with whites and (2) the effects on different Negroes of rapid changes in the quality of their relations with whites. An understanding of the personalities of different whites and of the changes in both race and class relations is essential to any full understanding of the personalities of Negroes.

It is also true that class and race are heterogeneous and variable, and in important ways one variable intervenes with another: race perceptions and identity are buffered by class. There have been numerous efforts recently to interrelate race, class, culture, and personality in order to explain and therefore to affect public policy and private opinion, wittingly or unwittingly, with respect to low-income Negroes, ghetto residents, the culturally deprived, and socially disadvantaged children. Among the better known works that postdate Frazier, Allison Davis, and Gunnar Myrdal are Clark's *Dark Ghetto,* Lewis' *La Vida,* Gan's *The Urban Villagers,* Moynihan's *The Negro Family,* Miller's various descriptions of lower-class culture, and Lee Rainwater and his associates' studies of lower-class behavior in St. Louis.[10]

One of the examples of the recent preoccupation of many students with lower-class Negroes' personalities and family behavior is in the research of Lee Rainwater and his associates, based mainly on the residents of a high-rise public housing project in St. Louis. Rainwater suggests that three kinds of survival strategies are encouraged in Negro slum worlds and they are represented as an ideal-typical sequence:

. . . *the expressive life cycle* . . . an effort to make yourself interesting and attractive to others so that you are better able to manipulate their behavior. . . . When the expressive strategy fails or when it is unavailable there is . . . the temptation to adopt a *violent strategy* in which you force others to give you

---

[9] Thomas F. Pettigrew, "Negro American Personality: Why Isn't More Known?" *Journal of Social Issues,* Vol. 20, No. 2 (April 1964), p. 5.

[10] Kenneth B. Clark, *Dark Ghetto* (New York: Harper & Row, 1965); Oscar Lewis, *La Vida* (New York: Random House, 1967); Herbert J. Gans, *The Urban Villagers: Group and Class in the Life of Italian-Americans* (New York: Free Press of Glencoe, 1962); Daniel P. Moynihan, *The Negro Family: A Case for National Action* (Washington, D.C.: U.S. Government Printing Office, 1965); Walter B. Miller, "Lower Class Culture As a Generating Milieu of Gang Delinquency," *Social Problems,* Vol. 9, No. 1 (Summer 1961); Lee Rainwater, "Crucible of Identity: The Negro Lower Class Family," in "The Negro American, Part 2," *Daedalus,* Vol. 95, No. 1 (Winter 1966).

what you need. . . . Finally, and increasingly as members . . . grow older, there is the *depressive strategy* in which goals are increasingly constricted to the bare necessities of survival.

Most lower-class people follow mixed strategies, as Walter Miller has observed, alternating among the excitement of the expressive style, the desperation of the violent style, and the deadness of the depressed style.[11]

This kind of analysis, although it purports to be ideal-typical, has many limitations, is likely to be misleading, and is of questionable use for guiding policy-making. It is questionable (1) if these are pervasive lower-class phenomena characteristic of most lower-class Negroes in the slums, (2) how this behavior really differs from that of other socioeconomic classes and other racial and ethnic lower classes, (3) whether "the temptation to adopt a violent strategy" is a social style or personality trait or the result of the interaction of a certain person with an objective condition, and (4) whether the time sequence of the strategies suggested is as empirically grounded as it should be (the onset of the depressive phase is related to growing older and to the constriction of goals "to the bare necessities of survival"; among people in poverty, the need for constriction of goals to the bare necessities of survival is a constant, recurrent thing, not necessarily correlated with age). What kinds of programs would be based on such ambiguous premises and propositions about Negro slum-dwellers and the Negro lower class, based mainly on life in a massive public housing project, except improvement in the amount and flow of income and possibly the breakup of the ghetto, beginning with the dispersion or reorganization of public housing?

Camille Jeffers, while a member of the Washington study staff, lived for fifteen months in a public housing project as a participant-observer. A number of prop-

ositions about the quality of life among the poor who have come to or are nearing the chronic feeling that their future is not theirs are presented in and suggested by her report. The following propositions are presented in the author's Introduction to Jeffers' *Living Poor:*

(1) In the main, parents who are poor know what they want for their children and themselves.

They want and prefer better food, shelter, clothing, education, and more stable family unions, geared to supporting and cooperative husbands and fathers; and they want the level and flow of money income that will enable them not only to get or achieve these things themselves, but that also will reduce their continuing vulnerability to little lacks—to poverty-contingencies involving food, shelter, and health.

(2) There is a pattern of social differentiation among the poor in public housing that is based more on differences in the extent to which families think they have the power or potential to change status—to escape public housing, than it is on life styles, education, and income level.

This is true despite indications that small absolute differences in income can make for relatively large differences in outlook and behavior in the poor category, in as well as out of public housing.

(3) The lack of sufficient money and its irregular flow restrict child rearing options and force a continuous shuffling and re-shuffling of priorities among food, shelter, clothing, health, educational, recreational, and other demands.

(4) The presumed inability of some poor parents to delay gratification is less a matter of weak will, small self-control, weak stamina, or lower class norms than it is a matter of realistic and rational responses to chronic uncertainty, of conditioned reflexes related to constant vulnerability to the big and little contingencies of poverty.

"I just have to let tomorrow take care of itself" is frequently more a matter of realism based on experience than an indication of irresponsibility and of freedom from caring about self and children.

Certain aspects of the behavior of many poor are therefore better characterized as contingency-oriented rather than present-oriented.

(5) The most rejected and frowned upon problem behavior of many poor parents is often less a matter of not knowing better, or

---

[11] *Op. cit.,* pp. 206–207.

of not having the ability to act differently, than it is a matter of fluctuating mood; mood is critically related to the presence and absence of money with which to satisfy wants— to exercise a minimum of self-determination.

(6) Many of the urban poor straddle poverty and affluence. They may exhibit complex, fluctuating, puzzling and sometimes what appears to be bizarre and aggressive mixtures of the living situations and styles, possessions and tastes of different classes; and they may have more linkages with relatives and friends who have "made it," or who are upwardly mobile via occupation and education than we are wont to think.

This suggests the crucial importance of understanding the open quality and very fluid aspects of the contemporary lower middle class among urban Negroes.

(7) To understand the influence of poverty it is necessary to examine the expansion and shrinkage of the repertory of family roles in response to poor parents' child rearing needs and to what is happening in the community.

There are indications that the older child in some poor families is in a particularly vulnerable position; that he is more likely to be isolated in the family and to have a less satisfactory relationship with the mother because of the relative absence of play experience, for example.

(8) The family environment of a poor family may fluctuate markedly over relatively brief periods of child rearing time. Opportunities for growth and development may vary markedly among children of different ages and ordinal positions; for example, speech patterns often vary markedly among children of the same family.

(9) The lives of parents in many poor families in and out of housing projects are marked by extreme loneliness.

The loneliness of the poor is accentuated by awareness of the lack of self-determination and of the disproportionate vulnerability to small lacks and to the unpredictable.

(10) Families in the housing project with the most inadequate and uncertain incomes "appeared to have the most extensive communication network in the project."

These are ad hoc networks, essential for survival. They facilitate the elementary exchange of small goods and services among people constantly caught with small lacks.[12]

---

[12] Hylan Lewis, Introduction to Camille Jeffers, *Living Poor: A Participant Observer Study of Choices and Priorities* (Ann Arbor, Mich.: Ann Arbor Publishers, 1967), pp. iv–v.

Implications

Understanding and solidly grounded action in this turbulent field of forces requires a perspective that is broad and flexible enough to accommodate the powerful extra-individual forces that are shaping and elaborating the definitions of race, class, and culture and that may become decisive in altering the tendency toward polarization of the Negro and the poor from the white and the middle class. The indication that there is "a large and growing group of educated people and they do not belong to either the old, or the new middle class" is of critical importance when attempting any prognosis of race relations and social welfare.[13] One has to weigh the probability that the new groups will seek to exercise strategic power and the possibility that they will use it to develop new formulas for the distribution of income and services, perhaps on behalf of disadvantaged poor and Negroes—especially the lower middle-class Negro.

One example of an explicit by-product of changes in perceptions of both race relations stances and roles and of social welfare functions is the emergence of the idea of the guaranteed minimum income as a matter of national interest and inquiry and its immediate adoption by increasingly politically conscious civil rights groups. Another is the affirmation and public implementation of the legal rights of the poor and the eventual translation of the idea into the concept and political strategy of welfare rights. The organization and strategy are designed to obtain the maximum the law permits and to enroll all those eligible on the welfare rolls, thus placing an impossible administrative and fiscal strain on the unsatisfactory system. The politicization of race relations is a part of the general tendency to attempt to reduce powerlessness

---

[13] Michael Harrington, "The Middle Class: Whose Camp Is It In?" *Village Voice*, June 1, 1967, p. 6.

—to increase options, personal competence, and the efficiency of local institutions through maximum participation and sharing in their control.

These developments raise important questions for which new research orientations and strategies might be developed. Approaches that more effectively penetrate the intrafamilial and intra-individual system and that accommodate the rich variability of life experience are needed. And if anything can be learned from our history, it is evident that more effective ways of communicating the results of our efforts must be found.

The public policy problems have been made more urgent, not changed in their essentials, by the recent surge of violent protest and destruction. We must learn how to achieve an optimum and efficient distribution of income, space, services, and, important now, social reputations for social adequacy, normal learning capacity, and disposition toward family stability. These are at once problems of race relations, class, and politics.[14] They indicate the new salience of race along with class in local decision-making processes.

---

[14] For an example of a major effort to describe and analyze the issues, stakes, and processes involved, *see* Lee Rainwater and William Yancy, *The Moynihan Report: The Politics of Controversy* (Cambridge, Mass.: MIT Press, 1967).

The metropolis is now a matrix of local political arenas loosely held together by transportation, the economic interdependence of unequal areas, races, and classes. Today's vigorous and fluid race relations are at once a test and an acute manifestation of the working out of the necessary formulas for local democratic participation and sharing in decision-making. Decisions about social welfare, income maintenance, and education are among the most critical. Specifically, research and experimentation to test the feasibility of various kinds of income maintenance and the validity of fears about the effects of direct income subsidy on motivation are especially needed. Similarly, experiments in local self-government and self-help are indicated. Some research is needed as well on the two most strategic classes on the urban scene— the lower middle class, both Negro and white, and the new middle class of educated, unaligned technicians, managers, and computer experts. The lower middle class is the real test of whether the mobility system with its capacity for conversion into middle-class status is working and of how it works for different groups at different times. The new middle class might move to exercise the balance of power in political decisions affecting social welfare. Whether it does or not can make a big difference in race relations and welfare.

Discussion

Discussion of the three papers that comprise Part I of this report of the Institute on Research Toward Improving Race Relations was aimed at finding a frame of reference that would clarify the nature of Negro-white transactions. With some reluctance, the institute participants were persuaded to accept a construction of race as the decisive social-psychological reality, a construction more relevant to the contemporary scene than the conceptions of class and minority status. Reluctance to adopt a racial conception of the problem stemmed, on the one hand, from aversion toward a viewpoint that has such an odious history and a lack of scientific support and, on the other, from the attraction of conceptions that highlight similarities among people and their social experiences.

BLUMER. The matter which confronts us in American society is, however, a racial problem—decidedly so!

Favoring adoption of a class context was the knowledge that Negro-white comparisons within class or economic strata regularly reveal greater similarities than differences. Through the introduction of control over the class variable, differences in mortality rates, educational achievements, and family structure and composition, for example, are eliminated or reduced to a point below socially, if not statistically, significant levels. And while there was no disposition among the participants to abandon the conception of socioeconomic status as a mediating variable, it was acknowledged that class formulations, in isolation, fail to identify some essential realities in the developing social scene.

Similar arguments were advanced about the conception of minority status. Without a doubt, Negroes constitute a minority group in America, but this perspective fails to explain the profound differences in the treatment of the Negro from the reception accorded other minority groups.

LONG. We have gotten out of the classical theoretical context of race relations in the case of every group but the Negro. I consider this too limiting and unfortunate. Race relations today in the popular conception are Negro-white relations.

Seen as central to the present circumstances was an evolving, socially imposed construction of race, the product of interaction between Negro and white. Blumer made the point bluntly:

BLUMER.   American white people are not ready to accept Negroes in the way they have accepted members of the European minority groups. There is no question at all that we draw a color line and, while that line is shifting, it is still there. It appears now to approach the most critical area, an area to which Negroes are most sensitive— being accepted in intimate and personal relations.

The response of Negroes to life in a racist society was widely and recurrently acknowledged by the participants to be an increasingly powerful force directed toward placing the problem in a racial context. It was observed that the Negro, having been saddled with racism, was in the process of finding ways to make an advantage of this. Negro militants in particular were seen to be seeking to elevate the status of the category "black."

BATCHELDER.   The Negro himself is now beginning to assert and to define the situation in his own terms, and this may really be the most important thing for us.

The transactional and evolving conception of race that participants were invited to adopt was distinguished from the static conception of race that had fostered the study of Negro characteristics. The attempt to define Negro characteristics was viewed by Long as "a kind of trap in which the Negro is made unique and thereby an aura of mystery becomes associated with him as a social entity." Challenged too was the assumption of independence among the variables in comparative studies of Negroes and whites. For most theoretical and practical problems, data purporting to locate Negroes as a group with respect to whites were regarded as irrelevant.

These ideas were examined against the experience of the participants in an effort to evaluate and qualify them. One discussant observed, for example, that the doctrine of self-help, central to other ethnic minorities, has not been prominent in the experience of Negroes. Because this led into what he could think of only as the special characteristics of the Negro, a uniqueness, he asked if this view were really inappropriate.

LONG.   Yes, because I think it is a dead end.

LEWIS.   It also exacerbates the problem.

JEROME COHEN.   But I think that this is a difficult question. I happen to be interested in social characteristics; it is part of my work. I think I can avoid seeing social characteristics outside social institutional changes, but rather as part of that whole complex of activities. To deny the existence of social characteristics, however, throws out my whole set of lenses.

BLUMER.   What I would very much urge be done, then, if you are going to use this conceptual equipment, is to recognize it as a developing social structure and not get trapped into the idea that it is already there and organized.

The conception of race as a product of social transactions served both to draw concern away from the subject of Negro characteristics and to highlight instead the participation of the white community in racial affairs.

HERZOG.   I think we know remarkably little about how to get people to change in the direction of perhaps giving up what they conceive as their self-interest.

Underlying this discussion was the assumption that the dominant white group, as the senior partner in the genesis of what are now termed racial problems, must accept a proportional share of the responsibility for finding solutions to these problems.

Perspectives on Change in Race Relations

With the evidence so abundantly at hand, it was not surprising that the view that race relations are in the process of changing was accepted unanimously. Because of the ongoing transformation in Negro-white relationships, it seemed less appropriate to establish in detail the exact nature of the present circumstances than to detect the major thrust of the movements and identify the forces likely to shape their course.

Divergent views were expressed about the relevance of available theory to the developing pattern of race relations. The dominant view was that the tides and currents in racial interactions highlight a vacuum in social science theory. Existing theory was believed by some to offer little insight into the dynamic processes of interest here. Psychological theory was cited, for example, as better attuned to explaining the transmission of culture than to its change.

NATHAN COHEN. Many of the theories . . . have nothing to do with the social change processes that we are involved in today.

Other participants saw the value of one or several theoretical contexts. Constellations of ideas about identity formation, organizational and social system analysis, power in the political arena, as well as socioeconomic and minority status were introduced in the effort to illuminate the changes in race relations.

Evolution or Revolution?

The riots and the rhetoric of the new leaders gave one participant the "sense of being in the middle of the French Revolution and sitting around talking about how we are going to research it." The term revolution was used occasionally by other discussants. The implication that social changes in race relations constitute a revolution was, however, sharply challenged:

NORTHWOOD. We are so unaccustomed to any kind of social change at all that we consider what is going on as a revolution. I don't think that there is any revolution going on.

If anything, it is a counter-revolution or consolidation of a conservative situation in this country. A revolution, to me, means a major transformation of our institutions. We are living through a series of rapid changes—automation and its effects. . . . But if we conceptualize what we are in as a political revolution, it shows how far we are from understanding things.

While no one seriously argued that a revolution is presently going on in this country, Lewis' view, that the tempo of change in race relations has quickened, was generally accepted. And in efforts to envision the future, the prospect of revolution could not be excluded summarily. One observer argued that our nation is at the beginning of something that could be revolutionary—an attempt to throw off colonial rule. In this view, we are presently on the borderline between a reform movement and a revolutionary movement, the course of which will be influenced by the capacity of the social system for making the kinds of adjustments needed. If the current expressive Negro violence should shift to organized political violence, it was speculated that a short-lived revolutionary period could ensue, to be terminated by military force. No participant was aware of serious systematic attempts to organize the Negro community for revolution. The point was made, however, that Negro communities are becoming more organized for change activities, perhaps for protest activities, and if concessions are not granted at the rate required to sustain this push, the same kind of organizational structure could shift to revolutionary activity.

LAUE. We see a sentiment growing among people who aren't connected with any group now, but who will emerge into groups as they find the situation getting more and more unbearable, as they find society stiffening, and as they find virtually no change in their life situation.

NATHAN COHEN. The evidence derived from the Watts riots indicates that there is a sizable percentage of people who may not belong to extremist groups but who have great sympathy for what those groups are doing.

Changing Negro Identity

In reviewing his paper, Long pointed to changes in orientation among different generations of Negroes by asking the following:

LONG. Why are young Negroes of this generation willing literally to take a chance with their lives, as no previous generations were? These young people have been taught quite opposite ways from the previous generations—taught that in a sense they are not Negroes. At the same time perceptually they are clearly Negroes, because they see evidence all around them that confirms their racial status. It is quite possible that there may be a kind of built-in conflict within the personality of the present generation because of this fact. . . . These young people have thus incorporated into their process of becoming conflicting dimensions of the process of identity.

Beyond confirming Long's observations, the ensuing discussion identified a number of social forces that were believed to have influenced the shifting identity of the Negro. Noted was the revolution in expectations that has occurred all over the world; the young Negro is rejecting the implication that there is any reason why he should not have a legitimate share in the fruits of society. The emergence of independent states in Africa and the struggle against colonialism were believed to have helped redefine the expectations of the Negro. An additional force cited was the sanctioned violence attending this country's present war footing. The limited opportunity to pursue social goals afforded by social institutions such as trade unions and the church was also seen to encourage the Negro to turn toward resources within his own community.

Negro Community, Leadership, and Representation

Lindsay objected to the use of the term "Negro community"; "There is no such thing." Community was seen to imply a nonexistent degree of homogeneity; the reality is that Negroes represent all socioeconomic levels, all shades of political opinion, and show all the diversity found in any other large grouping. Other participants were unwilling to abandon the conception of Negro community and sought ways to organize and grasp its heterogeneity. The chairman suggested differentiation into three component subgroups: *traditionalists*, in the DuBois talented-tenth conception, who have on the basis of individual talent and ability won a place in the existing culture; *survivalists*, the substantial minority who show up on the welfare rolls and in poverty surveys; and *militants and activists*, the 20–30 percent (chiefly urban youths) who see the value of collective rather than individual action. It was suggested that these subgroups differ in their concerns, in the responses they elicit from the white community, and in their relationship to social institutions, including social welfare. Laue subsequently introduced roughly comparable differentiations organized around the terms colored community, Negro community, and black community. Common to both formulations was the acknowledgment that the action today is in the militant black camp, and that Black Nationalism is growing.

LAUE. There is a great deal of intellectual activity in the ghettos and it is largely black oriented. [The movement is visible in] the black bookstores, the Afro-American societies, the way the kids are talking on the streets, the way they identify with what is going on in revolutions in other countries. They have become politicized in a way that most of the white community hasn't caught up with yet.

The conception of a Negro community, or Negro communities however differentiated, seemed to most participants inescapable. From his observation that increasingly Negroes are organizing and coming forward to assert a right to represent what they see as their interests, Gilbert concluded that the idea of Negro community, like the idea of race, is a current social reality: "I think that if we deny that Negroes have distinct interests, we are falling into a dangerous trap." Reed advanced the analysis by underscoring the transactional nature of the concept:

REED. There is, I think, a common set of problems that has evolved between whites and Negroes. Otherwise, I don't think there would be any purpose in a conference on race relations. All too often we don't really examine the components of either the white or Negro communities sufficiently.

The examination of Negro leadership followed a course parallel to that traced earlier. Viewpoints ranged from the position that Negro leadership is a fiction that exists only in the minds of white people to the position that Negro leadership is sufficiently stable and rationally achieved to permit it to be studied by general organizational or system theory.

Drawing from his study of post-Watts Los Angeles, Scoble introduced a distinction between Negro leaders and leaders of Negroes. Negro leaders are designated by the white community, either from ignorance of the sentiments present in the Negro community or through efforts to control or suppress the emergence of natural leadership. To illustrate, he cited the practice of some Los Angeles newspapers, which do not have any regular staff assigned to the Negro community, of identifying as a Negro leader anyone who chooses to pass out mimeographed statements from a downtown hotel suite. "The white news media are not concerned with the variety of experience in the Negro community." Interference by the white community in the development of leadership, as seen in the refusal of public officials to listen to indigenous leaders, was familiar to most participants.

Northwood referred to Weber's typology, which differentiates bureaucratic leaders, who occupy formal positions in established institutions, from charismatic leaders, who through the gifts of grace and influence are able to capture the imagination of people and assemble a following:

NORTHWOOD. It seems to me that there is a set of theories—some related to power, some to influence, some to position in organizations—that is relevant to the leadership of the Negro community.

Views of Negro representation ranged widely from an assertion of its unattainability to an assertion of its desirability as an action goal. It follows from the diversity of the Negro community that no one Negro can reasonably represent it. The symbolic value of the presence of Negro representation was regarded as important, however, since the board of a social agency, for example, speaks to the community generally and is part of the message transmitted by the agency. Orshansky observed that special interest representatives express a psychological principle: We believe we will be best understood by a person who is similar to us. A complication in the case of Negro representatives was recognized: In some segments of the Negro community distrust of the Establishment is so great that a representative would become suspect by virtue of his very association with an agency. Concern was expressed from one quarter that in attaining Negro representation an inadvertent form of co-optation could occur, thereby reducing the leadership available to and accepted by the Negro community.

Power

Concern with power permeated the discussion. If the analysis of the nature and dynamics of power was somewhat asystematic, conviction about the maldistribution of power and the salience of power for the problem of race relations was unanimous.

However conceived, the distribution of power was regarded as a problem, possibly *the* problem of our time. In the baldest terms, a majority group was seen to be holding down a minority group, giving it little in the way of resources or power. Since power is rarely surrendered willingly, the Negroes' efforts to acquire power were expected to create conflict. Manifestations of resistance to the transfer of power were seen in the disparity between the potential and actual achievements of the civil rights movement, and more dramatically in the responses of the Establishment to the 1967 riots.

The chairman introduced a view of a power elite that, through its manipulation of economic and other resources, operates in such a way as to restrict the development of programs and services that threaten established community interests. Termed the yo-yo theory, the withdrawal of support and suppression of power redistribution were said to have characterized local and national policy from Reconstruction to the present. Other discussants saw a more broadly spread institutionalized power network, inflexible and impenetrable by virtue of its complexity. For example, solidly entrenched and intricately operating city government can frustrate the development of desirable programs, and do so in a way that is impossible to trace. It was also observed that the American system exhibits a tremendous inertia, a tremendous capacity to resist change.

Power was seen to derive from money, organization, institutional position, weight of numbers, moral-ideological position, and protest and violence. Since the Negro lacks economic power and will foreseeably remain a minority in this country, organized sociopolitical lines seemed to offer the most promising avenue for expanding his power position. Wider community support for acquisition of power by the Negro seemed uncertain; gains elicited by ideological considerations and evoked by fear might be canceled by losses deriving from these identical circumstances. The course

through which a significant redistribution of power could be achieved, other than movement within the Negro community itself, was not clearly envisioned. Another of the interlocking forces that at every turn seemed to hamper action was encountered here. It was observed that mistrust on the part of the Negro is general enough to create skepticism about efforts by the white community to promote the growth of Negro power.

Conflict versus Consensus

In a lengthy and technical paper not reproduced in this monograph, Northwood and Reed included an historical review of sociological conceptions about the course of social change:

The Course of Social Change

Comte and Spencer, early systems thinkers, rejected any serious proposals for man to change the body politic as forms of interference with the inevitable and progressive laws of social development. For them, society was based on consensus, order, and equilibrium, "best understood as a contractual or informal agreement made between equals to secure a common goal." [1] Consensus was viewed as a necessary condition for the emergence of social structure, the allocation of positions in society, the establishment of group cohesion, collective representations, and common traditions. On the other hand, conflict was seen as extraneous to social structure. "In short, consensus differs from conflict as organization differs from deviance." [2]

Positivistic organicism could hardly maintain "its claims as a form of science," according to Martindale, in view of its "failure to account for the facts of conflict that turn up

---

[1] I. L. Horowitz, *The War Game: Studies of the New Civilian Militarist* (New York: Ballantine Books, 1963), p. 149. *See* especially his cogent essay on "Conflict, Consensus and Cooperation," pp. 147–169.

[2] *Ibid.*, p. 152.

at every point. . . . Every society has its conflicts. No society can survive without individuals who face up to them." [3]

The first serious challenge to the naïve and untenable propositions of Comte and Spencer came at the time of the mid-nineteenth-century revolutionary struggles with the theories and polemics of Marx and Darwin and their followers. Thus began the dialogue between the conflict theorists and the consensus theorists about the nature of organization and change, a dialogue that is very much with us in the present.

The conflict theorists essentially view organization as the process and product of struggle and compromise among conflicting interest groups. It is part of an ever dynamic, evolutionary institutionalization that goes on at all times in society. The function of theory is to describe the process by means of concrete historical and sociological studies, especially the working of political and economic institutions. For Marxists, the theory must also serve as a polemic to guide the masses toward class-conscious activity to shape their own destiny.

What, then, are the concepts and orientations of the conflict theorists that contribute to the analysis of organization and change? These have been summarized generally in terms of notions that have characterized the theory for the hundred years since Marx. To be sure, much is left out in this listing, and the reader must turn elsewhere for amplification.[4]

> Proposition 1. *Social structure emerges not as an act of God or as the result of public consensus; it comes from the process of living together and interacting together.*

A social structure should be considered as a "dynamic balance of disharmonious parts subject to endless change and redefinition. . . . Thus, conflict situations are intrinsic and organic to social structure." [5] The function of conflicts is that they "tend to make possible the readjustment of norms and power

relations within groups in accordance with the felt needs of its individual members or subgroups." [6]

> Proposition 2. *Men who work together and who share common conditions of life develop a consciousness of kind. They become interest groups directed toward changing the environment in line with their own interests.*

The phenomenon of conflict cannot be properly understood without incorporating into the theory concepts and propositions concerning the dynamic properties of value systems, or ideologies. The opportunity structure of different social strata varies; large numbers of workers cannot achieve their aspirations. This leads inevitably to the development of working-class ideology, which in turn fosters class consciousness and class conflict. Sociologically, this may be viewed as a kind of intergroup relations—a set of social events or processes. Ratzenhofer and the early conflict theorists saw the domain of sociology as determining the laws that govern such intergroup processes.[7]

> Proposition 3. *"Conflict, no less than consensus, operates within the social structure, within the system of mutually established laws, norms and values."* [8]

That is, within conflict there are recognized norms and rules that allow for control of the situation. Even in political regimes in which terror is used as an instrument of control, some boundaries are established.[9] All social systems provide for specific institutions that serve to drain off hostile and aggressive sentiments.[10]

> Proposition 4. *So long as there are unequal and unsatisfactory life conditions, there will be a struggle among the interest groups for control of the economic and political institutions of society.*

---

[3] Don Martindale, *The Nature and Types of Sociological Theory* (Boston: Houghton-Mifflin Co., 1960), p. 129.

[4] Brief versions of the sociology of conflict are found in Lewis A. Coser, *The Functions of Conflict* (Glencoe, Ill.: Free Press, 1956); *ibid.*, pp. 127–210 and 525–542; and C. Wright Mills, *The Marxists* (New York: Dell Publishing Co., 1962).

[5] Horowitz, *op. cit.*, p. 153.

[6] Coser, *op. cit.*, pp. 151–152.

[7] This was an idea advanced first by Gustav Ratzenhofer, according to Martindale, *op. cit.*, p. 185. Martindale notes that, as of 1960, the works of this acknowledgedly important German sociologist had not been translated into English.

[8] Horowitz, *op. cit.*, p. 161.

[9] E. V. Walter, "Violence and the Process of Terror," *American Sociological Review*, Vol. 29, No. 2 (April 1964), pp. 248–257.

[10] Coser, *op. cit.*

Institutions are not just "moral entities." They become the arena for contests for power. "Conflicts of interest are seen as endemic in all social systems which 'institutionalize' power relationships because power (authority) over others is the most general form of 'scarce resource' and one that is inherent in society itself." [11]

Proposition 5. *Societies and their institutions grow and change at different rates of development. This leads to conflict and instability in the system, and under certain conditions to revolutionary action.*

Revolutionary action, essentially, is an act of collective desperation, when one social class feels that it cannot obtain its "ends" within the state as it is constituted. Revolutionary action comes at the end of a long process after the masses have become organized and class conscious and after they have developed "correct" leadership by a revolutionary party that epitomizes their goals.[12]

Many of these concepts have become so much a part of sociological analysis that they frequently are not seen as conflict theory. Theories of organization usually take these ideas into account, even if they do not give them a central place.

The warfare between consensus theorists and conflict theorists has about run its course. Several attempts are now being made to synthesize the two approaches.[13] What kinds

of "agreements" have been reached about the nature of social change by those who synthesize the approaches? [14]

Primarily, they agree that organization must be seen as a dynamic, changing social process. The writers have tried to capture this orientation by calling the phenomenon "process-event-organization." Changes are seen as occurring in society at four levels simultaneously, all of which occur during the process of institutionalization. The four analytical levels are personal, organizational, cultural, and ecological.

Behavior at the personal level involves a meaningful exchange of information among two or more persons via social transactions. The resultant of the exchange, expressed in interaction, is *organization* of social structure. For the symbolic interactionist, society is sometimes defined as "an organization of meanings." [15] The ego may perceive some transaction as an innovation although its counterpart does not; thus, perceptions of change may vary among the members of any organization. The changed behavior or attitudes that are seen in the individual may be characterized as a *personal change*. Every personal change in ego, to some extent, affects the alter ego. It also brings about a change in the group organization. When this occurs, it is called an *organizational change*.

An organization may be said to have become institutionalized when a stabilized reciprocal pattern of activity has emerged and when individuals may leave and join without changing the pattern in any essentials. Organiza-

---

[11] David Lockwood, "Social Integration and System Integration," in G. K. Zollschan and Walter Hirsch, eds., *Explorations in Social Change* (Boston: Houghton-Mifflin Co., 1964), pp. 246–247.

[12] V. I. Lenin, *State and Revolution* (New York: International Publishers, 1937). A revolutionary change is an irreversible "transformation in the core institutional order of a social system." Lockwood, *op. cit.*, p. 244.

[13] *See*, for example, R. N. Wilson, "Patient-Practitioner Relationships," and S. Polgar, "Health Action in Cross-Cultural Perspective," in Howard E. Freeman, Sol Levine, and L. G. Reeder, eds., *Handbook of Medical Sociology* (Englewood Cliffs, N.J.: Prentice-Hall, 1963), pp. 277 and 399 respectively. Wilson, in a clinically oriented discussion, found this mode of conceptualizing of the sick person as a "deviant" very "incisive"; it made it "natural to think of the practitioner first as an agent of social control." Polgar, on the other hand, thought the usefulness of the analysis "quite restricted" because it tended to un-

derplay the role of personal motivation in behavior and because it was inadequate for describing the organized behavior of people aimed at health promotion.

[14] Walter Buckley, *Sociology and Modern Systems Theory* (Englewood Cliffs, N.J.: Prentice-Hall, 1967); Martindale, *op. cit.*; Zollschan and Hirsch, *op. cit.*; Pierre van den Bergh, "Dialectic and Functionalism: Toward a Theoretical Synthesis," *American Sociological Review*, Vol. 28, No. 5 (October 1963), pp. 695–705. *See* the answer to van den Bergh by A. G. Frank, "Functionalism, Dialectics and Synthetics," *Science and Society*, Vol. 30, No. 2 (Spring 1966), pp. 136–148. To be sure, there are variations among these people, but they also agree on many concepts.

[15] G. H. Mead, *Mind, Self, and Society* (Chicago: University of Chicago Press, 1934), pp. 6–7.

tional theorists tend to be more concerned with the action itself during the institutionalization process than with the study of the cultural values that are the residue of the process. They ask such questions as these: What are the sources for organization and institutionalization in society? Under what conditions does change in organization and institutionalization take place? How does the mobilization for change occur? How are changes maintained and consolidated? They are also concerned with the long-term ecological developments of the community, that is, the reciprocal impact of the physical and social environment with the organized and evolving forms of community life.[16] Some changes at the ecological and cultural levels are viewed as evolutionary. The Marxists, for example, have attempted to specify the preconditions necessary for the transition from slavery to serfdom to capitalism to socialism. Parsons, who in 1949 held that no "competent modern sociologist" could hold this evolutionary view, by 1964 had reversed his position and had become one of the leading spokesmen for "evolutionary universals." [17]

For example, four features of human societies at the level of culture and social organization (ecology) are described as "prerequisites" for sociocultural development: technology, kinship organization based on an incest taboo, communication based on language, and religion. Four others are "fundamental to the structure of modern societies: bureaucratic organization of collective goal attainment, money and market systems, generalized universalistic legal systems, and democratic association with elective leadership and mediated membership support for policy orientations." Analysts of current social movements apply similar theory when they discuss the prerequisites that are needed in the state of organization for the transformation of a "protest group" into a resistance movement into a revolutionary party.[18] A protest group attempts to achieve change in a program it opposes through the regular channels of the host society available to protesters. A resistance movement emerges when protest by itself does not accomplish a desired end; resistance may use means of achieving change that are not sanctioned by the host society, such as sabotage or civil disobedience. A resistance movement wants a drastic change in society, but this may be in the practice rather than the institutionalized form. A revolution, on the other hand, develops among the protesters and resisters and is aimed at a transformation in the core institutional order—usually the political institution—of a society.

The advantage of viewing organization as process was a liberating one in the mid-nineteenth century. It turned attention away from futile speculations about the ultimate origins and ends of mankind and returned it to the consideration of ongoing life. It has the same effect today. It focuses on the description of sequences of present behavior. If projections are extended into the future or predictions are made to any time period, this can be related to the present series of real events. Explanation in terms of correlation or cause, rather than telesis, is encouraged. Conceptually, the only fixed linkage in process pertains to events in time. This encourages the use of open system models to describe the structure of social action.

---

[16] Amos H. Hawley, *Human Ecology: A Theory of Community Structure* (Ann Arbor: Roland Press, 1950). For a discussion of ecological factors in change *see* Walter Firey, "Sentiment and Symbolism as Ecological Variables," *American Sociological Review*, Vol. 10, No. 2 (April 1945), pp. 140–148; E. S. Deevey, Jr., "General and Urban Ecology," in Leonard J. Duhl, ed., *The Urban Condition* (New York: Basic Books, 1963), pp. 20–33; O. D. Duncan and L. F. Schnore, "Cultural, Behavioral and Ecological Perspectives in the Study of Social Organization," in Seymour M. Lipset and Neil J. Smelser, eds., *Sociology: The Progress of a Decade* (Englewood Cliffs, N.J.: Prentice-Hall, 1961), pp. 311–331.

[17] Talcott Parsons, *Essays in Sociological Theory, Pure and Applied* (Glencoe, Ill.: Free Press, 1949), pp. 23–28; Parsons, "Evolutionary Universals in Society," *American Sociological Review*, Vol. 29, No. 3 (June 1964), pp. 339–357. "An evolutionary universal is a complex of structures and associated processes, the development of which so increases the long-run adaptive capacity of living systems in a given class that only systems that develop the complex can attain certain higher levels of general adaptive capacity."

[18] David Willer and G. K. Zollschan, "Prolegomenon to a Theory of Revolutions," in Zollschan and Hirsch, eds., *op. cit.*, pp. 125–151; Carl Oglesby and Richard Shaull, *Containment and Change* (New York: Macmillan Co., 1967), pp. 140–156; W. I. Waskow, *From Race Riot to Sit-In* (Garden City, N.Y.: Doubleday & Co., 1966).

Relevance of This Analysis

The relevance of the foregoing conceptual analysis to the contemporary world was challenged. Blumer proposed that the utility of the scheme be tested by analyzing the institute itself. In his opinion, the institute involved far more than consensus or conflict:

BLUMER. We are trying to establish communication with one another. It is neither consensus nor conflict. We talk past one another; we don't understand one another. We feel each other out in all kinds of ways to try to get some sort of common stance; if not a common stance, to orient ourselves as individuals, to take perspective on what is going on. This is merely one of the multitudes of different facets of human group life that go on—a group life that to my mind just cannot be meaningfully squeezed inside the scheme you have. We are confronted here with an area of fluid activity that is in the process of formation. I don't think one can understand this by trying to make some kind of systematic analysis from factors and variables supposed to be present, on the assumption that having identified these factors you have caught the whole scheme.

To the observations that human society consists of people, not organizations, and that people actively interpret the situations they encounter and behave in ways that influence those situations, Northwood replied:

I think we have to deal with persons. There is no choice. But we can't explain [behavior] simply in terms of a set of persons and personal motivations, needs, desires, and so on.

Other participants pointed out that the test of a formulation is not its capacity to explain everything, but its capacity to explain anything. Interest was expressed in Northwood's plan to utilize his guide toward describing social processes in a recently initiated study; this experience was expected to help clarify the merits of his idea system.

Suggested in the limited enthusiasm with which Northwood's ideas were received was disappointment because the scheme seemed to offer little in the way of guidelines for action. The studies couched in these terms seem to describe what has happened rather than provide any basis for projecting the course of future events. There was no absence of concern with the issue of conflict; indeed, the discussion disclosed an interest in grasping the thrust of the present conflict so keen as to dominate appraisals of proposed formulations.

Part II

Perspectives on Practice, Program, and Change

Research Perspectives on Interracial Adoptions

ANDREW BILLINGSLEY AND JEANNE GIOVANNONI

The practice of interracial adoption—that is, the adoption of a child of one race by adoptive parents of another race—although limited, is apparently growing.[1] In the writers' view, interracial adoption can most appropriately be examined within the context of what is happening in the broader field of adoptions generally, and indeed within the framework of what is happening in society. Within this context, some of the major parameters of the interracial adoption movement can be appreciated. Review of the experience accumulated to date suggests some generalizations about this new practice, including some of the underlying assumptions embodied in it, and stimulates consideration of some alternatives to interracial adoption.

Andrew Billingsley, Ph.D., is Associate Professor, School of Social Welfare, University of California, Berkeley, California. Jeanne Giovannoni, Ph.D., is Associate Professor, Department of Social Work Education, San Francisco State College, San Francisco, California.

Recent Trends in Adoptions

Despite the recent decline in the proportion of adoptive applicants to the number of children available for adoption, the field of adoption is a large and expanding enterprise.[2] The adoption of children is a relatively recent phenomenon in the United States and was not recognized in English Common Law. In 1851 Massachusetts was the first state to pass enabling adoption legislation. It was not, however, until the Civil War—which gave tremendous impetus to adoptions because of the large numbers of homeless infants—that many states be-

[1] For present purposes, the authors will follow common usage and consider persons of Caucasian, Negro, American Indian, and Oriental ancestry as representing different racial groups. Interracial adoptions mainly involve people of these backgrounds.

[2] Lydia F. Hylton, "Trends in Adoption, 1958–1962," *Child Welfare*, Vol. 44, No. 7 (July 1965), pp. 377–386.

gan to pass legislation permitting and protecting the practice. By 1929 all the states had such laws.[3]

There are currently about 1.5 million adopted children under 21 in this country, which means that roughly two out of every hundred minors are adopted. There has been a 100 percent increase in the annual number of adoptions in the past fifteen years. Child welfare statistics compiled by the U.S. Children's Bureau indicate that in 1964 a total of 135,000 children were adopted. This represents about a 25 percent increase over the number of adoptions tabulated for 1960.[4]

Despite the gross overrepresentation of non-Caucasian children among those available for adoption, they have continued to comprise only about 10 percent of the adoptions completed each year. There were still in 1964 between ten and twenty non-Caucasian children available for every adoptive applicant, while the demand for Caucasian babies continued to outstrip the supply.

Sources of Children

There is little doubt that illegitimate children are the major resource for adoptive placement. It is of considerable importance to observe, however, that the degree of reliance placed on this specific source depends on a number of variables, including time, place, and manner of adoption. Over the past few years, despite a slight decline in the proportion of children adopted who *were* born in wedlock, legitimate children still accounted for 39 percent of all children adopted in 1964.[5]

Children born in wedlock who are relinquished for adoption come principally from four subsources: (1) Young, newly married couples whose first child was conceived prior to marriage. (It has been estimated that nearly a quarter of all firstborn children were conceived prior to marriage.)[6] (2) Young couples who conceive early in their marriage and before they are ready to assume the responsibilities of parenthood. (3) Women who are "technically" married, such as those who are separated, divorced, or widowed. (4) Women whose husbands are not the fathers of their children.

The relative importance of these two sources of adoptive children—those born in and out of wedlock—varies somewhat not only over time, but by type of adoption: that is, adoption by a relative or nonrelative and through an agency or independently of agencies. For children adopted by relatives, including stepparents—which account for nearly half of all adoptions—in-wedlock births are the major source, while the opposite is true for adoptions by persons not related to the child. Non-Caucasian children are more highly represented in relative than in nonrelative adoptions.[7]

Types of Adoptive Placements

Adoption practice in the United States, where it is much more highly developed than in any other country, is a highly varied enterprise. Thus, there are not only relative and nonrelative adoptions, but within the latter category there are the further subdivisions of agency and independent adoptions. Among the 135,000 adoptions that were approved by the courts

[3] Alfred Kadushin, *Child Welfare Services* (New York: Macmillan Co., 1967), p. 436.
[4] *Child Welfare Statistics* (Washington, D.C.: Children's Bureau, U.S. Department of Health, Education, and Welfare, 1960, 1961, 1962, 1963, 1964).
[5] *Ibid.*

[6] Ethel Branham, "Coping with Change: More Children than Adoptive Homes." Paper presented at the Northwest Regional Conference, Child Welfare League of America, Seattle, Wash., 1966.
[7] *Child Welfare Statistics.*

in 1964, 71,600, or 53 percent, were non-relative adoptions. Of these, 67 percent were agency adoptions and 33 percent were independent adoptions. Twenty years before, a slight majority of all nonrelative adoptions were independent.[8]

Agency adoptions are supervised by recognized child welfare agencies that usually charge the adoptive parents a fee for their service. Independent adoptions have no such continual agency supervision of the total process of adoption, although in some states, such as California, even independent adoptions must undergo a certain social agency home study and limited supervision. The controversy surrounding agency versus independent adoptions has often generated more heat than light. Professional adoptions workers, the social work profession, and most state legislation favor agency adoptions. The argument is that this arrangement affords greater protection for the child, the adoptive parents, and the natural parents. Yet it has not been clearly demonstrated that agency adoptions are superior in effectiveness to independent adoptions.

Among agency adoptions, the private voluntary agencies still do the lion's share of adoption practice. Thus, in 1964, 41 percent of all nonrelative adoptions were supervised by voluntary child welfare agencies, while 26 percent were supervised by the vast network of public welfare agencies located in virtually every county in the country.[9] There are implications in this distribution for the adoption of non-Caucasian children that will be discussed later. There are two major categories of persons arranging independent adoptions: (1) the child's own family and (2) physicians and attorneys (who arrange the bulk of them).

The trends and patterns in adoption practice just outlined suggest several hypotheses that relate to a concern for interracial adoption and the adoption of non-Caucasian children that is the focus of this new movement. The writers hypothesize that non-Caucasian children have a significantly greater chance of being adopted (1) through relative than through nonrelative adoptions, (2) through independent nonrelative adoptions than through agency adoptions, and (3) through public agencies than through private voluntary agencies. Sufficient data are not available to test these hypotheses, although some support for the first has already been suggested.

Regarding the second hypothesis, there is an apparent high correlation between percentage of independent adoptions and percentage of non-Caucasian adoptions. U.S. Children's Bureau data for 1963 show that Washington, D.C., and Minnesota have relatively high proportions of non-Caucasian adoptions despite a low proportion of independent adoptions. But in all the other states in which non-Caucasian adoptions account for more than 10 percent of all adoptions, independent adoptions are also relatively high, accounting for from 30 to 50 percent of all nonrelative adoptions. Both independent and non-Caucasian adoptions tend to be high in the southern states and in such other selected places as Puerto Rico, Washington, D.C., and Hawaii.

Critical to social work is the possibility that non-Caucasian adoptions are differentially effected by public and voluntary agencies. The evidence at this point is mixed. Helen Jeter found that in 1961, 24 percent of children served by public agencies were Negro and 3 percent other non-Caucasian races, while in private agencies the respective percentages were 14 and 2.[10] She also found that among all children in adoptive homes under public agency auspices, 15 percent were Negro and 3 percent

---

[8] *Ibid.*
[9] *Ibid.*

[10] Helen R. Jeter, *Children, Problems, and Service in Child Welfare Programs* (Washington, D.C.: U.S. Department of Health, Education, and Welfare, 1963).

non-Caucasians of other races; in private agencies these proportions were 10 and 2 percent respectively.

Other figures from Jeter also bring out in another way the underrepresentation of Negro children among those receiving adoption services. Among both public and private agencies the principal problem of children receiving preadoption services was "parents not married to each other." (These were 37 percent of public agency children and 83 percent of private agency children.) While for both public and private agencies there was less than a 10 percent difference between all of the Negro and all of the Caucasian children receiving preadoption services, there was a dramatic difference in the percentage of both groups whose principal problem was "parents not married to each other." This was especially true in the public agencies. This was the principal problem for 43 percent of the Negro children being served, but for only 16 percent of the Caucasian children. Thus, if the potential pool of adoptive children is actually most likely to come from those whose principal problem is "parents not married to each other," then it would appear that the Negro children in this potential pool were highly underrepresented among those actually receiving preadoption services. Recent figures from the San Francisco Department of Social Services indicate that even among public agencies non-Caucasian children are underrepresented in adoptive placements, with Negro children constituting only 5.5 percent of all the children placed.[11]

Should these hypotheses be substantiated, they would help to explain in part the predicament faced in the adoption field today. Such data would surely suggest that there is something about the structure and function of the adoption field itself that helps

to account for the backlog of non-Caucasian children available but not adopted and at the same time helps to account for both the interest in and resistance to interracial adoption.

Experience with Interracial Adoption

Interracial adoption is a relatively new and fledgling, but apparently growing, practice. Reports in the literature to date, summarized in Table 1, have been extremely fragmentary. They reflect, of course, only a small portion of the actual practice. Some agencies have not judged it advisable to publicize their activities in this field. No effort has been undertaken to date to bring together the total range of this experience.

It must be said at the outset that child welfare workers in Hawaii, Alaska, Puerto Rico, and the Virgin Islands must wonder what the fuss is all about in the rest of the country. Interracial adoptions are not new to them. They are so extensive and apparently well accepted that there are no special reports in the literature on interracial adoptions in those states and jurisdictions. Any comprehensive study of interracial adoption from cultural and psychological perspectives, although not necessarily from the broader perspective of social climate and general attitudes of the population, might well start with these places that have an appreciable body of experience. Such data, however, are not yet available. It is known that over half of all adoptive placements in Alaska are non-Caucasian children placed with Caucasian families and that a majority of placements of the Child Welfare League of America member agency in Hawaii may also be described as interracial adoptions.[12]

---

[11] Non-Caucasian adoptions have comprised less than 16 percent of the adoptions reported for 1962–66 inclusive.

[12] Myron C. Chevlin, "Adoption Outlook," *Child Welfare*, Vol. 46, No. 2 (February 1967), p. 75.

TABLE 1. REPORTS OF INTERRACIAL ADOPTIONS

Author and Date	Auspices	Number and Ethnicity of Children Adopted	Ethnicity of Adoptive Parents
Graham 1957	International Social Service, New York	959 Japanese (1946–57)	Caucasian
Valk 1957	International Social Service, New York	75 Korean-Caucasian 14 Korean-Negro 11 Korean, 4 Korean-Mexican	Caucasian Negro Caucasian
Pettiss 1960	International Social Service, New York	208 Chinese (1958–59)	Chinese 75 percent Caucasian 25 percent
Gallay 1963	Children's Service Society, Montreal	72 Negro, 22 Oriental, 21 Canadian Indian (1951–63)	Caucasian
Branham 1966	Alaska Department of Social Service	Fifty percent of all adoptions; ¼ to full-blooded Aleutians, Eskimos, and Indians	Caucasian
	Children's Service Centre, Toronto	77 Negro (1954–63)	Caucasian
	Los Angeles County Department of Adoptions	118 Oriental 41 Negro 52 other, mixed (1953–65)	Caucasian Caucasian Mixed
Fanshel 1966	CWLA and U.S. Bureau of Indian Affairs	250 American Indian (1958–67)	Caucasian
Fricke 1966	State Department of Welfare, several county welfare departments, seven (of thirteen) private agencies, Minnesota	20 Negro 71 other non-Caucasian races	Caucasian Mostly Caucasian
Chevlin 1967	Boys and Girls Aid Society, Oregon	12 Negro, 33 other non-Caucasian races (1957–63)	Caucasian
	Children's Home Society of California	177 Negro (January-June 1967)	Negro and Caucasian
	CWLA member agency, Honolulu	Majority of adoptive children are of mixed race	Unspecified
	International Social Service, New York	1,600 non-Caucasian (1960–67)	Caucasian

In the rest of the country and in Canada, the newest concern with interracial adoption centers chiefly around the adoption of children with one Caucasian parent and one parent who is Oriental, American Indian, Negro, or Puerto Rican. The chief novelty and interest of this new movement is the extent to which these children are adopted by Caucasian couples. For, in the past, when such children have been adopted by non-Caucasian couples, the adoption has not been considered interracial. In Los Angeles County even today, the adoption of a child who has one Oriental and one Caucasian parent is considered interracial if he is adopted by a Caucasian couple, but not if he is adopted by an Oriental couple. The same is true with Negro adoptions. The problem, however, is that there have not been sufficient non-Caucasian couples applying and accepted for adoptions and the new movement is a partial outgrowth of that fact.

Some of the accumulated experience with interracial adoptions according to these large ethnic groupings will be described, first considering Oriental, then American Indian, and finally American Negro children.

Oriental Children

In 1957 Margaret A. Valk wrote a report for the Child Welfare League of America on 104 children from Korea adopted by American families.[13] The report covered one aspect of the intercountry adoption program that was made possible by the Refugee Relief Act. She reported that a large number of Oriental and mixed Oriental-American children have been adopted by American families under the provisions of this program. According to her report, Korean-American orphans actually comprise the second largest group of foreign children placed by International Social Service in co-operation with the U.S. government and local child placing agencies in this country. At the time of this report, 104 such children had been placed in American homes. The ethnic parentage of these children was as follows: 75 were of Korean-Caucasian ancestry, born to Korean women and American white servicemen; 14 were of Korean-Negro ancestry, born to Korean women and American Negro servicemen; 11 were apparently of purely Korean parentage; 4 were probably of Korean–Mexican-American parentage.

At the time of placement these children ranged in age from infancy to 10 years. About a third of them were between 3 and 4 years of age and another fifth were between 4 and 5. The fourteen children with Negro fathers were all placed in Negro homes. All the other children were placed in Caucasian homes.

In general, the families who adopted these children met the usual standards for adoptive parents promulgated by CWLA. They were predominantly middle class. Two-fifths of the Caucasian families and half of the Negro families were professionals, with teachers, social workers, and ministers predominating. Their incomes were rather modest, falling mainly in the neighborhood of $6,500 a year with only one or two earning above $10,000. In half of these families the parents were between 30 and 40. The rest were mainly in their late twenties or early forties. They did depart, however, from the usual standard of infertility. Nearly half the families had children of their own. All families were carefully screened by local child placing agencies.

A second early experience with Oriental children was reported by Lloyd B. Graham.[14] He conducted a study of 779 chil-

---

[13] *Korean-American Children in American Adoptive Homes* (New York: Child Welfare League of America, 1957).

[14] "Children From Japan in American Adoptive Homes," *Casework Papers, 1957* (New York: Family Service Association of America, 1957), pp. 130–145.

dren from Japan adopted by American families between 1946 and 1955. He reported that an additional 180 such children had been placed with American families by 1957 through the auspices of International Social Service. The author reports that the bulk of these children were of Japanese mothers and American Caucasian fathers. The next largest group had Japanese mothers and American Negro fathers; a relatively small number were of pure Japanese ancestry.

Of the 779 children studied, 366 were boys and 413 were girls. They ranged in age from infancy to 12 years old. The average age for both boys and girls was about 3 years.

There were 674 American families involved in the adoption of these 779 children. Six families adopted three or four children each, 91 families adopted two children each, and 577 families adopted one child each. Of the 217 families who responded to the questionnaire sent out by Graham, 74 already had one or more of their own children. Fully 99 percent of these adoptive families were American, non-Japanese in origin, and 90 percent were physically present in Japan with American military and civilian agencies at the time adoption took place. Most of these children were chosen personally by the adoptive parents through private arrangements with the children's mothers or guardians or with the child care institutions in which they had been placed. Fifty-nine of these children were placed directly by public agencies in Japan; the bulk of them were placed either through private or independent adoptions. The vast majority seem to have been placed independently.

The average age of the adoptive fathers was 36.5 and of the mothers, 35.5. Among the 143 couples who had no children of their own, the average ages at the time of adoption were 33.5 and 32.5 respectively.

A third major experience with the adoption of Oriental children was reported by Susan T. Pettiss in a symposium on the adoption of Oriental children by American Caucasian families held in May 1959.[15] This symposium was primarily concerned with Chinese children. Unlike the two experiences with Oriental children just described, in which most of the children were only half Oriental, having had American fathers, the Chinese children under consideration were of purely Chinese parentage. It was this very fact that prompted CWLA to hold the seminar, which brought together experts on genetics, psychology, anthropology, and social work to examine problems of assimilation and adjustment.

It was reported at this symposium that between 1954, when the Refugee Relief Act was passed, and 1956 only 4 Chinese children arrived in this country for adoption from Hong Kong. However, with the passage in 1958 of a more liberalized law permitting the entry of adopted children from China, the number increased appreciably. In that year 57 Chinese children came to this country from Hong Kong under the sponsorship of International Social Service and in 1959, 151 came in. Again, unlike the Korean and Japanese children, these Chinese children were placed mainly with Chinese families in America. Of the 151 Chinese children adopted in this country in 1959, 117 were adopted by Chinese and 34 by Caucasian families.

A great deal of leadership in the new area of adoption across racial lines has come from Canadian agencies. One Protestant agency, the Children's Service Centre of Montreal, has gradually increased the number of non-Caucasian children adopted by Caucasian families from 1 in 1951 to 29 in 1962.[16] Among 94 adoptive

---

[15] "Some Facts About ISS Placements," *Adoption of Oriental Children by American White Families: An Interdisciplinary Symposium* (New York: Child Welfare League of America, 1960), p. 10.

[16] Branham, *op. cit.*

placements, 19 children (or more than one-fifth) had one Oriental and one Caucasian parent, and one had two Oriental parents. Altogether, 77 of these 94 adoptive couples already had children of their own. Sixty had natural children and 17 had adopted Caucasian children prior to adopting an Oriental child. A majority of these applicants specifically requested a non-Caucasian child.

In Montreal, the volume of applicants who specify an interest in adopting a child of Indian or Oriental extraction is such that these children have been removed from the hard-to-place category.[17] Among the 115 non-Caucasian children placed with Caucasian families between 1951 and 1963 by Children's Service Society of Montreal were 22 Oriental children. The new challenge in Canada is the placement of Negro children with Caucasian families.

A final set of experiences with the interracial adoption of Oriental children comes from California, which is the leading state in total volume of adoptions. In 1963 nearly 16,000 children were adopted in California, more than twice as many as were adopted in New York, the next closest state. This represents a marked increase over the 14,764 adopted in 1962. California also has the largest Oriental population of any of the states. Still, in California, as in the rest of the nation, adoption is essentially a Caucasian institution. Nevertheless there is some experience to report with the adoption of Oriental children, and some limited experience with the interracial adoption of such children. The Los Angeles County Department of Adoptions has a vigorous new program of interracial adoptions. Of the 150 adoptions completed each month in this giant agency, at least 50 are adoptions of non-Caucasian children. A large share of these are Or-

iental children, several of whom have been adopted by Caucasian families. During the period 1953–65 at least 115 children with one Oriental parent had been adopted by Caucasian families.[18]

American Indian Children

While the distribution of children with at least one American Indian parent is probably not limited to a specific geographic region, the greatest activity in placement of these children has been in the far northern United States and in Canada. A large proportion of the children adopted by Caucasian families in Alaska have Indian parentage.[19] The Children's Service Society of Montreal reported that 21 of the 72 non-Caucasian children adopted by Caucasian parents between 1951 and 1963 had Indian parentage.[20] The most celebrated experience with the adoption of American Indian children by Caucasian families, however, is the program jointly supported by CWLA and the U.S. Bureau of Indian Affairs, whereby 250 American Indian children were placed with Caucasian families, mainly on the East Coast, between 1958 and 1967.

The most unique aspect of this program is the ongoing research being conducted under the direction of David Fanshel on a group of 100 of these adoptive families and the children. Owing to the longitudinal and developmental nature of this investigation, the compendium of information obtained is not yet fully available. However, preliminary reports provide some interesting insights into the motivations of these parents and their social characteristics.[21] As with other interracial programs

---

[17] Grace Gallay, "Interracial Adoptions," *Canadian Welfare*, Vol. 39, No. 6 (November-December 1963), p. 248.

[18] Branham, *op. cit.*

[19] *Ibid.*

[20] Gallay, *op. cit.*

[21] Edgar F. Borgatta and David Fanshel, "Self Reports of Parents Who Have Adopted American-

the usual restrictions on age and infertility were relaxed, and there is a slightly higher representation of blue-collar workers (10 percent) in the sample of 100 under study than in the usual agency adoptive families. As for motivation, the preliminary reports indicate that the primary impetus for taking an Indian child was simply a desire for a child. Contrary to many assumptions, these people did not seem to be predominantly motivated out of a humanitarian concern for the minority child. They did not appear as a group to be especially liberal in their views and in the majority of cases their acceptance of an Indian child did not indicate a generalized acceptance of minority group children. Seventy-eight percent expressed some strong reservations about adopting a part-Negro child. Of course, since these parents had specifically chosen American Indian children, this finding cannot be generalized to all parents involved in interracial adoptive placements. The question "Would you adopt a Negro child?" would, of course, be irrelevant to those who already had done so. This research undertaking, when completed, promises to be a source of considerable enlightenment to the field of interracial adoption.

Negro Children

The experience of placing Negro children with Caucasian adoptive couples is, perhaps, the most novel feature of the interracial adoption movement. It also, however, has the greatest potential for expansion both because of the relatively large numbers of Negro children available

for adoption, with no adoptive parents in sight, and the relatively large numbers of Caucasian couples who wish to adopt children, with no Caucasian adoptive children in sight. But perhaps because these adoptions bring into contact the two polar races in our society, Negro and Caucasian, they are fraught with a high degree of ambivalence on the part of the child's own parents, the adoptive parents, the professional worker, and the agency.

One example of the complexity of the obstacles involved in the situation stems from the experiences of a Jewish agency in the East, reported by Werner J. Cahnman.[22] Of 400 non-Caucasian or mixed children considered for placement by this agency since 1953, 30 were American Indian; the remaining 370 children had Jewish mothers and fathers whose races were as follows: 5 Oriental, 65 Puerto Rican (including some Negro), and 300 Negro. In addition to these 400 children of mixed or non-Caucasian background, the agency has also received 56 children— 50 of Negro and 6 of Caucasian parentage —who were not necessarily born of Jewish mothers but were referred to the agency under the system of rotation of placement of children to sectarian agencies by the authorities when the religion of the mother is not known. Of these 56 children, the agency placed the 6 apparently Caucasian children with Jewish families; the 50 apparently Negro children were placed with gentile Negro families.

Cahnman speaks specifically about the situation of the 320 children born of Jewish mothers but of non-Jewish and non-Caucasian fathers. He underscores the point that in Jewish law the religion of the mother is the religion of the child. In spite of this, of the 320 children who were considered Jewish by reason of their

---

Indian Children Compared to Those Who Have Adopted Caucasian Children," and David Fanshel, "The Indian Adoption Research Project: A Preliminary Report." Papers presented at the Mid-West Regional Conference, Child Welfare League of America, May 1966.

---

[22] Werner J. Cahnman, "The Interracial Jewish Children," *Reconstructionist: A Jewish Bi-weekly,* Vol. 33 (June 9, 1967), pp. 7–12.

mother's religion, only 4 were adopted by Jewish couples—these 4 were all part Oriental; none was part Negro. With reference to this situation, Cahnman states: "It is abundantly clear that color, not religion, is the determining factor in the adoption of interracial Jewish children." [23] It is also known, however, that in other instances a relatively high proportion of Caucasian families adopting part-Negro children have been Jewish. There are, then, already a large number of variations and complexities in this small practice of interracial adoption, reflecting, no doubt, variations in the prevailing social norms about interracial contact at the family level. In this respect, both the policies and procedures of the agencies and the attitudes of their workers are influenced by these prevailing social norms.

In the following reports of placement of Negro children with Caucasian families, most placements have been of children with one Negro and one Caucasian parent.

Some of the earliest experiences with placement of these Negro children were in Canada. The Children's Service Centre of Toronto placed 77 Negro children with Caucasian adoptive parents between 1954 and 1963. The number of such placements increased beginning in 1960 from a previous average of 5 per year to over 15 per year.[24] Child welfare agencies in Montreal had placed 80 Negro children with Caucasian families by 1964.[25]

Perhaps the most celebrated experience reported in the literature comes from Minnesota, where seven of thirteen private adoption agencies in collaboration with the State Department of Social Welfare and several county welfare departments undertook a massive campaign to recruit families, including Caucasian families, for the

adoption of non-Caucasian children. In the process they placed 20 Negro children with Caucasian families over a 2½-year period ending in 1965.[26]

In California the statewide private agency, Children's Home Society, has developed an intensive recruitment and placement program in this area during the past few years. In the first six months of 1967 they placed a total of 177 children of Negro parentage, many of whom were adopted by Caucasian couples.[27]

Another experience with the adoptive placement of Negro children with Caucasian parents is that of the Los Angeles County Department of Adoptions, which made its first such placement in 1955 and by 1965 had placed 47 children who had one Caucasian and one Negro parent. Thirteen of these placements were made in 1965. Most of these children had Caucasian mothers and Negro fathers. Among the 34 Negro children placed with 28 Caucasian families as of 1964, only 2 had Negro mothers and Caucasian fathers. The other 32 had Negro fathers. Of these, 27 had Caucasian mothers and the other 5 mothers were either Mexican-American or Oriental.[28]

Among the 28 Caucasian families who adopted Negro children up to 1964, Jews were heavily represented, followed by Unitarians and nondenominational Protestants. Eleven families were Jewish, 8 were either Unitarian or nondenominational, 6 were Catholic, and the other 3 were associated with various Protestant denominations.

---

[23] *Ibid.*, p. 7.
[24] Branham, *op. cit.*
[25] Gallay, *op. cit.*

[26] Harriet Fricke, "Interracial Adoption: The Little Revolution," *Social Work*, Vol. 10, No. 3 (July 1965), pp. 92–97.
[27] Minutes of the May 25, 1967, meeting of the Children's Home Society Minority Adoption Committee.
[28] Ethel Branham, "Transracial Adoptions: When A 'Good' Family Is Not Good Enough." Paper presented at the National Conference on Social Welfare, Los Angeles, Calif., May 1964.

Eleven of these families had one or more natural children of their own (10 had more than one such child) and 9 other families had adopted one other child. Eight had not been able to have children of their own. Four of these families had served as foster parents for the children subsequently adopted. The average age of the adoptive fathers was 37 and of the mothers, 29. All these families had expressed an interest in adopting a child of mixed racial background.

These adoptive parents also tended to be of relatively high socioeconomic status. Sixteen of the 28 fathers were college graduates, including 8 who had advanced degrees. Nine had attended college for periods between one and three years, and only 3 had not graduated from high school. The mothers had a similar level of education. The men were mostly employed in professional occupations that involved a high degree of interpersonal interaction.

A number of agencies in other cities have undertaken a small number of such adoptive placements. Among the cities where such placements have occurred are Seattle, Portland, San Francisco, Yonkers, and New York. In addition, a number of organizations devoted especially to the encouragement of adoption of Negro children by Caucasian parents have emerged. Among these are the Open Door Society of Montreal, the Open Door Society of Minnesota, and the Council on Adoptable Children of Ann Arbor, Michigan. In addition, many states are developing statewide exchanges for hard-to-place children in order to increase the total resources for them beyond the local level.

Evaluative Studies

There is indeed a paucity of evaluative studies of all kinds of adoption, not only interracial. As Maas has noted, while there has been no dearth of work among social scientists interested in adoption because it offered a "natural experiment" for testing theories of child development and socialization, it is only recently that practice-oriented research, including evaluative research, has been initiated.[29] Thus there really is little systematic knowledge concerning ordinary adoption, even of Caucasian-Caucasian placements, to use as a yardstick for purposes of comparison in evaluating the outcome of interracial adoption. Just what would be an appropriate comparison group for interracially adopted children is, of course, questionable, since in reality the alternatives to interracial adoption are limited and the outcomes of such adoptions should be measured against these alternatives rather than some theoretical ideal in making practice-oriented decisions.

While there are many defensible reasons why evaluative research in adoption practice has lagged, including practical matters such as the inaccessibility of families, nonetheless it should be remembered that there is little systematic knowledge to substantiate the principles and values that dictate current adoption practices. Further, since there is such a paucity of evaluative research in general adoptions, there is consequently no ready yardstick available by which to compare the relative success of interracial adoption.

The limited research that has been done cannot yield any generalized statements owing to the size and variability of the different groups used and to the variation in the questions studied. Not all have been primarily concerned with outcome evaluation. Three broad areas can be delineated as having attracted research attempts in the field of interracial adoption. These are (1) the motivation of adoptive parents, (2) social psychological consequences for

---

[29] Henry S. Maas *et al., Perspectives on Adoption Research* (New York: Child Welfare League of America, 1965).

the child, and (3) social psychological consequences for the adoptive parents. Underlying the raising of these questions is the probably valid assumption that interracial adoption adds a dimension to the adoption situation that requires special understanding. It is known, however, that there are some adoptive parents and prospective adoptive parents who hold that such differences are exaggerated.

Motivation of Parents

That part of Fanshel's reports on the motivation and characteristics of families adopting American Indian children has already been discussed. The finding that these parents were not especially motivated by social consciousness in adopting or characterized by liberal sentiments is somewhat contrary to what others have reported. Perhaps some of the differences, however, are explained by sample differences, these parents having selected American Indian children while those in some other studies adopted Negro children.[30]

Gallay in Montreal reviewed 100 case records of Caucasian applicants who had agreed to take non-Caucasian children and concluded:

It is obvious that the same motivations are present in "matching" and "interracial" adoptions, that is, infertility, love of children and desire to enlarge the family. The significant difference is the strong expression of religious and humanitarian motivation by the people who wished to adopt children of a racial background different from their own.[31]

Alma J. Hill, whose sample did not include those adopting Negro children, came to a similar conclusion from her study of 17 interracial adoptions in Los Angeles.[32]

An interesting survey was conducted in Boston by the Arffas among a group of parents who had adopted interracially and had initiated their own study group.[33] Replies to the portion of the Arffas' questionnaire dealing with motivation for adopting revealed humanitarian values were equally as influential in the parents' choice as was the desire for a child.

While further research on motivation is certainly needed, the work to date might be construed to indicate that there are parents who are not resistant to the idea of interracial adoption but, on the contrary, are sincerely desirous of such adoption *in preference to* adoption of a child of their own race. It is interesting to note that there is no work available concerning the attitudes of adoption workers themselves toward interracial adoption. Such work would be helpful in ferreting out where the greater resistance to interracial adoption actually exists, in the applicants or in the agencies. Several parents in the Boston group, for example, noted that their initial request for a child of a different race was greeted with suspicion by the agency personnel with whom they dealt. The writers have also found a great deal of worker resistance to interracial adoptions.

Psychosocial Adjustment of Children

The available studies of the psychosocial adjustment of interracially placed children all suggest there are no observable untoward results. DiVirgillo in Boston and Bahan in Los Angeles, both dealing with relatively small samples of Oriental children, report no unusual incidence of behavioral maladjustment in these children.[34]

---

[30] Fanshel, *op. cit.*
[31] *Op. cit.*, p. 4.
[32] This study is reported in Branham, *op. cit.*

[33] Marvin and Elissa Arffa, "Questionnaire Survey of Parents of Interracial Children." Unpublished manuscript, Boston, Mass., April 1967.
[34] Letitia DiVirgillo, "Adjustment of Foreign Children in Their Adoptive Homes," *Child Welfare,* Vol. 35, No. 9 (November 1956), pp. 15–21;

Less systematic observations by agencies involved in these placements would corroborate these impressions. As noted earlier, the ideal model for evaluating psychosocial effects of interracial placement on children is itself fraught with many problems, such as the selection of a suitable comparison group and the choice of proper measurements of adjustment, not to mention the accessibility for study of a sufficiently large number of placements of a similar nature. Furthermore, the ideal type of study here is the longitudinal one, which is expensive and difficult to maintain. In view of these problems, while it seems unfortunate, research that is focused on the effects on the child, especially of an evaluative nature, will probably remain sparse and inadequate for many years to come. A more likely avenue of child-centered research is that which, at a more descriptive level, is focused on special problems of adjustment that the situation may present to the child and variations in parental and child handling of these problems.

Psychosocial Adjustment of Parents

A final area receiving increasing systematic attention is that of the psychosocial impact on the adoptive parents. Many agencies have given numerous case reports of how parents handle the racial difference between them and their child. However, recent work, especially at the University of Washington, has been more systematic and has covered larger numbers of cases. Such research has been concerned with the implications of racial differences for the performance of the parental role in general.[35] Hiatt, for example, has suggested

from her work with 24 couples who had adopted interracially that these parents were high in their "role confidence" as parents.[36] Some positive aspects of the interracial situation for parents have also been pointed to by Pepper, who reported that cross-racial adoptive parents may more easily cope with their adoptive status through the acknowledgment of differences inherent in the situation than by trying to deny such differences.[37]

Research in the area of parental adjustment, of course, has many problems parallel to those already mentioned for children that may restrict its progress. Interest in the positive as well as potentially negative consequences of interracial adoption for the parents, while of theoretical interest, would not seem to have great practical value. It seems highly unlikely that even if advantages over "same race" adoptions were demonstrated there would be extensive impact on practice. However, it is quite possible that such research might lead to new information that would be helpful in assisting all adoptive parents in coping with their role, which is indeed one that exceeds the parameters of the biological parental role.

One point concerning all research on interracial adoptions deserves considerable

Rita Bahan, "Adjustment of Foreign-Born Oriental Children Adopted by Caucasian Families," unpublished MSW dissertation, University of Southern California, Los Angeles, June 1963.

[35] *See,* for example, Patricia Denny, "A De-

scriptive Study of Eight Cross Racial Adoptions," unpublished master's thesis, University of Washington, Seattle, 1964; Evelyn Hoover *et al.,* "A Cross Racial Adoption Study," unpublished master's thesis, University of Washington, Seattle, 1965; Doris Cooper *et al.,* "Cross Racial Adoption: An Extension of Earlier Studies," unpublished master's thesis, University of Washington, Seattle, 1966.

[36] Michelle A. Hiatt, "An Empirical Measure of Role Confidence in Adoptive Parents." Unpublished master's thesis, University of Washington, Seattle, 1967.

[37] Gerald Pepper, "Inter-Racial Adoptions: Family Profile, Motivation and Coping Methods." Unpublished doctoral dissertation, University of Southern California, Los Angeles, 1966.

attention and may have great implications for the field of adoptions in general. As frequently noted, most interracial adoptions have necessitated the relinquishment of many of the usual standards set by agencies for adoptive parents. In the event that the adoptive placements so made may be demonstrated to have no or few ill effects for the parents concerned, and perhaps even more benign effects, then this research would certainly raise considerable question about the validity of the present general standards. Without this growing number of placements made beyond the pale of these standards, there could not have been a population available for study to test the validity of assumptions underlying standards. In sum, the ultimate value of research on interracial adoptions may well not be in direct application to this specific practice, but rather in the general information it might yield about parent-child relationships in general and especially the adoptive parent-child situation.

General Trends in Interracial Adoptions

Considering the available reports on interracial adoptions and the existing research, there are ten general trends that seem to characterize the movement to date:

1. The initiative for interracial adoptions seems to have come from the experience and aftermath of World War II, the Korean War, and the Chinese Civil War. Thus, the first interracial adoptions were international as well, with children coming from Japan, Korea, and Hong Kong.

2. A fairly high proportion of these interracial adoptions have been on an independent basis.

3. A very high proportion of these children have had one Caucasian and one non-Caucasian parent.

4. The vast majority of adoptive par-

ents involved in interracial adoptions have been Caucasians.

5. Interracial adoption has necessitated the relaxing of long-established agency standards for adoptive parents.

6. A large number of these children have been older than Caucasian children placed for adoption and many have had previous placements in foster homes and institutions.

7. While little research has been done, the agency reports on these adoptions describe them as in general highly successful.

8. The higher volume and longer history of placement of Orientals with Caucasians indicates that the resistance to interracial adoption probably follows a continuum based on skin color, reflecting the situation in the larger society. This would seem to apply both to applicants and agency personnel.

9. The term interracial with reference to adoption is an elastic one and any comparison of programs must take into account the specific groups involved.

10. There appears to be little systematic reporting available concerning independent interracial adoption. This omission must be borne in mind in considering the field, since we may be best informed about the smallest volume of this type of adoption.

Assumptions

The institution of interracial adoption implies lack of existing alternative resources for these children. The fact that agencies have seen fit to alter standards for the adoption of minority group children while maintaining a different set of standards for adoption of Caucasian children further indicates that agencies anticipate Caucasian parents will want these minority group children only as a second choice to a Caucasian child. Some data have been presented to suggest that the latter may not always be the case and that some parents may, in fact, prefer a child of a different race. Quite conceivably, then, it may be the agencies' own placement of value on racial matching that underlies their notion of the undesirability of these children rather than the reality demand for them. Thus, it is possible that the institution of interracial adoption has, in fact, arisen as much out of the demand by Caucasian parents for these children as it has out of the children's need for adoptive parents.

The placement of non-Caucasian children with Caucasian parents further assumes that there is an insufficient supply of potential parents of their own race, or at least parents who meet agency standards. While there may be some validity to this assumption, this paper will deal later with some of the unexplored possibilities of developing the resource of parents of the children's own race, specifically with reference to Negro children.

Interracial adoptions are based on further assumptions that underlie all adoption practice. They stem from the explicit assumption that nonadoptive placements are less desirable than adoptive placements. Further, there is the same striking upward mobility assumption accompanying interracial adoptions as accompanies other adoptions in which agencies are involved. The assumption is that children from lower status, minority racial, foreign country origins will be best off and happiest in the adoptive homes of Caucasian, middle-class American families. Finally, these interracial adoptions assume that the functional consequences of these adoptions (unspecified) by far outweigh the dysfunctional ones for the natural parent, the child, and the adoptive parent. This is reflected especially whenever discussions of psychological adjustment and development and cultural assimilation are considered. It may be said that these discussions—without much data, but a great deal of thought and consideration—reflect the optimistic bias associated with adoptions in general.

The writers' own perspective on the institution of interracial adoption is essentially a child-focused one. As such it can be viewed only in the context of an entire array of child welfare services to meet an ever increasing need of minority group children—and especially Negro children—for care and protection that are not or cannot be provided by their biological parents. The urgency of their need demands that all forms of child care be given ever increasing attention.

Interracial adoption obviously meets some legitimate needs of parents who wish to adopt children and at the same time provides families and homes for a few children who would otherwise be denied them. But the general interest in interracial adoption seems considerably out of proportion to its magnitude and its potential for meeting the needs of children without parents able and willing to rear them. For example, when one thinks of the enormous problems faced by the ever increasing numbers of children in countries devastated by war, the adoption of a few thousand children by American families is virtually not a solution at all, although it is, of course, a worthwhile undertaking on other grounds. And in the same vein, when one views the problems of large numbers of Negro children in need of stable and permanent families, the adoption of these children by Caucasian families must take its proper place as a miniscule effort and more of an indication of socal change in the broader area of intergroup relations than an adoptive resource for these children. For the child welfare field in general, more fruitful and imaginative efforts might well be devoted to finding homes for children in their own country and their own ethnic subsociety and doing whatever is necessary to strengthen the fabric of those homes while carefully researching the totality of these alternative child care arrangements.

Alternatives to Interracial Adoption

In the following sections alternative plans that can be developed for meeting the needs of these children will be discussed. It is not the writers' intention to imply that the practice of interracial adoption should be replaced by any one plan. Rather, our perspective is that interracial adoption can fulfill its greatest potential only when it is integrated into an array of services adequate to meet the need. No plan can be the plan of choice until there are honest choices to be made. Until that time arrives, decisions as to the fate of these children cannot be truly child focused; they will simply get what is available, whether it is in their best interest or not.

In considering alternatives to interracial adoption two things will be looked at: (1) other adoption alternatives and (2) alternatives to adoption itself. In considering other adoption alternatives, focus will be specifically on alternatives for Negro children, since this is by far the group with the largest and most pressing need. Reference is specifically to the adoption of Negro children by Negro parents.

Stimulating Adoption by Negro Families

Common practice has been to attribute the large numbers of unadopted Negro children to the lack of interest in adoption on the part of Negro families. There have been general notions of a culturally determined reluctance to adopt illegitimate children at the same time as there has been a notion that illegitimacy was highly sanctioned among the Negro people. While neither of these assertions has been supported by careful research, it is the contradiction between the two that has long gone undetected. It is now fairly clear,

based on rather careful analysis, that Negroes who meet agency standards for adoption adopt children at a somewhat higher rate than similar Caucasian families do. Among Negro husband-wife couples without children who earn $3,000 or more per year—that is, among those barely above the poverty line—the adoption ratio is 4.9 per 1,000, while the ratio for Caucasian families of similar status is 3.4.[38] Four other studies among middle-income Negro families in Buffalo and Rochester, New York, Washington, D.C., and Baltimore, Maryland, have found a relatively high level of awareness of and interest in adoption.[39]

Perhaps the most striking feature of the general effort to get Negro families to adopt Negro children has been the consistent and wide discrepancy between the expression of interest and availability on the part of these parents and the number who have actually received children from agencies. Three large-scale efforts indicate the dimensions of this phenomenon.

The first is that of the Family and Children's Service of Pittsburgh, which early showed an interest in the recruitment of Negro adoptive applicants.[40] The number of applicants who expressed interest in adoption and the number of adoptive placements actually made for the years 1951–55 are shown in Table 2. The second report is from the large-scale and highly successful efforts of six children's agencies in Chicago under the co-ordination of the Wel-

[38] Elizabeth Herzog, "A Reappraisal of Evidence: Why So Few Negro Adoptions?" *Children*, Vol. 12, No. 1 (January-February 1965), pp. 14–18.

[39] Irving Fowler, "The Urban Middle-Class Negro and Adoption: Two Series of Studies and Their Implications for Action," *Child Welfare*, Vol. 45, No. 9 (November 1966), pp. 522–524; Leila C. Deasy, "The Urban Negro and Adoption of Children," *Child Welfare*, Vol. 41, No. 9 (November 1962), pp. 400–410.

[40] David Fanshel, *A Study in Negro Adoption* (New York: Child Welfare League of America, 1957).

fare Council of Metropolitan Chicago.[41] Their experience is shown in Table 3. A third observation of recruitment of Negro adoptive families comes from the experience of Minority Adoption Recruitment of Children's Homes (MARCH) in San Francisco.[42] Working closely with a number of adoption agencies in the San Francisco Bay Area, this project successfully recruited 801 applicants for minority group children, most of them Negroes. By the end of the project only 49 placements had been made.

In all these projects the voluntary withdrawal of Negro couples after making contact with the agency was extremely high. The reasons for withdrawal and the reasons for rejection by the agency were varied and complex. Among them, however, were a few that are as simple as they are effective: agency requirements that adoptive applicants prove their infertility, that adoptive applicants pay a fee, and that the wives not work; agency restrictions that only married couples can adopt children; and age and health restrictions. Whatever the psychosocial validity of other standards of adoption agencies, it seems clear that these take an undue toll on the applications of Negro couples for adoptions. It also seems fairly clear that these standards were developed at a time when their major function was to help agencies screen out some of the many Caucasian applicants who were applying for the few available Caucasian babies. They seemed wholly dysfunctional for the adoption of Negro children. The requirement of a married couple, for example, underestimates the extent and functions of extended families among Negroes.[43]

TABLE 2. NEGRO APPLICANTS AND ADOPTIVE PLACEMENTS, FAMILY AND CHILDREN'S SERVICE OF PITTSBURGH, 1951–55

Year	Negro Couples Interested in Adoption	Negro Children Placed in Adoptive Homes	Percentage of Adoptions (assuming one child per couple)
1951	31	4	13
1952	43	7	16
1953	37	9	24
1954	75	10	13
1955	67	18	27

TABLE 3. NEGRO APPLICANTS AND HOMES APPROVED, SIX CHICAGO AGENCIES, 1956–58

Year	Adoption Applications from Negro Couples	Homes Approved	Percentage of Approval
1956	324	56	17
1957	271	84	31
1958	249	60	24

One of the Negro adoptive placements made by an agency in Jamestown where 70 percent of adoptive parents were middle-class white-collar professionals bears considerable relevance for some observations that have been made here:

Kathy was a three year old Negro girl, adopted by Mr. and Mrs. Elmer Barker, a Negro couple in their mid-thirties who had one other child, aged fifteen. Neither parent had been to school beyond the ninth grade and both worked in the fields for a combined annual income of $3,000 to $4,000. Mr. Barker's high blood pressure was a problem which he let only moderately restrict his daily living.

The Barker home was in a tenant house without plumbing; there was an outdoor toilet. Although Kathy had her own bedroom, this was made possible only because Mr. and Mrs. Barker now used the living room as their bedroom. In spite of these factors, the agency, acknowledging that it was making some exceptions to its standards, decided to

---

[41] Rita Dukette and Thelma G. Thompson, *Adoptive Resources for Negro Children* (New York: Child Welfare League of America, 1959).

[42] *Adoptive Placement of Minority Group Children in the San Francisco Bay Area* (San Francisco: MARCH, 1959).

[43] Andrew Billingsley, *Black Families in White America* (Englewood Cliffs, N.J.: Prentice-Hall, 1968).

use this home since there was no other available Negro couple with dark skin and it was thought Kathy was greatly in need of a permanent home, having been in foster care almost all her life. . . . Currently, at the Barkers, Kathy's symptomatology included difficulties in social adaptation and ready crying, but her almost twelve months of continued living with one set of parents seemed to have made Kathy less frightened and more certain of the grown-ups in her immediate world.[44]

The relaxation of restrictions ordinarily placed on couples adopting children has been experimented with by several agencies wishing to increase the number of Negro adoptive parents. The waiving of age limits, restrictions on employment of the mother, the infertility requirement, and even the limitations on single parents have all been successful in increasing the actual number of placements and without any apparent hardship for the children involved. However, the simple relaxation of restrictions and revisions in agency policies regarding acceptance of applicants would not seem to be as far reaching in its effects as might be hoped. The relaxation of restrictions will not affect the loss of the couples who drop out after the initial contact or certainly of those who never approach the agencies. Whatever emphasis may be placed on the specifics of the situation such as restrictions and rules, the simple fact remains that while the clientele of children and the wished-for clientele of adoptive parents is increasingly becoming Negro, the agencies remain essentially Caucasian-dominated institutions. This is no less true for the field of adoptions than for any of the other fields in social welfare. Thus, some of the more basic solutions will, no doubt, require basic changes in both agency policy and structure. The need for Negro social workers is apparent. Equally important is the need for imaginative and innovative approaches for insuring Negro

---

[44] Henry S. Maas and Richard E. Engler, Jr., *Children in Need of Parents* (New York: Columbia University Press, 1959), p. 212.

lay representation at the policy-making level of these agencies, in order to insure a true integration of the services into the Negro community and at the same time to bring about changes that are consonant with the values of the group being served.

In summary, the new departures in adoption practices with respect to Negro families and children that a number of agencies such as the Los Angeles County Department of Adoptions and the Children's Home Society of California are already finding valuable include the following:

1. Changing adoption standards to take into consideration the structure and function of Negro family life in America. Some of the specific changes involve eliminating arbitrary restrictions on (a) age, (b) financial status, (c) fertility, and (d) marital status (e.g., marriage unbroken by divorce, adoption by single persons). The most easily achieved change that could immediately be brought about concerns fees charged by adoption agencies. Fees certainly need to be made more flexible. In some instances, not only should the fee be waived, but the agency should actually pay a fee to the adoptive parents.

2. Subsidizing adoptive homes. The potential of this is virtually unexplored. The United States is probably the only major nation in the world without some system of family allowances. Thus, the paying of people to be parents is not without precedent. With specific reference to Negro adoptive parents, it should be pointed out that even middle-income Negro families are frequently not in the same position to undertake parental financial responsibility as are their Caucasian counterparts with the same earned incomes. This is because the volume of inherited wealth among Negroes is not nearly that among Caucasians. Thus the parental financial help so often available to Caucasian couples when they begin a family is far less frequently available to Negro couples. In addition, most Negro families in the middle- and upper-income ranges maintain this status only

through employment of wives. Thus, the need to assist Negro couples—even those in the middle-income bracket—in some financial way in order to stimulate adoption cannot be overemphasized.

The task would seem to be to undertake these changes based on a realistic assessment of both the needs of children and the alternatives to adoption. Flexible and reality-oriented standards are already in practice on a selective basis, as the previous illustration suggests.

3. Recruiting a truly racially integrated staff and board.

4. Actively recruiting Negro families for adoption and treating them as clients in a sellers' market rather than in a buyers' market.

5. Co-ordinating agency practices with the new standards and recruitment efforts so that discrepancies between recruitment and placement might be minimized.

6. Training and reorienting adoption agency staffs to function in accord with this new direction. Nonprofessional trained workers should be used for tasks that do not require professional skill, thus releasing the professional workers.

7. Carefully researching both the process and outcomes of these changes.

8. Using volunteers, especially adoptive parents, more extensively for recruitment and interpretation.

Alternatives to Adoption Itself

Beyond simply making changes within the basic structure of the adoption process, alternatives to adoption itself need to be explored. The two to be discussed here—subsidized permanent foster homes and guardianship—while not approximating a parental relationship identical to the biological one, are both intended to insure the child some measure of permanence and stability.

The institution of the "permanent foster home" is now in operation in the Los Angeles County Welfare Department, Lutheran Social Service of Minnesota, and the Children's Aid Society of Philadelphia. These homes may be distinguished from both usual foster homes and adoptive homes in several ways. There is a psychological commitment on the part of both the agency and the foster parents to consider the placement a permanent one. At the practical level, the child is no longer considered for an adoptive placement and the home no longer as having that child's place available for others.

Legally, of course, unlike adoption, the agency retains accountability for the child. Economically, although there is wide variation in the homes, the agency can continue varying levels of economic support as in normal foster care. All three of the programs in operation report a favorable increase in the number of such permanent placements for children and favorable effects for both the foster parents and the child ensuing from this sense of permanence. These placements have been both inter- and intraracial.

An unexplored avenue of adoption alternatives that would indeed insure greater permance of status for a child is that of legal guardianship. It is used, however, on a limited basis by some agencies. While the legal entanglements involved are complex, especially concerning parental consent and the relationship to relinquishment, guardianship offers some measure of security to those for whom adoptive homes cannot be established. There are, of course, other complexities with guardianship that need to be resolved in order for it to be an effective alternative to adoption.

While the status of wardship is not unusual for many children under child welfare services, such children have been almost exclusively wards of the juvenile court. This impersonal kind of guardianship is not referred to here. Rather, reference is to the appointment of an *individual* by the court to be the guardian of a child. Such an individual then has all the rights and responsibilities of a parent save financial responsibility. While a guardian is subject to the control of the court, his relationship to his ward is far more responsible and autonomous than that of a foster parent, whose relationship to the child is always contingent on the third party, the supervising agency. Guardianship, of course, is a legal entity that insures the child a much more definite status in society than does foster care. The ward also enjoys a more clearly defined relationship to his guardian than does the foster child to his foster parent. While guardianship is an old and established legal entity, it has remained virtually unused by child welfare practitioners. At least two prominent figures in the welfare field, Charles Schottland and Hasseltine Taylor, have called attention to the potential of guardianship in child welfare.[45] The field has been dominated by the practice of foster care, in which the agency retains responsibility for the child. This, of course, has been true for all children, not only minority groups, which are the focus here.

The potential of legal guardianship as a resource, especially for minority group children, is now being experimented with by a few agencies. One agency in California at present obtains permission for this routinely from Negro mothers who are also relinquishing their child.

Guardianship might have the following advantages, especially for minority group children: (1) Since it does not entail financial responsibility as does adoption, but does entail all other parental rights and

obligations, the potential source of guardians for these children may well expand the present restricted resource of adoptive parents for them. (2) Legal guardianship may be preferable to ordinary foster care or even permanent foster homes, since it insures the child a legal status that the foster child does not have. (3) It might be a means of strengthening and expanding the resources of the extended family in the Negro subsociety for the Negro child in need of parental substitutes.

While guardianship, like the other solutions to the needs of these children, is by no means without problems, it certainly does seem to be a resource that deserves considerably more attention from the child welfare field than it has received to date.

In sum, the alternatives to interracial adoption, for Negro children especially, concern the stimulation of Negro adoptive placements and the exploration of alternatives to adoption itself. While it seems doubtful that the interest in interracial adoptions will outstrip either of these alternatives in the near future, a more immediate and basic social policy issue may be at stake. The resources of adoption institutions are not unlimited. In the face of the limitations on resources, where should the available energy be put—in simply pursuing Caucasian applicants for interracial adoptions or also in spreading resources to pursue alternatives to this solution? Hopefully such an issue might be decided, not on the basis of unsubstantiated values and principles, but rather on the basis of documented evidence of which course is most beneficial to the child's welfare.

In arriving at such decisions, we are truly faced with a pitiable amount of knowledge. This lack of knowledge is not limited to information concerning the evaluation of various kinds of placements; rather, and perhaps more important, there is a great deal that is not known about these children, their mothers and fathers, and their general

---

[45] Personal communication from Charles I. Schottland, Waltham, Mass.; Hasseltine B. Taylor, "Guardianship or 'Permanent Placement' of Children," in Jacobus Tenbroek and the Editors of the *California Law Review*, eds., *The Law of the Poor* (San Francisco: Chandler Publishing Co., 1966).

welfare. For all the studies that have been made of Negroes, for example, none has specifically focused on the structure and function of Negro family life as it seeks to adapt to the conditions imposed on it by history and contemporary social forces. Not much is learned about these families by measuring social pathology in them as compared with Caucasian middle-class families. And it must be said frankly that social work researchers have failed the field as other social researchers have. What is needed is not one study, of course, but a whole series of studies of Negro family and community life with a variety of research methods designed to learn something about the value systems, patterns of adaptation, and other aspects of the structure and function of Negro family life. Perhaps then something might be learned about the causes, consequences, and meaning of differential strategies of survival not only among Negro families but among American families in general.

Such studies will need to be pursued within explicitly formulated theoretical frameworks. But we shall have to create our theories as we go. The ones we have, have not served us well.

Summary

In this paper the emerging practice of interracial adoption has been discussed from a research perspective. The general context of adoptions within which this practice takes place has been described, the accumulated experience in interracial adoptions has been discussed, some suggestions have been made about the general parameters of this practice together with some of its underlying assumptions, and, finally, some alternatives to interracial adoptions have been discussed briefly. Throughout the paper questions have been raised about areas of adoption practice that are in need of systematic research.

The writers' general assessment of the interracial adoption movement is that it creates much more public interest than is warranted by either its place in child welfare practice or its potential for meeting the needs of children in need of families. While it might appropriately be viewed as reflecting social change in intergroup relations in the larger society, it can hardly be hailed as contributing major solutions to current child welfare problems. The writers have thus concluded with a discussion of some underdeveloped alternatives to the interracial adoption of non-Caucasian children. Chief among these, with respect to Negro children, is expansion of adoptions by Negro families. This task calls for a greater understanding of the structure and function of Negro family and community life and the reformulation of adoption standards, agency practices, agency staffing and board composition, and reorientation of adoption agency staffs according to this new standard. Long-term foster care and legal guardianship were also briefly discussed as alternatives to adoption.

Racial Discrimination and Diagnostic Differentiation

JOSEPH W. EATON AND NEIL GILBERT

The current state of race relations in social welfare institutions is marked by a confusion between *discrimination* and *diagnostic differentiation*. Both involve the classification and segregation of individuals, but whereas one is morally repugnant in a democratic society, the other documents its capacity to serve diverse groups, each in accordance with its needs. Social workers, as well as the general public, often fail to make the appropriate distinction between these concepts, although they are quite different in their meaning and their operational consequences.

Discrimination can be said to occur when services, opportunities, or resources are allocated to people strictly on the basis of

Joseph W. Eaton, Ph.D., is Director, Advanced Program, and Professor of Social Work Research and Sociology, Graduate School of Social Work, University of Pittsburgh, Pittsburgh, Pennsylvania. Neil Gilbert, Ph.D., is Research Director, Mayor's Committee on Human Resources, Pittsburgh, Pennsylvania.

irrelevant status characteristics, i.e., skin color, sex, legal status, ethnic background, and the like. Diagnostic differentiation involves the allocation of these social commodities on the basis of *relevant* social and psychological characteristics in conformity with each person's individual (rather than status) attributes.

Diagnostic differentiation can result in what looks like discrimination. Quasi-segregated programs develop when a status group has a high incidence of distinct interests or personal characteristics requiring special services. For instance, in the Pittsburgh Community Action Program there is an educational-medical service for pregnant school-age girls. The agency that operates this program has a policy of nonpreferential treatment for those who need it. Although it serves an area that is more than 50 percent white, the agency's clientele is about 90 percent Negro. This is a reflection of the fact that proportionately fewer white girls in the area get pregnant out of wedlock; those who do may receive enough support from home so that they do not need the agency's service or they go outside their community for help more often than do Negroes. To label this program discriminatory would obscure these social realities.

Diagnostic differentiation may also lead to *preferential* treatment. This involves the granting of an advantage in the competition for a social role or for scarce resources on the basis of a status characteristic. Veterans get a ten- to fifteen-point credit in their civil service examinations. Why is this done? It is viewed as a form of compensation for past contributions to their country. It also makes allowance for the loss of time during which to acquire relevant technical training and experience that others could obtain because no military service interfered with their career development. The added points serve as a means of equity restoration.

But what if this credit were raised to eighty points? In this case the opportunity for employment would be allocated totally on the basis of one's status as a veteran. The applicant's actual abilities would become nearly irrelevant. What would emerge is *discrimination in reverse.*

It is difficult to pinpoint in the abstract the line separating discrimination in reverse from preferential treatment. But in practice it is often possible to tell when this line has been crossed—when, for example, the directorship of a community action agency is assigned on the basis of race to an individual who has no prior experience or technical qualifications for running a multimillion-dollar operation.

Preferential treatment may operate on two levels. It can be quite explicit when reasons for preference are generally acceptable. For example, few will argue against special treatment for veterans, the handicapped, or children. A local residence preference was written into the job description for the co-ordinator's position in each of the eight target neighborhoods

of the Pittsburgh CAP. This was generally acceptable because of the belief that local candidates have a superior insight into the neighborhood problems and as a bonus it provided employment for neighborhood people. However, when the program was launched only one of the eight co-ordinator's positions had been filled with a local resident because no suitable candidates were available.

When the degree of consensus is less, preferential treatment may be realized by informal agreement. This is what often occurs when special provisions are made for those handicapped by the consequences of past racial discrimination. Race is a more controversial criterion for preferential treatment. In spite of their informality, unofficial agreements for preferential treatment can be quite binding. None of the Pittsburgh neighborhoods had a racial preference written into the co-ordinator's job description. But in three neighborhoods with large and vocal Negro populations a Negro co-ordinator was hired. This implicit form of preferential treatment accounts for the fact that across the United States more and more key jobs in the human relations field are going to Negroes even when equally or better qualified whites are available and are interested in the jobs.

The four concepts just outlined are key variables in rendering welfare services. Discrimination, diagnostic differentiation, preferential treatment, and discrimination in reverse become relevant whenever minority groups get or want specialized services. These concepts are especially useful for analyzing contemporary treatment programs and the delivery of services to Negroes. Briefly, they may be defined as follows:

Discrimination: the allocation of services, opportunities or resources strictly on the basis of irrelevant status characteristics (e.g., skin color).

Diagnostic differentiation: allocation of the above-mentioned commodities by relevant social and psychological characteristics (e.g., to unmarried mothers or persons with special learning problems).

Preferential treatment: a social policy favoring a status category in the allocation of services, opportunities, and resources in compensation for past services, past or present injustices, handicaps, or other characteristics (e.g., the assignment of a ten- to fifteen-point advantage to veterans on civil service examinations).

Discrimination in reverse: a social policy favoring a status category in the allocation of services, opportunities, and resources to so high a degree as to result in the exclusion of other variables that should also be given some weight (e.g., the unwritten policy of many community action agencies to hire only Negro directors).

The civil rights movement is concerned with the elimination of discrimination. Few people would advocate that its intent be to prevent diagnostic differentiation or preferential treatment for past disadvantages and injustices. And most would draw a line separating preferential treatment from discrimination in reverse. Theoretically, this position is quite clear. However, in actuality problems often arise that tend to blur the distinctions when efforts are made to apply these concepts to the day-to-day allocation of welfare resources.

Confusing Discrimination and Diagnostic Differentiation

Confusion arises easily between discrimination and diagnostic differentiation because on the surface the practical consequences of both policies are often quite similar. Both can result in segregated services.

Camouflage of Discriminatory Policies

Clever racists have for a long time camouflaged discriminatory policies in the rhetoric of diagnostic differentiation. A sterilization law—which was directed at Negroes—was advocated in North Carolina by rationalizing it as a means of curbing illegitimacy. An extraordinarily offensive sentiment of racism was thus cloaked in a pseudo-diagnostic guise. Those making the seemingly diagnostic case for a sterilization law took care to avoid mention of race. Illegitimacy was analyzed as a lack of individual morality rather than a lack of structural supports for family life. From this perspective, sterilization was advocated as a scientific solution for persons unable to exercise control over their sexual impulses. It might not restore morality, it was argued, but it could in one swoop eliminate the pregnancy risks. There was no public mention of the fact that such a sterilization program, if widespread, would also serve to reduce what those who favored the legislation would call the "problem" of a growing Negro population.[1]

An apparently nonracial characteristic (illegitimacy) was thus used as a cover to rationalize practices that would in both intent and consequences be essentially discriminatory. This proposal could not touch the socioeconomic roots of illegitimacy. Instead, it offered a seemingly diagnostic basis for surgically reducing the capacity of an outgroup to bear children. Members of the ingroup would face fewer risks that their daughters would be sterilized since they could rely on tradition to insure that in practice a policy of this nature would be stringently applied only to Negroes.

The type of camouflage noted can be misleading in two directions. A valid distinction between racial discrimination and diagnostic differentiation may be deliberately obscured for political reasons. Some political leaders point to differential allocation of services, opportunities, or resources as

---

[1] *See* Joseph Morrison, "Illegitimacy, Sterilization and Racism," *Social Service Review*, Vol. 39, No. 1 (March 1965), pp. 1–10.

an indication of discriminatory policies. Actually, when the facts are carefully checked it may be found that the differentials reflect—largely or entirely—the consequences of a process of diagnostic differentiation. Not all those who voted in favor of censuring Congressman Adam Clayton Powell can be dismissed as racists, delighted to discriminate against a Negro. While this case no doubt provided some with an opportunity to strike at a political figure they would have protected had his skin been white, those who defended the congressman against all charges might not have taken so morally compromising a position had he been a politician from the deep South. They expressed a preference for discrimination in reverse.

Opposition to Preferential Treatment

The controversy surrounding the Moynihan Report suggests another basis on which the distinction between these concepts is obscured. Diagnostic differentiation may be rejected when it punctures the wishful notion that essentially all groups are equal in their educational, social, or psychological attributes. Although special services based on differences unrelated to past caste conditions, such as segregated or near-segregated gym classes for boys and girls or speech correction classes for non-English-speaking students, are readily accepted, special services needed to correct for delicate variables reflecting past racial discrimination may be discredited for social-psychological reasons. As Moynihan indicates:

Family is not a subject Americans tend to consider appropiate as an area of public policy. For that very reason to raise the subject in terms of public policy is to arouse immediate interest: edged with apprehension, but interest nonetheless.[2]

---

[2] Daniel P. Moynihan, "The President and the Negro: The Moment Lost," *Commentary*, Vol. 43, No. 2 (February 1967), p. 35.

As Moynihan found out, this edge of apprehension was quickly honed to cut razor sharp after the publication of his carefully written and scholarly analysis. He was personally charged, among other things, with encouraging a new form of subtle racism. In an article on the report, *Newsweek* clearly expressed the dilemma:

The Negro family problem was scarcely news to social scientists. But its very intimacy has excluded it from the public dialogue of civil rights; it reaches too deep into white prejudices and Negro sensitivities.[3]

Preferential treatment aimed at correcting past handicaps can be seriously undermined by such opposition. An example is provided by the programs of compensatory education in urban schools. An overwhelming proportion of those who need such special education are Negro children. Of 629 elementary schools in twelve major city school systems in 1966 using compensatory education funds, 435 served student populations in which Negroes outnumbered whites. Although the findings of the study undertaken by the U.S. Commission on Civil Rights indicate that these programs have as yet made little impact on the quality of education in predominantly Negro schools, it is plausible that in the future a more intense economic and social commitment to compensatory education would produce more salutary results.[4] Yet many civil rights advocates are opposed to extending this form of preferential treatment. Robert Carter, general counsel for the National Association for the Advancement of Colored People, views it as a manifestation of the "separate-but-equal doctrine." He states that the commission's report "makes

---

[3] As quoted in Lee Rainwater and William L. Yancey, "Black Families and the White House," *Trans-Action*, Vol. 3, No. 8 (July–August 1966), p. 48.

[4] U.S. Commission on Civil Rights, *Racial Isolation in the Public Schools* (Washington, D.C.: U.S. Government Printing Office, 1967), pp. 115–140.

clear that we are deluding the public, both Negro and white, when we offer compensatory education instead of mainstream education." [5] This view of preferential treatment fails to acknowledge its intent when compensatory education is passed off merely as a guise for maintaining the status quo.[6]

The confusion that arises between these concepts may be inspired by prejudice or by corrupt political considerations. But often the misunderstanding is based on the imputation of fraudulent motives without regard for the actual circumstances. The civil rights movement has no simple problem in attempting to separate out the differences between racial discrimination and diagnostic differentiation, between preferential treatment and discrimination in reverse. Men are not born equal. Within all races there are great variations in terms of aptitude, health, and other individual characteristics. These differences cannot be politically abolished for either the white man or the black man. What can and must be accomplished politically is equalization of the opportunity structure. To achieve this there has to be a program of preferential treatment to compensate for past inequalities. But it must be organized in such a way as to avoid becoming discrimination in reverse. This may often lead to quasi-segregated services. Attempts will also have to be made to strengthen diagnostic tools in order to provide more meaningful services and normatively equitable treatment.

The utility of any conceptual framework, such as the distinctions drawn here between racial discrimination and diagnostic differentiation and between preferential treatment and discrimination in reverse, depends on what can be clarified when it is applied. Do the concepts help one focus on the normative meanings of social conditions that are analytically relevant to a program of civil rights enforcement? The authors will try to answer this question by reference to the treatment of Negroes in two institutional settings that operate with captive populations. In too many such settings the treatment accorded minority groups tends to perpetuate the sense of futility and powerlessness often felt by the black man in America.

Negroes in the Armed Forces

The National Advisory Commission on Selective Service cites a disturbing fact in a recent report: 22 percent of the army troops killed in action during the first eleven months of 1966 were Negroes.[7] This was almost twice their proportion in the total population of the United States and in the population of army personnel serving in Vietnam at that time. Are Negroes being sent out on dangerous assignments more often than white soldiers? Is Negro blood less valued than that of other citizens of the United States? Racial discrimination of a most heinous type could reasonably be inferred if no other information were available, all the more since the army has been desegregated only a few decades. But while plausible, this interpretation does not provide an adequate explanation.

To begin with, in the selection of recruits diagnostic differentiation rather than dis-

[5] *New York Times*, March 10, 1967, p. 38.

[6] A cogent argument supporting the idea of preferential treatment for Negro institutions is presented by Frances Fox Piven and Richard A. Cloward, "The Case Against Urban Desegregation," *Social Work*, Vol. 12, No. 1 (January 1967), pp. 12–21. For the opposing view, *see* Clarence Funnye and Ronald Shiffman, "The Imperative of Deghettoization: An Answer to Piven and Cloward," *Social Work*, Vol. 12, No. 2 (April 1967), pp. 5–11.

[7] National Advisory Commission on Selective Service, *In Pursuit of Equity: Who Serve When Not All Serve* (Washington, D.C.: U.S. Government Printing Office, 1967), p. 26.

crimination seems to be the major process for determining who shall serve.

Of all those examined [for induction into the armed services] almost 50 percent of the non-white men aged 26 to 29 years in 1964 had been found unfit for service as opposed to almost 25 percent of the white male population of the same age group.[8]

This high Negro rejection rate is not consistent with any theory that the military prefers Negroes or that they are less valued. Rather, it reflects the unfortunate reality that membership in a disadvantaged group, aside from economic consequences, has distinct social and physical effects on the individual.

Then why is the Negro casualty rate so high? The casualty statistics correspond closely to Negro representation in army combat units. In 1965, 22.8 percent of the enlisted men in combat units in Vietnam were Negro. Their disproportionate representation in these units in part reflects the Negro soldiers' record of heavy volunteering for such duty, because combat units provide a superb opportunity for rapid advancement into noncommissioned officer positions. Also, the combat situation allows Negroes the opportunity to "prove to themselves, and to their white colleagues that they are men capable of as much skill, courage and sacrifice as any man alive." [9] But equally—if not more—important is the fact that educational deficiencies and lack of skills disqualify a disproportionate number of Negroes from admission to specialized (noncombat or limited combat) units that often require some technical knowledge or advanced education. As the report indicates, even for those Negroes who pass the induction examination "sometimes the

path leading to an infantry division is the only one entirely open." [10]

While induction and placement within the army appear to be based on diagnostic variables, the National Advisory Commission on Selective Service also found data that suggest discrimination at the point of recruitment. Three out of ten Negroes judged qualified for service by the armed forces were actually drafted as against fewer than two out of ten (18.8 percent) of the qualified whites. The report explains this discrepancy in part by the fact that few Negroes are admitted into the state-controlled reserve programs. In 1964 only 5.4 percent of the qualified nonwhites as compared with 20.6 percent of the qualified whites had experience in the reserves. The implication of this discrepancy was bolstered by seemingly justified complaints that "men are recruited into the Reserve Programs for qualifications other than those which determine entry into the regular forces." This finding had a major bearing on the recommendation of the commission that the current reserve program be fundamentally revised.[11]

Another ingredient that has bearing on discrimination at the point of entry is the composition of the nation's draft boards. In 1966 only 261 (1.5 percent) of the 17,123 local board members were Negro. Since these boards are invested with a great deal of local autonomy, the lack of Negro representation is especially relevant in the southern states.[12]

Discrimination also appears to be a factor in explaining the small number of Ne-

---

[8] *Ibid.*, p. 22.

[9] Whitney M. Young, Jr., "When the Negroes in Vietnam Come Home," *Harper's* (June 1967), p. 66.

---

[10] National Advisory Commission on Selective Service, *op. cit.*, p. 26. *See also* Morris Janowitz, "American Democracy and Military Service," *Trans-Action*, Vol. 4, No. 4 (March 1967), pp. 6–8.

[11] National Advisory Commission on Selective Service, *op. cit.*, p. 53.

[12] *Ibid.*, p. 19.

groes who get into officer training programs. Only 0.4 percent of the qualified nonwhites were officers as contrasted with 4.3 percent of the qualified whites. A strong case might be made for introducing a procedure of preferential treatment aimed specifically at Negro applicants who meet at least the minimum requirements for officer training. A more intensive effort at recruiting Negroes into the regular officer training programs might also help. It is highly likely that qualified Negroes fail to apply because they are unaware of this program or assume that they will be discriminated against as is true in so many areas of American life. One could even consider providing special training programs structured to help candidates overcome the impact of past educational deficiencies. A preferential program of this nature would, however, have to guard against discrimination in reverse. Officers lead men in battle. The consequences of commissioning an unqualified officer would be potentially more perilous than those of employing an incompetent foreman.

Strongly circumstantial evidence exists of discrimination against Negroes by the draft board, the reserves, and the officer training programs. Yet the evidence provides only a partial explanation for the high rate of Negro casualties in Vietnam. For many individuals of lower-class origins a military career presents an excellent path for upward social mobility.[13] As the 1963 U.S. Commission on Civil Rights report concludes: "Negro service men believe that the armed forces offer them greater career opportunities than they can find in the civilian economy."[14] This statement is supported by the high re-enlistment rates among Negroes. These facts—along with discrimination—also have a bearing on casualty rates.

Treatment of Negroes in Penal Institutions

The most insidious forms of racial discrimination are manifested in the courts and penal institutions of the United States. Discriminatory practices there affect not only the basic rights of the individual but threaten the very essence of democracy. Life itself is affected, as is so tragically evident in the differential applications of the death penalty. The harsh statistics reveal that between 1930 and 1961, 85 percent of the robbers and burglars and 90 percent of the rapists who received the death penalty were Negro. These sentences were exacted largely in southern states for crimes committed against whites.[15]

In other areas of life such as housing, education, and employment, discrimination functions to reduce the Negro opportunity structure. It limits available alternatives for achieving the "good life." Gifted and well-organized Negroes can sometimes triumph in spite of such special disabilities. Whatever the restrictions may be, some alternatives often exist for those who are unusual. With respect to discrimination in the courts and penal institutions, these alternatives are nearly closed. When Negroes are inequitably kept behind bars, their opportunity to organize for counteraction is nullified.

Prejudice and discrimination in the administration of justice have to be expressed subtly, otherwise the higher courts would have too much cause to intervene. Con-

---

[13] *See*, for example, Charles H. Coates, "America's New Officer Corps," *Trans-Action*, Vol. 3, No. 4 (March 1966), pp. 22–24.

[14] As quoted in National Advisory Commission on Selective Service, *op. cit.*, p. 26.

[15] Thomas F. Pettigrew, *A Profile of the Negro American* (Princeton, N.J.: D. Van Nostrand Co., 1964), p. 139.

sequently, these manifestations are often difficult to distinguish from the operation of diagnostic differentiation concerning the most appropriate disposition of criminal offenders. These latter judgments tend to be based on social characteristics that are associated with race, i.e., stability of employment and residence, credit ratings, family stability, and so on. As a result, the refusal of probation to a Negro, for instance, although seemingly biased, could also occur on the basis of a professionally sound process of diagnostic differentiation.

A study of delinquency in Los Angeles indicated that Negro male offenders were institutionalized more often and at an earlier age than white offenders. But is this difference necessarily the result of a policy of discrimination? The Los Angeles Probation Department was led by personnel who were ideologically opposed to discrimination. Its staff included Negro personnel. Except perhaps for a rare case, it is doubtful that racial status was a factor in determining disposition. Differences in the frequency of institutionalization could well be explained by such facts as the type of delinquent offense. The percentage of Negroes committing acts involving actual or threatened bodily harm was more than three times that of whites. Also, family composition was given a good deal of diagnostic attention in determining the outcome of any case. Those coming from broken homes, both Negro and white, were institutionalized more frequently than persons from homes in which both parents were present, irrespective of category of offense. And among all the delinquents seen by the Los Angeles courts, approximately 57 percent of the Negroes came from broken homes as compared to 36 percent of the whites.[16]

---

[16] For a more complete analysis of the data *see* Joseph Eaton and Kenneth Polk, *Measuring Delinquency* (Pittsburgh: University of Pittsburgh Press, 1961).

The juvenile court system in Los Angeles is strongly oriented toward treatment and sentences are justified more in these terms than on the basis of punitive action. Few would seriously charge this system with discrimination. In any case, the harshness of life for most Negroes—even in sunny California—and the long-range impact of lack of opportunity result in dispositions of Negro cases similar to what might occur if a discriminatory policy were in force.

The case for discrimination rather than diagnostic differentiation is much stronger in the adult prison field. Although serious efforts are being made to develop treatment programs in many state institutions, the state systems for the adult prisoner retain an orientation around punishment. And once again racial differentials exist that need to be explained. The data in Table 1 indicate that in state prisons throughout the country Negro felony prisoners are detained longer before first release than white prisoners for almost every category of offense. While the difference between median months served by Negroes and whites is, in most cases, small, the direction is quite consistent. There are only six out of sixty possible cases in which Negroes served less time than whites. When the population breakdown for each category of offense is considered, the difference becomes even more severe. Ninety percent of the population fall in the first ten categories in which in only three out of forty possible cases did Negroes serve less time than whites in terms of median months.

Statistical data are crude. They can provide only a rough comparison of the differential that probably exists in the adult parole treatment accorded to Negroes and whites. But the statistics strongly suggest that in every part of the nation the Negro offender is somehow handled more punitively in the administration of justice. Few black faces are found among the judges who pass sentence, the wardens who control penal institutions, and the officials who sit on parole boards. The color of American justice is largely white. In view of the fact that available evidence indicates that Negro felons adjust to prison better than do whites—incurring fewer rule infractions and less often attempting escapes—their poor parole record lends further credence to accusations of discrimination.[17] But before the charge of discrimination becomes accepted without qualification, other factors need to be considered.

The Negro offender is distinctly disadvantaged in presenting himself as a good risk for probation or parole. As with the case of juvenile offenders, the variables used to make a diagnostic disposition favorable to institutionalization also happen to correlate with race. This is even more true in the case of a punishment-oriented system with special concern for the protection of society. The Negro offender comes before the parole board with an inferior education that, coupled with discrimination, has led to a poor employment record. This, among other things, has hampered his ability to maintain a stable family life. The disability spiral locks him into a state of poverty and despair and out of mainstream—middle-class—America. These factors in combination serve to reduce the possibility for parole even when no racial discrimination is intended.

To insure social justice in penal institutions one must go beyond diagnostic differentiation. What is called for is some form of preferential treatment whereby those who have suffered past disadvantages owing to discrimination are allowed equal opportunities for parole. A compensatory program might have to be built into the system by allowing even some of those who present poor risks to be released early under a program of more intensive parole service to facilitate improvement in the parolee's chances for employment, family

TABLE 1. DIFFERENCE IN MEDIAN MONTHS SERVED BETWEEN NEGRO AND WHITE FELONY PRISONERS BEFORE FIRST RELEASE FROM STATE INSTITUTIONS, BY REGION AND OFFENSE, 1953 [a]

Offense	Region			
	North-west	North Central	South	West
Murder	−60	−69	+7	+11
Manslaughter	+ 3	+ 2	+8	+ 6
Robbery	+ 4	0	+4	+ 2
Aggravated assault	+ 1	+ 2	+2	+ 1
Burglary	+ 5	+ 2	+5	+ 6
Theft, except auto	+ 3	+ 2	+3	+ 5
Auto theft	+ 2	+ 3	−2	0
Embezzlement/ fraud	+ 6	+ 3	+1	+ 3
Forgery	+ 2	+ 3	+1	+ 4
Rape	+10	+ 3	+5	+13
Other sex offenses	+ 2	0	+3	− 6
Drug laws	+ 1	+ 4	+2	+ 2
Weapons	+ 1	+ 3	−7	0
Escape	0	+ 1	+1	− 6
Other	+ 1	0	+1	+ 2

[a] Data are calculated from U.S. Department of Justice, Bureau of Prisons, *National Prisoner Statistics: Prisoners Released from State and Federal Institutions 1952 and 1953* (Washington, D.C.: U.S. Government Printing Office, 1957), p. 33.

adjustment, and the like. Such a program would require a drastic reduction in the size of the parole officer's case load. Also, halfway houses could be established to provide a physical and emotional shelter against parole failure.[18] Opportunities such as these must be provided if the penal system is to avoid compounding past inequities.

---

[17] Pettigrew, *op. cit.*, p. 140.

[18] For a discussion of these procedures *see* Joseph W. Eaton, *Stone Walls Not a Prison Make* (Springfield, Ill.: Charles C Thomas, 1962), pp. 174–176; and National Council on Crime and Delinquency, "Correction in the United States," *Crime and Delinquency*, Vol. 13, No. 1 (January 1967), pp. 209–224.

Conclusion

In the field of race relations careful distinctions must be drawn between policies that tend to perpetuate or aggravate patterns of inequality and those that attempt to counteract them. Both can lead to segregated or semisegregated services.

Discrimination cannot be presumed simply on the basis of statistical differences in the way Negroes and whites participate in the social system. Disparities often do reflect the consequences of deeply rooted policies of racial discrimination. But they can also arise from diagnostic differentiation largely as a reflection of the cumulative effect of injustices that prevailed in America for more than three hundred years. Special services that have as their objective the abolition of differences that exist must not be confused with those that are the outcome of discriminatory policies. Such preferential treatment is usually required if one wants to undo the cumulative consequences of discrimination.

In developing such programs it is necessary to distinguish between those that are ideologically and politically feasible and those that create a system of discrimination in reverse. There can be much room for argument about where this line might be drawn. It may be a matter for negotiation. Conceptual tools such as diagnostic differentiation and discrimination, as well as discrimination in reverse and preferential treatment, may help the social scientists and social practitioners identify and traverse the pathways toward social justice.

Race in Social Welfare

The antidiscriminatory policy of the National Association of Social Workers, as expressed in its Code of Ethics, has been anticipated or echoed by numerous national and local agencies in both the public and voluntary sectors.[1] From the absence of any protest against such forthright pronouncements, it might be concluded that discrimination has happily been excluded from social welfare. Or, conversely, it might be concluded that the need for such policy statements indicates the field's failure thus far to exclude discriminatory practices. At the very least, the official policy leaves open the question of whether social welfare is discriminatory.

The ambiguity in the implications of public policy statements is unfortunately not easy to resolve. On the one hand, social welfare enjoys nothing like the wealth of documentation of discrimination that is found in education or housing. But on the other hand, this circumstance may be the result of the lower visibility of the field's clients and service operations in comparison with other social institutions. It is also possible that discrimination, if it occurs in social welfare, is more subtle than has often been true in organized labor or religion, for example. While the absence of widespread evidence of discrimination is encouraging, it is not an entirely reassuring state of affairs.

The issue of discrimination, especially against Negroes, has been the subject of a few investigations and the results of this research merit attention. Because of the paucity of direct research findings, however, it seems important to pursue the examination beyond such evidence. Therefore, data picturing the prevalence of Ne-

Charles T. O'Reilly, Ph.D., is Professor and Dean, School of Social Welfare, State University of New York at Albany, Albany, New York.

[1] "I will not discriminate because of race, color, religion, age, sex, or national ancestry, and in my job capacity will work to prevent and eliminate such discrimination in rendering service, in work assignments, and in employment practices."

groes among the client population and on the staffs and boards of social agencies will be examined as well. While this examination is recognized as capable only of screening out gross expressions of discrimination, there is reason to believe that even such a crude approach might help to appraise the field's present stance in relation to discrimination.

Studies of Discrimination

It is difficult to find up-to-date, specific information about allegedly racially inspired deficiencies in the operation of the welfare system. About all that exists are articles that urge policy changes after a general overview of discriminatory practices.[2] Such articles do not fall within the scope of this paper although they provide excellent background for understanding the problems confronting clients and agencies.

Sterner's *The Negro's Share*, which dates from the early 1940's, revealed that at that time social services did not reach Negroes, especially in the South.[3] He reported considerable segregation in the Civilian Conservation Corps and noted that federally supported programs for youths during the Depression did not care for Negroes in proportion to their needs, although Negroes were represented proportionally on the basis of their numbers in the population. During the same period Johnson reported:

Organized relief, both public and private, is controlled by white people. This exclusion from policy making and execution opens the way for far-reaching discrimination and a great deal of complaint and misunderstanding.[4]

Other examples of discriminatory practices were documented in a study conducted

in Pittsburgh in 1929, which found some agencies with segregated facilities and meager services for Negroes, and in a 1927 survey in Richmond, Virginia, which found that although 29 percent of the population was Negro, they received only about 10 percent of the services provided by the community fund.[5] The National Urban League surveyed forty-three member agencies in the mid-1950's and found:

. . . not a single social agency, eleven months after the Supreme Court decision, was reported having made any changes in either policy or practices with respect to Negroes.[6]

Two relatively recent studies attempted to explore the possibility of discriminatory practice by comparing the case records of whites and Negroes receiving Old Age Assistance and Aid to Families with Dependent Children. A 1960 study compared the problems of and services provided to 161 white and 141 Negro OAA recipients in Chicago. Workers identified about the same number of problems for each and found that services were provided for 48.9 percent of the problems confronting Negroes and 52 percent of those facing whites.[7] Another study of 80 OAA and 80 AFDC cases in Chicago and Gary, Indiana, in 1961 assessed the worker's ability to identify and treat the problems of white and Negro clients.[8] Some differences were found

---

[2] *See,* for example, Joseph Golden, "Desegregation of Social Agencies in the South," *Social Work,* Vol. 10, No. 1 (January 1965), pp. 58–67.

[3] Richard Sterner, *The Negro's Share* (New York: Harper & Bros., 1943).

[4] Charles S. Johnson, *Patterns of Negro Segregation* (New York: Harper & Bros., 1943), p. 36.

[5] Ira De A. Reid, *Social Conditions of the Negro in the Hill District of Pittsburgh* (Pittsburgh: General Committee on the Hill Survey, 1930); June C. Guild, *The Negro in Richmond, Virginia* (Richmond: Richmond Council of Social Agencies, 1929).

[6] M. Leo Bohanon, "Social Work and Public School Desegregation," *Minority Groups: Segregation and Integration* (New York: Columbia University Press, 1955), p. 94.

[7] Charles T. O'Reilly and Margaret M. Pembroke, *OAA Profile: The Old Age Assistance Client in Chicago* (Chicago: Loyola University Press, 1961).

[8] Charles T. O'Reilly and Constance E. Kellam, *Factors Underlying Case-weighting in Public Assistance* (Chicago: Loyola University School of Social Work, 1962).

in the number of problems identified, depending on the client's race, but no consistent patterning was discovered. White OAA clients received more help than did Negroes with financial, self-care, and health problems, but Negroes received more help with housing—which was also more of a problem for them. Although differences in problem identification and handling existed, they could be explained in terms of the characteristics of the clients and the situation in the broader society.

At the present time probably the best documentation of racial discrimination in the social services appears in statements such as the following:

About half of the child caring institutions have now fully desegregated or are in the process of desegregating their admissions and services for children and families.[9]

An indication of the continued existence of discrimination in the South comes from a Civil Rights Commission survey:

Few opportunities for care or service previously denied to Negro welfare clients have in reality been opened to them as a result of Title VI. . . . Child care, nursing homes, private medical care and training, where welfare departments have a major responsibility, are areas in which State and local directors had taken the least action. . . .[10]

Nothing similar is available for the North, probably because the limited resources of the civil rights commission preclude such an investigation.

Taken collectively, these findings suggest that discrimination was and is a social welfare problem. Discrimination was formerly conspicuous enough to be identified recurrently, and no dramatic changes in

practice are described, but at least some contemporary discriminatory practices have been brought to light. The indication that there was no obvious differentiation in public welfare service rendered to Negro and white clients in the Midwest suggests the possibility of regional differences in discrimination. Thus far, the indications are that the antidiscriminatory clause in the NASW Code of Ethics describes a goal rather than an achievement for at least some social welfare programs.

Racial Composition of Clienteles

Considerable information exists about the presence of Negroes in the public welfare system. Racial breakdowns of public assistance case loads are usually available in the reports of state welfare departments and of those in large cities, and frequently appear in federal publications. A random selection of studies of AFDC, for example, reveals that Negroes are overrepresented in it, that they tend to have more illegitimate children than whites, and so forth.[11] It is well known that Negroes collectively carry more than their share of the burden of social problems; their high incidence of service use would only become interpretable if level of social need were controlled. Such studies, therefore, although they can be useful within the welfare system for planning, in-service training, and many other purposes, tell us nothing about the

---

[9] Martin Gula, "Quest for Equality," Children's Bureau Publication No. 411–1966 (Washington, D.C.: U.S. Government Printing Office, 1966), p. 1.

[10] "Title VI, One Year After: A Survey on Health and Welfare Services in the South" (Washington, D.C.: U.S. Commission on Civil Rights, 1966), p. 23.

[11] Robert H. Mugge, *Characteristics and Financial Circumstances of Families Receiving Aid to Dependent Children, Late 1958*, Public Assistance Report No. 42 (Washington, D.C.: U.S. Department of Health, Education, and Welfare, 1960); Jerome L. Schwartz, *Statistical Survey of the Aid to Needy Children Program in Imperial Valley California* (El Centro, Calif.: Imperial Valley Family Health and Welfare Project, 1961); "Facts, Fallacies and Future: A Study of the Aid to Dependent Children Program of Cook County, Illinois" (New York: Greenleigh Associates, 1960).

presence or lack of discrimination in programs.

Does the fact that some Negroes and members of other minorities who have demonstrable need are not receiving assistance mean that the system is discriminating against them? There is presumptive evidence that many more persons are eligible for public assistance than receive it. Some may be excluded by positive action; others may simply not be knowledgeable about their rights. If needy people who belong to racial minorities are not allowed in the system they may be victims of "the poorhouse state." [12] Once in the system they may be even more victimized, but there is no systematic evidence that the functionaries or the policies of the welfare system discriminate on racial grounds. The pervasive depreciation of the person and his rights that occurs in some welfare agencies could well be the subject of intensive research, but it is likely that in most places it falls impartially regardless of race.

Racial Composition of Boards

Statements similar to the following one of the Philadelphia Health and Welfare Council have been widely adopted by welfare councils:

It is the operating policy of the Health and Welfare Council to work actively with and assist all health, welfare and recreation agencies and other community institutions providing human services to the end that they shall operate without racial discrimination. . . . Implicit in this policy of service without racial discrimination are the following: no one to be denied service because of race; service be provided on an integrated basis; the hiring, assignment, and promotion of staff and employees be done without racial discrimination; agencies seek representation on their boards

and committees from all segments of the community or area served.[13]

In a survey conducted by the author in the spring of 1967 five national agencies were asked about the racial composition of their boards. It was found that the average board had 38 members, with an average of 1.5 Negroes per board. None of these agencies had information about the racial makeup of the boards of their member agencies.

Morris and Rein noted that although "minority groups have assumed a new position of influence in our urban centers . . . these groups . . . are grossly underrepresented in our health and welfare planning structures." [14] This echoed Berry's contention in 1955 that social work needed to move toward the integration of clients, staffs, and boards.[15] At that time, however, social work was no more ready to move to implement the spirit of the Supreme Court's decision on school desegregation than was the educational system. The lack of minority representation on the boards of social agencies was again criticized almost a decade later when Whitney Young said that it

. . . perpetuates not only the great social distance between policy maker and client group but also continues the practice that Negroes deeply resent, of doing *for* rather than doing *with* the Negro citizen.[16]

To obtain current information about

---

[12] Richard M. Elman, *The Poorhouse State* (New York: Pantheon Books, 1966).

[13] Statement on racial discrimination adopted by the Board of Directors, Health and Welfare Council, Inc., Philadelphia, Pa., January 7, 1964.

[14] Robert Morris and Martin Rein, "Emerging Patterns in Community Planning," *Social Work Practice, 1963* (New York: Columbia University Press, 1963), p. 163.

[15] Edwin C. Berry, discussion of Esther M. Taylor, "Segregation, Desegregation and Integration in a Social Agency," *Minority Groups: Segregation and Integration* (New York: Columbia University Press, 1955), p. 91.

[16] Whitney M. Young, Jr., "Racial Discrimination," in Nathan E. Cohen, ed., *Social Work and Social Problems* (New York: National Association of Social Workers, 1964), p. 359.

local agency practices, the author, as part of the survey mentioned earlier, asked the welfare councils in twenty-one cities with populations of more than 500,000 and sizable Negro populations about the racial composition of their boards. Sixteen of the twenty-one councils replied. The median board had thirty-six members, three of whom were Negro. Few Negroes were officers, the average being less than one per council. Only two councils had information about the racial composition of their constituent agencies. This lack of information about board composition might be taken as an indication of the nonsalience of race as a factor in the building of agency boards in local communities.

Another piece of evidence that race is not a factor in welfare planning is found in a thorough analysis of the Indianapolis Community Chest made in the 1950's.[17] It only incidentally mentioned the role of Negroes or any other minority in the community welfare system, or the roles social agencies or the chest saw for themselves vis-à-vis Negroes. Yet in 1960, 97,736, or 20.5 percent, of the city's residents were Negro.

One of the few available studies of the racial composition of boards was made by the Eastern Massachusetts Chapter of NASW in 1965.[18] Questionnaires were sent to 318 public and voluntary agencies in the metropolitan Boston area and information about board membership was obtained from 102 of them. Sixty percent had no nonwhites on their boards, 24 percent had one nonwhite board member, and 7 percent had two or more. (In 1960 Negroes comprised 3 percent of the population of the metropolitan Boston area and 9 percent of the population of the city itself.)

Policy pronouncements about minority representation on boards abound, but there is no indication from the available studies that they are implemented. The issue of Negro board membership apparently has little salience for most communities with organized welfare systems, in spite of the statements of national agencies and "spokesmen" for the profession.

Race and Social Agency Staffs

The 1960 census found that 11.5 percent of the 123,621 persons in social welfare and related jobs were Negro.[19] Since about 10.5 percent of the nation's population were Negro, they were slightly overrepresented in social welfare positions. As noted earlier, however, Negroes are grossly overrepresented as victims of societal dysfunction and as clients of the welfare system. A communication gap between whites and nonwhites often can occur in treatment and in the provision of other services; this gap can best be bridged by nonwhite workers. For these and other professional and social policy reasons that need not be detailed here, Negroes are needed as practitioners and administrators.

An important reason for knowing something about the racial composition of agency staffs is that such knowledge can be helpful in the planning and evaluation of services. As in the case of boards, however, staff composition has not received much attention. The following are a few recent examples of important studies in which race is the missing dimension.

A large-scale study of correctional manpower published in 1966 said nothing about

[17] John R. Seely *et al.*, *Community Chest: A Case Study in Philanthropy* (Toronto: University of Toronto Press, 1957).

[18] "Survey of Non-White Participation in Health and Welfare Programs" (Boston: Eastern Massachusetts Chapter, NASW, February 1967). (Mimeographed.)

[19] U.S. Bureau of the Census, *U.S. Census of Population: 1960, Vol. I, Characteristics of the Population* (Washington, D.C.: U.S. Government Printing Office, 1964).

the race of corrections personnel.[20] Similarly, a 1964 Arden House conference on correctional manpower did not mention race as a possible factor in staffing.[21] This happened in spite of the fact that in 1960, 37.3 percent of the men in state prisons and 26 percent in federal prisons were Negroes.[22] The high percentage of Negro offenders should raise questions about the number of Negro correctional workers available to work with them, but this received no attention in documents intended to influence decisions about correctional manpower.

Corrections is but one area of social work that has not articulated the problem. A 1966 study of selected characteristics of NASW members did not mention race, nor did a similar study of 1967 social work graduates.[23] Neither did the 1965 manpower report of the Department of Health, Education, and Welfare deal with the racial characteristics of social work personnel, or the 1965 Council on Social Work Education report on social work education and manpower.[24] Although CSWE has not re-ferred to race in its statistics on enrollment in schools of social work, it did gather racial data for students and faculty in 1966.[25]

Although the profession has not been alert to the implications of racial characteristics in the manpower area, the situation is changing rapidly. Both in its annual meeting and in special projects CSWE is reviewing its responsibilities for the education of minorities. The Civil Rights Act of 1964 undoubtedly played a role in alerting social work educators, but CSWE's tendency is to go beyond compliance and seek affirmative action to realize the spirit of the act. That a significant reorientation has occurred is evident when one notes that only a few years ago Pins advocated selective recruitment of "men, individuals from upper socio-economic homes, and students with high undergraduate records. . . ."[26] Recently Dean Jackson of the Atlanta University School of Social Work called for "a crash recruitment program [for] qualified Negro applicants."[27] His observations and those of Wilcox about social work education for Negroes lend support to a radically different recruiting emphasis for professional social work education.[28]

At first glance, recruitment of Negroes into the social work profession may not seem to be a problem. In 1960, 11.8 per-

[20] Herman Piven and Abraham Alcabes, *Education, Training, and Manpower in Corrections and Law Enforcement: A Digest of Data,* Source Books I through IV (Washington, D.C.: U.S. Department of Health, Education, and Welfare, 1966).

[21] Charles S. Prigmore, ed., *Manpower and Training for Corrections* (New York: Council on Social Work Education, 1966).

[22] Charles T. O'Reilly *et al., Men in Jail* (New York: LePlay Research, 1966).

[23] Deborah Golden, "Selected Characteristics of NASW Members: The Third Study," *Personnel Information,* Vol. 9, No. 2 (March 1966), pp. 1, 46–47; and Alfred M. Stamm, "1967 Social Work Graduates: Salaries and Characteristics," *Personnel Information,* Vol. 11, No. 2 (March 1968), pp. 1, 50–54.

[24] *Closing the Gap in Social Work Manpower* (Washington, D.C.: U.S. Department of Health, Education, and Welfare, November 1965); and Ellen Winston *et al., Social Work Education and Social Welfare Manpower: Present Realities and Future Imperatives* (New York: Council on Social Work Education, 1965).

[25] Kay L. Dea, ed., *Statistics on Social Work Education: November 1, 1965, and Academic Year 1964–65* (New York: Council on Social Work Education, 1966).

[26] Arnulf Pins, *Who Chooses Social Work, When and Why?* (New York: Council on Social Work Education, 1963), p. 153.

[27] William S. Jackson, "The Civil Rights Act of 1964: Implications for Social Work Education in the South." Paper presented at the Fourteenth Annual Program Meeting, Council on Social Work Education, New York, January 1966.

[28] Preston R. Wilcox, "Social Work Education and the Negro Student, the Northern View." Paper presented at the Fourteenth Annual Program Meeting, Council on Social Work Education, New York, 1966.

cent of the first-year students in schools of social work were Negroes.[29] This about equaled their representation in social welfare-related jobs. Because Negroes are so overrepresented as clients of the welfare system, however, their roughly proportionate representation among welfare workers and new professionals masks the need for many more of them.

Fugitive Status of Racial Data

Why is there such a paucity of data about the racial factor? Perhaps because the welfare system stems from a liberal, humanitarian philosophy in which it is assumed without question that the system is nondiscriminatory and color-blind. In addition, enough criticisms of welfare programs have an element of racial prejudice —such as the recurrent claims that AFDC fosters high Negro illegitimacy rates—to make welfare staffs protective and reluctant to furnish racial information about clients. Some hide behind regulations or laws intended to prevent discrimination. But perhaps the most important reason is the widespread belief that the social problems of minorities are only facets of more general problems.

Thus the child welfare problems of Negroes are seen as part and parcel of those of all children and broad child welfare programs are assumed to be the answer to the need for more and better services for Negro children. They will get the services, not because they are Negroes, but because they are children. In the same manner, the housing problems of Negroes are thought to be met best by over-all programs focused on the needs of all low-income people.

Political considerations sometimes play a part in the suppression of the racial dimension. Long before the Moynihan episode, people knew the delicacy with which it was necessary to tread in the area of race relations.[30] Even more cautious movement may be indicated in the future because of increased Negro militancy. There may be good reasons (although these are not in evidence) why race is not considered in the reports recently issued by the President's Commission on Law Enforcement and Administration. Neither the summary volume nor the one on corrections, which is especially important to social welfare, has more than incidental references to race.[31] Since there can be no question about the utility of racial data in the planning and programming of correctional services, it is difficult to understand why attention was not given to the race of the clientele of the correctional system or of its staff, unless policy dictated its omission.

The lack of attention to the racial factor, both in the identification of problems and in the provision of services, is not limited to social work. The national survey results of the Joint Commission on Mental Illness and Health, for example, provide no racial breakdowns.[32] As a result one has the impression that there are no racial

---

[29] Pins, *op. cit.*, p. 34. Two schools of social work with large Negro enrollments accounted for about one-third of these Negro students.

[30] Daniel Moynihan's "The Negro Family: The Case for National Action" (Washington, D.C.: Office of Planning and Research, U.S. Department of Labor, May 1965) is better known as the Moynihan Report. This analysis of the Negro family created a furore among some Negro and white sociologists. *See* Lee Rainwater and William L. Yancy, *The Moynihan Report and the Politics of Controversy* (Cambridge, Mass.: MIT Press, 1967), for a detailed account of this minor *cause célèbre*.

[31] President's Commission on Law Enforcement and Administration of Criminal Justice, *Task Force Report: Corrections* (Washington, D.C.: U.S. Government Printing Office, 1967).

[32] Gerald Gurin, Joseph Voroff, and Sheila Feld, *Americans View Their Mental Health* (New York: Basic Books, 1960).

differences in attitudes toward mental
health. There actually may be none, but
the question is not yet moot, especially in
terms of operationalizing programs in the
urban ghetto. Another survey of the commission found no relationship between the
supply of community resources for mental
health and the proportion of nonwhites in
the county populations.[33] It is noted, however, that this report did not say how nonwhites fared with respect to the supply of
resources in a given place and implied that
the supply would be less in the South.
This clue to a potential obstruction in the
mental health delivery system was not exploited. Its long-range implications for
the provision of services to Negroes need
much more investigation.

Another reason for limited information
is the fact that for many years it was believed inappropriate to gather information
about the race of clients and staff, since
such information had been and could be
used to facilitate discrimination. Therefore, together with the schools, business,
and other organizations, social agencies
adhered to a color-blind policy. Eventually, however, the reasons for eliminating
racial identification come into conflict with
the need to know whether organizations are
open to members of minorities. Now it is
generally recognized that lack of data about
race can severely handicap programs to
aid minorities. The White House Conference on Civil Rights noted:

. . . experience has amply demonstrated that
"color blindness" has served as a shield for
racial discrimination and a cover for the
preservation of the status quo.[34]

---

[33] Reginald Robinson, David F. DeMarche, and
Mildred K. Wagle, *Community Resources in
Mental Health* (New York: Basic Books, 1960).

[34] *The Report of the White House Conference
"To Fulfill These Rights"* (Washington, D.C.:
U.S. Government Printing Office, 1966), p. 61.

Areas for Further Research

The professional manpower situation in
social welfare has been surveyed repeatedly, but data covering race have not regularly been collected or reported. A secondary analysis of existing data, if they
contain identifying information about race,
could answer some of the questions about
manpower that were raised earlier. If this
cannot be done, research should be undertaken to determine the role of racial minorities in welfare manpower. In spite of the
limitations of census data, the 1970 census
could be a source of invaluable information if analyzed in reference to welfare
needs, including manpower. National social welfare organizations should promote
such manpower research.

Cities with various proportions of minority groups in their populations should
be examined with explicit attention to the
role played by racial groups at all levels
of their welfare systems. The ad hoc, fragmentary, and fugitive material now available is inadequate for understanding or
coming to grips with what may be a major
problem of de facto discrimination in the
welfare system.

Toward this end community welfare
councils should regularly gather information about the racial characteristics of the
clients, staffs, and boards of their member
agencies. Such information is essential in
order to monitor compliance with the principles of nondiscrimination to which councils and agencies subscribe. Failure to do
this and to take remedial action when appropriate lays the welfare system open to
the valid criticism that it has a merely
formal commitment to nondiscrimination.

The internal operations of welfare agencies must be examined carefully to determine whether discrimination exists. The
subtleties of discrimination cannot be
ascertained through the crude methods

described earlier. Because it can be identified by skilled case reviewers, discrimination often tends to be camouflaged. Subtle discrimination can be every bit as much an interference with service as gross and overt discrimination, yet immeasurably more difficult to detect.

In spite of occasional articles in professional journals and normative statements at conferences and in policy pronouncements, the average social worker may not be especially conscious of the problems connected with race. A recent study in a midwestern city with racial tensions making it one of the most potentially explosive cities in the country found that social agency executives gave a low rating to the importance of racial problems in the community.[35] Such findings suggest the need to learn how much social workers understand the racial situation. This form of color blindness may mask insidious discriminatory practices.

Finally, more must be learned about the minorities' perceptions of the welfare system. It is known that many eligible people make no effort to avail themselves of services. Bailey's study tells us something about how the man on the street sees the system, but whether he believes the system discriminates is not known.[36] A 1964 study of Negro residents of Milwaukee found that only 17.6 percent believed that social agencies discriminated against Negroes, 51 percent thought that they treated everyone alike, and the remainder either did not know or did not answer.[37] That half the sample thought agencies did not discriminate hardly balances the fact that the other half thought otherwise or were unsure about the practices of local social agencies. Scattered studies like this do no more than hint at the scale of the problem facing efforts to convince Negroes that they have a right to social services.

Social work research must be color conscious and push its analysis of the racial dimension whenever possible. Present statistics about race only tantalize because of what they promise but cannot fulfill. Their more imaginative use could help answer some of the problems raised in this paper.

---

[35] Charles T. O'Reilly, unpublished study of the opinions of community influentials, winter 1966.

[36] Margaret B. Bailey, "Community Orientations Toward Social Casework," *Social Work,* Vol. 4, No. 3 (July 1959), pp. 60–66.

[37] Charles T. O'Reilly, Willard E. Downing, and Steven I. Pflanczer, *The People of the Inner-Core North* (New York: LePlay Research, 1965), chap. 6.

Race As a Factor in Social Work Practice

JEROME COHEN

Race exerts a pervasive and powerful influence on the delivery of professional services. In complex ways, race or the effects of race are visible in the answers that have been developed to some basic questions: Who needs help? What help is needed? Who can extend the help? For in current social work practice, which constitutes the profession's collective answer to these questions, race is a mediating factor.

The barriers to effective integration of the Negro into social service efforts probably run the gamut from overt, active, and deliberate expressions of discrimination to subtle, passive, inadvertent, or unwished-for arrangements that tend to exclude the Negro. If overt discrimination is rare, a quiet, unintentional dissuasion commonly may operate against the Negro. No social service efforts are entirely free from distortion by the variable of race.

Jerome Cohen, DSS, is Associate Professor, School of Social Welfare, University of California, Los Angeles, California.

Examined here are some of the inadvertent general forces that reduce the likelihood that accommodation will be found between the needs of the Negro and the operation of the service network. Considered are some of the restrictive effects of American culture on the Negro's orientation toward service and the congruence of practice arrangements with these orientations. The material suggests that the Negro encounters numerous obstacles in the path to service that conspire against his seeking help, against finding it offered under acceptable conditions, and, perhaps most tragically, against his utilizing it fully.

The 'Reality Principle'

Malcolm X described in his autobiography the advice a school counselor gave him concerning his ambition to be a lawyer. The counselor attempted to persuade him that this was an unrealistic goal for a Negro, and counseled him to be something he *could* be:

You're good with your hands—making things. Everybody admires your carpentry shopwork. Why don't you plan on carpentry? People like you as a person—you'd get all kinds of work.[1]

Such efforts by people to be of "help" are duplicated innumerable times in the life of the average Negro youngster. They serve eventually to grind ambitions down to a level of reality imposed by the structure of limited opportunity rather than by the limitations of individual capacity.

Perhaps the counselor was attempting to help him avoid the shame of failure and rejection he might encounter in seeking a status that the counselor thought unattainable for a Negro in our society at that time. He urged substitution of a goal that was perhaps less desirable, but more likely to result in success. In other words, he helped Malcolm X adjust to the "reality of his social situation." This is a common orientation expressed in the methodology of the various helping professions. It derives from the goal of promoting adjustment to existing conditions that appear beyond change and is generally viewed as appropriate to social realities. It is this unintended and passive element of discrimination that is frequently revealed by an examination of social work practice.

Structure of Discrimination

Discrimination that is an action of differential treatment of individuals belonging to a specific human group may be present with or without a prejudicial attitude. The relationship between prejudiced attitudes and discriminatory behavior is a complex one with innumerable patterns. Yinger

has developed a field theory of prejudice and discrimination.[2] He suggests that it is only by virtue of combining individual levels of prejudice and situational influences that we can gain a more accurate understanding and prediction of discriminatory behavior. He developed a paradigm that combines individual tendencies and structural supports that lead to active discrimination. It suggests the possibility that a social worker who possesses a low individual tendency toward prejudice but works in a situation with strong institutional supports for discriminatory behavior may engage in such behavior himself. Such analysis enables one to understand the nature of social work practice and its relationship to factors of race in a manner that reflects more accurately the profession's person-in-situation model of behavior.

The Power of Symbols

Along with the strong emotional basis of prejudiced attitudes is found an important cognitive dimension. Belief, perception, and symbolic language tend to mold attitudes as well as behavior. Allport has described the power of linguistic factors in the nature of prejudice.[3] Words enable us to form categories, generalize, reflect, and recall. Racial and ethnic labels are often powerful stimuli of this type. The symbols frequently tune out the finer discriminations that could otherwise be perceived. A category once formed with the aid of a symbol of high potency tends to be tenacious and to attract an increasing number of attributes for which it becomes a referent. The label then may become an indiscriminate referent of the original at-

---

[1] Malcolm X with Alex Haley, *The Autobiography of Malcolm X* (New York: Grove Press, 1965), p. 37.

[2] J. Milton Yinger, *Toward a Field Theory of Behavior* (New York: Hill Book Co., 1965).

[3] Gordon W. Allport, *The Nature of Prejudice* (New York: Doubleday & Co., 1958).

tribute, probable attributes, and highly imaginative and nonexistent attributes.

The Whorfian hypothesis suggests that language not only serves as a means of communicating the various aspects that make up a culture but also serves as a critical component of socialization that directs its members to the reality of their cultural perspective.[4] The language of social work practice then becomes a critical issue not only in the description of the reality but also in the shaping of the reality the practitioners—and especially students—will see and believe. This is, of course, a condition common to all professional education. It is recognized here as a reflection of the way in which a limited view of a problem may be maintained and thus increase the possibility of stereotyping both the client and the social condition that underlies his problem.

It is ironical that while language enables man to describe and generalize the complexity of reality, it also enables him to distort it. Psychiatric labels attached to certain behavioral disorders continue to call for inappropriate responses from both the public and the professional practitioner. The same eccentric aunt who lived with reasonable comfort in her family surroundings is no longer accepted after being labeled schizophrenic.[5] Likewise in social work, when social differences are labeled in pathological terms, a new formula for action is required. How frequently do these professional terms lead to a self-fulfilling prophecy?

Orientation to Service

In the variously global or microscopic analyses of the plight of the Negro, at least one common consequence is discernible: His life experiences fail to provide a foundation conducive to the unfettered use of social resources, including social work services. Instead, orientations are induced that impede or complicate the use of social resources.

Consequences of Discrimination

Duncan has succinctly characterized some of the consequences of discrimination against Negroes:

Negroes, in disproportionate numbers, (1) experience unstable family situations and depend on meager family resources; (2) attain less than average amounts of education; (3) are employed in lower level jobs; (4) secure low incomes; (5) have an inefficient pattern of expenditures; (6) in consequence, are characterized by inferior life chances, low levels of living and welfare, and impaired satisfactions. Each of these handicaps operate to set up the handicaps at later stages; schooling is terminated early partly because family support is inadequate; job opportunities are inferior partly because educational preparation is not good; low income is partly due to poor job opportunities; expenditures are inefficient and insufficient partly because of low income; Negroes get less out of life partly because of cumulative inadequacies at each stage of the life cycle.[6]

Locked into such circumstances of life for generations, a large segment of the Negro population has come to be justifiably suspicious of contacts with members of the majority who represent the forces that have brought about the dilemma.

A more detailed analysis of the impact of these abrasive social forces on the development of the Negro was presented by Kenneth B. Clark. He concluded that as minority group children learn the inferior status to which they are assigned and observe the fact of segregation, they often react with feelings of inferiority and a

---

[4] Benjamin L. Whorf, *Language, Thought and Reality* (New York: John Wiley & Sons, 1956).

[5] Elaine Cumming and John Cumming, *Closed Ranks* (Cambridge, Mass.: Harvard University Press, 1957).

[6] Otis D. Duncan, "Discrimination against Negroes," *The Annals*, Vol. 371 (May 1967), p. 88.

sense of personal humiliation. Many become confused about their own personal worth. Under these conditions, they are thrown into conflict with respect to their feelings about themselves and their group. This conflict and confusion frequently lead to self-hatred and rejection of their own social group.

Various patterns of coping with this conflict develop, depending on a number of interrelated factors, e.g., stability and quality of family relations, social and economic class, cultural and educational background of parents, personal characteristics, intelligence, and the like. Some children, usually those of lower socioeconomic status, react with overt aggression and hostility directed toward their own group as well as toward the majority group. Middle-class minority group children are more likely to react to frustrations and conflicts by withdrawal and submissive behavior or by compensatory and rigid conformity to prevailing middle-class values and standards. Many develop a determination to succeed in spite of the handicap of minority status. However, many minority group children react with generally defeatist attitudes and lowering of personal ambitions. They tend to be hypersensitive and anxious about their relations with the larger society. There is a heightened tendency to see hostility and rejection even in those areas where it might not actually exist.[7]

This cross-sectional look at the variety of feelings about self and others and of the disposition of aggression elaborates the conception of mistrust as a barrier to service. The overdetermined pursuit of success or renunciation of aspiration and the pull toward conflict or overconformity define stances that influence the decision about seeking help and that are carried to that situation.

The attempts to describe the Negro have been extended in a number of different directions. For example, the Negro child's rejection of his own color and group, cited in innumerable studies, appears to be changing with the development of a new pride in self and group consequent to the civil rights movement and the various nationalistic sentiments that surround it.[8] A study by Grossack reports an increasing amount of positive feelings associated with being Negro.[9] More than 90 percent of his 183 Negro respondents were able to find some good things in being Negro. Pride was evidenced in the progress Negroes have made and are making in all fields. Personal characteristics such as tolerance of frustration, remaining a loyal citizen despite inequality of treatment, and capacity to maintain ability to learn despite serious deprivation were cited frequently. The negative responses were not of the self-hatred type but rather reflected the conditions under which Negroes must still live. Perhaps it is this new ability to direct aggression outwardly that has reduced the amount of inward aggression that in the past led to self-hate.

Significant Social Worlds

A recent study by Thompson suggests that Negro identity can best be understood in relation to a distinct social segment of their social world.[10] He found that the

---

[7] Kenneth B. Clark, "Social Scientist's Brief to Supreme Court," in *Prejudice and Your Child* (2d ed.; Boston: Beacon Press, 1963), Appendix III, pp. 166–184.

[8] *See* Melvin Seeman, "Skin Color Values in All Negro School Classes," *American Sociological Review*, Vol. 11, No. 3 (June 1946), pp. 315–321; and Bingham Dai, "Some Problems of Personality Development Among Negro Children," in Clyde Kluckhohn *et al.*, eds., *Personality in Nature, Society and Culture* (New York: Alfred A. Knopf, 1962), pp. 545–566.

[9] Martin M. Grossack, "Group Belongingness Among Negroes," in Grossack, ed., *Mental Health and Segregation* (New York: Springer Publishing Co., 1963), pp. 18–29.

[10] Daniel C. Thompson, "Development of Attitudes in Respect to Discrimination: Formation of

individual responds to a much smaller psychological reality than social class or color caste. Among the New Orleans Negro community he located the following significant social worlds: (1) the middle class, (2) the matriarchy, (3) the gang, (4) the nuclear family, and (5) the marginal.

Among the *middle class* he cited the value placed on respectability and the need for success as an indicator of self-validation. There was ambivalence about skin color and evidence of deep feelings of self-hate.

In the *matriarchy* category he discovered a high degree of inner solidarity among the females, men being regarded as enemies. While he found some persons of this type in all social levels, the majority were among the lower class. There was a high degree of mutual dependency between mother and daughter and girls early regarded themselves primarily as women, all other roles being secondary. The outside world is of little concern and there is not much evidence of self-hate. Marked ambition or striving to succeed are limited. The high degree of dissatisfaction with segregation is connected to economic and sexual exploitation. Males in the family must conform to female patterns or renounce the home. Under these conditions they are forced to identify with the gang and become "men."

The *gang* is the place that articulates the male principle in society. Matriarchy and gang are natural enemies in this respect. Each owes allegiance to mutually exclusive ideologies. Manhood is defined in terms of independence, secretiveness, progressiveness, and sexual prowess. There appear to be a high degree of fear of women, scorn for middle-class standards, and hatred of outside authority. There is little in the

value scheme of this group that provides a basis for the establishment of a stable family life. Ties are necessarily temporary and loose. Members have almost no interest in community affairs unless these threaten their way of life. There is considerable sensitivity about race and great bitterness about discrimination.

The *nuclear family group* is most characteristic among lower middle-class Negroes. For this subgroup the family roles are regarded as central in members' lives, all others being secondary. Strong "we" feelings tend to limit concern for outside persons or institutions unless these contribute something to the family welfare, e.g., church or union. Most tend to value the skin color characteristic of their families. Attitudes toward discrimination varied considerably but all thought of it as a personal, individual phenomenon, the result of evil people's actions. There was high occupational ambition.

Finally, those who lived in conditions of *marginality* shared no satisfactory self-identity. Some attempted to develop an organized "bohemian" philosophy of life, but this was inconsistent and fell short of a meaningful choice.

Research that uncovers the conditions that mediate the broad category of race reveals the complex network of constraints that impinge on the utilization of services and programs. Whether social work is providing opportunities and resources or helping individuals to use the resources that are available, it is necessary to understand the way in which the client views himself and these services, and it is necessary to organize the delivery of services to articulate this view.

Structure of Social Work Practice

The structure of social service delivery systems is critical to the understanding of race and social work practice. The slogan "You can't eat civil rights" is heard in-

Social Attitudes," *American Journal of Orthopsychiatry,* Vol. 32, No. 1 (January 1962), pp. 74–85.

creasingly in lower-class Negro communities. It may be equally true that one cannot resolve some of the complex problems of service effectiveness by good will alone. Skill, understanding, and positive intention may be thwarted by the conditions under which service is given.

A pervasive problem exists in the assumptions about Negro problems and the action following these assumptions. Herzog cites the issue of unmarried parents as a reflection of this condition:

If he is a member of the middle-class . . . he is likely to be viewed as one who is troubled . . . and needs help . . . the help is likely to be offered under the auspices of a voluntary agency staffed by professional caseworkers. Efforts will be made to understand the individual's background and circumstances, and to work out the problems involved in a situation viewed as a unique constellation of factors. On the other hand, if the unmarried father comes from a deprived background, characterized by low income and poor education, the paramount question is not how the pregnancy came about and how he can be helped but how he can be made to shoulder his share of the financial burden.[11]

A differential approach to out-of-wedlock children can be documented adequately. In low-income families, especially Negro families, the problem is viewed as a cultural phenomenon and the parties are seen as public charges. Little can be found in the literature describing the complex emotional entanglements that prevail in the case of Negro parents of out-of-wedlock children.

An intensive case study of one family agency in southern California over a ten-year period offers further evidence of these perceptual distortions.[12] The Negro population in the geographic area served by this agency is not characterized by the extreme poverty found in the urban ghetto. Although the agency had always been underused by the Negro population, the ten years between 1950 and 1960 showed a further decline. Case records revealed that psychological problems presented by Negroes were frequently ignored, with attention focused mainly on concrete service. This can be as inappropriate as the opposite approach. For example, premature judgment about the treatability of marital problems occurred frequently, referrals were made for public assistance with little attempt to deal with other concrete or emotional problems, arrangements were made by the agency for child care placement with little attention paid to such matters as one parent's comment that her son had "bitten a neighbor child's penis." In general, the authors give evidence of a mechanical and superficial approach to service for Negroes rather than the more fully developed treatment given to others.[13]

Service Use in South-Central Los Angeles

The existence of social services does not in itself insure their meaningful use by the population requiring assistance. Various factors such as the style of delivery, accessibility to the client's residence, agency policies, and staff attitudes are known to influence the effective and appropriate use of services. An opportunity to inquire into these matters was found in conjunction with a large interdisciplinary study developed in the aftermath of the 1967 Los Angeles riots.[14] The availability and usa-

[11] Elizabeth Herzog, "Some Notes About Unmarried Fathers," *Child Welfare*, Vol. 45, No. 4 (April 1966), p. 195.

[12] Ruth Anderson and Rosalee Shaw, "Utilization of a Casework Agency by Its Negro Community." Unpublished master's thesis, School of Social Welfare, University of California, Los Angeles, 1963.

[13] *Ibid.*, p. 39.

[14] Jerome Cohen, "A Descriptive Study of the Availability and Usability of Social Services in the South Central Area of Los Angeles," in "Los Angeles Riot Study" (Los Angeles: Institute of Government and Public Affairs, University of California, June 1967).

bility of social services in the south-central area of Los Angeles revealed in this research suggest the kinds of impediments to service that may be general.

Interviews of two to three hours' duration were conducted in order to collect data from agency executives and line workers in a stratified random sample of all agencies in the area providing direct social services to clients. These included (1) primary agencies such as public assistance and family agencies, (2) social service departments or branches of host settings such as schools, hospitals, and courts, and (3) other agencies providing a variety of general welfare services. Excluded from the study were organized committees not giving direct service and agencies serving the area but based outside it. Forty-two agencies offering both public and private health, education, or welfare services were examined. The interviews were carried out by second-year graduate social work students.[15]

To be available, an agency must not only be located within reasonable distance of the population using its services, but must also be recognized as a resource for its potential users. On the whole, agencies were not engaged in a concerted effort to make their services known or to reach out with case-finding techniques to the population located within their service boundaries.[16] It was on word of mouth, unproductive referrals from other agencies, and the client's ingenuity that the agencies

relied. These are not methods that bring people in need to agencies in large numbers. The area covers forty square miles and the cost of transportation was often prohibitive to a family living at a subsistence level or below the poverty line.

Approximately half the agencies had provisions for emergency service. A number of the other agencies reported emergency services, but the social workers had to provide them on their own time without compensation. It should not be surprising that these agencies were rarely open after hours. In the public income maintenance programs social workers had to use their own time if they were to meet the emergency needs of their clients. The most serious gap in emergency service was found in the social service component of hospitals or in outpatient physical and mental health clinics. Finally, a large number of youth-serving agencies seemed to be without resources to help youngsters in times of emergent distress outside the usual agency hours.

Eligibility requirements for income and residence were not a barrier to the use of most agency services. However, among the eight agencies that did have such requirements were found the most basic services being offered—income maintenance and medical care. Other kinds of eligibility requirements proved to be more restrictive. These were the requirements of specialized agencies governing the conditions under which service can be offered. A number of highly specialized agencies required client stability in areas other than those covered by their specific service and would not accept persons with multiple problems.

Immediacy of service is an important factor in working with low-income clients. Most of the agencies had no waiting period and staff would see clients immediately, even when they came without an appointment. The new poverty program agencies did not, in fact, use an appointment system.

---

[15] The following UCLA graduate social work students participated in the research project: Diana Bechler, Dorothy Ferri, Sylvia Gressit, Audrey Gunther, Constance Haskell, Valarie Hastings, Jean Mack, and Sonia Zipperman.

[16] It should be noted that the absence of outreach efforts was due, at least in part, to the common circumstance that service resources were taxed by clients who did find their way to the agency. Whether these are the most appropriate claimants of scarce resources is unclear. That a population is underserved by agencies relying on substantial client initiative is, however, perfectly clear.

The agencies with waiting lists were those offering a highly skilled professional service in health, mental health, and family service programs.

The advantages of client participation in the planning of agency services have been stressed in the literature. Only four of the forty-two agencies included representatives of the client population on their policy-making boards. However, a much larger number reported indirect methods of client contribution to the determination of agency policy. It should be said that some were very indirect indeed.

Knowledge of the local community and sufficient autonomy to respond to the needs of the community's population are considered important factors in the effectiveness of agency services. Fewer than one-third of the agencies reported that the majority of their workers lived in the south-central Los Angeles area. Eighteen agencies, primarily poverty program agencies, reported the use of indigenous workers. Professional practitioners are not generally expected to live in the locale in which they practice. However, when the population served is locked in a community by virtue of the existence of a ghetto, the impression of the social worker is of a "visiting professional." In other than poverty program agencies, only one sectarian family agency took an official position on some aspect of the civil rights movement. Apparently the accusations of aloofness of the social care-takers are not always ill founded.

To avoid dividing the client, co-ordination of services is essential. To avoid gaps in service, planning is necessary. Most of the agencies reported maintaining contact with other agencies serving the same client. Nearly all agencies also reported that they plan jointly with other agencies in the community. It is unclear whether the rhetoric of planning is followed by integrated social services. It appeared that the major condition of meaningful co-operation in planning was absent in this community of agencies—the willingness to relinquish a small degree of autonomy for the advantage of over-all planning.

In general, the study found that the majority of agencies did not seem to block access to their services with excessive intake demands and long waiting lists. However, there was limited case-finding or reaching out for clients who could not connect without some additional help. Little effort was made to bring back those who failed to keep appointments or dropped out of treatment. As with most agencies, if the client does not have the strength to get there and stay there, he goes unserved. Some agencies located in the same geographic area are frankly not serving the population. These agencies—several with widespread reputations in their respective fields—were doing work of exceptional excellence, and their services would be a valuable asset to members of the local community. The study replicated the findings of many other investigators that the highest level of expertise is frequently not available to the low-income family. This may lead to an increased sense of relative deprivation, which is the seed of violence.

Stigma of Welfare Services

Coser, building on Simmel's work, characterizes the process of granting public assistance as an act of degradation. "To receive public assistance means to be stigmatized and to be removed from the ordinary run of men." [17] In order to be eligible for public assistance, a person is obligated to open his private life to public inspection. Such an invasion of privacy is often experienced as humiliating and degrading. Further, when moneys are allocated, the disposition of their use is limited. In essence, the poor are treated like children who have to account to parents for

---

[17] Lewis A. Coser, "The Sociology of Poverty," *Social Problems*, Vol. 13, No. 2 (Fall 1965), p. 144.

the wise use of their money. Through such procedures, the public assistance recipient is infantilized and dependency is insured rather than resolved. The point is made that the process of being helped assigns the recipient to a career that impairs previous identity and becomes a stigma marking his intercourse with others. The good will of the social worker, the administrator, or the volunteer does not eliminate degradation. There is no way of eliminating the power that the social worker has over the client under conditions of service in the current public welfare situation. Clark recognizes a similar estrangement between client and agency:

Agencies that encourage their clients to accept dependency or to accept transparent "make-work" contribute to the perpetuation of the pathology of ghetto communities. It is reasonable to assume that people who have not already been severely damaged want wholesome work. When the client cannot find such work, the professional cannot have wholesome work of his own either. This necessarily leads to a mutually protective estrangement of the client and worker; to the "flight from the client" illustrated by the exodus of most of the family service agencies out of Harlem.[18]

Negroes of the urban ghetto are so frequently involved in such transactions that these become a critical part of their self-definition.

Race and Relationship

Relatively little has been written about the factor of race as it influences the relationship between client and social worker in the common pursuit of problem-solving. What has been written involves descriptions of practice experience with little attempt to collect and analyze these data systematically. Periodically an attempt is made to describe empirically the nature of these relationships. The only experimental work in this area pertains to the effect of race on examiner bias in various diagnostic testing and research situations. Nearly thirty years ago, in a paper describing the socialization patterns of Negro children and adolescents, Allison Davis suggested:

If we then wish to do anything to change this group's behavior, (1) we must make it possible for a much larger proportion of Negroes to obtain the kinds of occupations, income, education, and legal protection necessary for middle-class training, which means that the caste-system must be gradually changed, and (2) we must learn to do a new kind of remedial work with individuals, in which we direct them toward new goals and show them the techniques for reaching these goals. . . . It is not to be expected that lower-class children will be especially hopeful about social mobility, or be especially responsive to efforts of remedial workers along this line. The first step in the retraining of children, by teachers or social workers, therefore, is to stop punishing lower-class children by contempt or condescension. The second step is to make them understand that the social rewards of higher status are satisfying enough to justify hard work. . . .[19]

This theme is to be found time and time again in the current literature of class, race, and social work practice.

A growing literature is addressed to understanding the social and cultural factors that underlie behavior of the client group in question, in an attempt to reduce the strangeness between helper and client.[20]

---

[18] Kenneth B. Clark, *Dark Ghetto* (New York: Harper & Row, 1965), p. 49.

[19] Allison Davis, "The Socialization of the American Negro Child and Adolescent," *Journal of Negro Education*, Vol. 8, No. 3 (July 1939), pp. 264–274.
[20] *See* Fred R. Crawford, Glen W. Rollins, and Robert L. Sutherland, "Variations Between Negroes and Whites in Concepts of Mental Illness and Its Treatment," *Annals of the New York Academy of Science*, Vol. 84, No. 17 (December 8, 1960), pp. 918–937; Hugh McIsaac and Harold Wilkenson, "Clients Talk About Their Caseworkers," *Public Welfare*, Vol. 23, No. 3 (July 1965), pp. 147–154; Seaton W. Manning, "Cultural and Value Factors Affecting the Negro's Use of Agency Services," *Social Work*, Vol. 5, No. 4 (October

There has also been a concern with the attitudes of both Negro and white professionals as these affect the relationship with both Negro and white clients in various combinations. In the mental health field, a series of articles and investigations have been cast in the form of transference and countertransference mechanisms and their distortions when client and professional are of different races.[21] Some suggest that race prejudice may be used as an unconscious defense to conceal more basic conflicts in the life of the individual. They warn against allowing racial differences to blind the clinician to the more central problem.[22] Others warn against interpreting as transference the reality of the therapist's behavior toward the client owing to their racial difference. In these cases, the behavior of the client is seen as a reality reaction to the attitudes or behavior of the professional rather than as a reflection of the client's experience with earlier significant figures.[23]

Negro Client, White Worker

Similar concerns have been voiced directly in relation to social work practice. In 1938 DuVinage reported a study of responses of Negro clients to the casework relationship when the caseworker was white. She noted a considerable amount of accommodative behavior under these conditions and suggested that such behavior interfered with the effectiveness of the casework intervention.[24] Submissiveness based on fear and distrust of white persons, along with circuitously expressed aggressions, blocked treatment. She reported that the clients able to make good use of the casework relationship had caseworkers whose feelings toward Negroes were both comfortable and positive.

The following year Hart replicated the DuVinage study but used Negro caseworkers and Negro clients.[25] She found some of the same accommodative and secretive behavior on the part of the clients, but to a lesser extent. This early study was predictive of later ones indicating that all problems are not solved by the use of a professional of the same race as the client. The Negro social workers were warned not to be too demanding of their Negro clients or to foster dependency in them by taking for granted that discrimination is their problem.[26]

1960), pp. 3–13; Elizabeth Meir, "Social and Cultural Factors in Casework Diagnosis," *Social Work*, Vol. 4, No. 3 (July 1959), pp. 15–26; Lois Pettit, "Some Observations on the Negro Culture in the United States," *Social Work*, Vol. 5, No. 3 (July 1960), pp. 104–109.

[21] *See* Andrew E. Curry, "Some Comments on Transference When the Group Therapist Is a Negro," *International Journal of Group Psychotherapy*, Vol. 13, No. 3 (July 1963), pp. 363–365; Curry, "The Negro Worker and the White Client," *Social Casework*, Vol. 45, No. 3 (March 1964), pp. 131–136; Janet Kennedy, "Problems Posed in the Analysis of Negro Patients," in Martin Grossack, ed., *Mental Health and Segregation* (New York: Springer Publishing Co., 1963), pp. 199–221; and John P. Speigel, "Some Cultural Aspects of Transference and Countertransference," in J. H. Masserman, ed., *Individual and Familial Dynamics* (New York: Grune & Stratton, 1959), pp. 160–182. Maas developed a short review of the treatment variations between Negroes and Caucasians in cases of mental illness, highlighting the major findings of some recent studies and commenting on the difficulties in comparing data. *See* J. P. Maas, "Incidence and Treatment Variations Between Negroes and Caucasians in Mental Illness," *Community Mental Health Journal*, Vol. 3, No. 1 (Spring 1967), pp. 61–65.

[22] Walter A. Adams, "The Negro Patient in Psychotherapy," *American Journal of Orthopsychiatry*, Vol. 20, No. 2 (March 1950), pp. 305–310.

[23] Alexander Thomas, "Pseudo-Transference Reactions Due to Cultural Stereotyping," *American Journal of Orthopsychiatry*, Vol. 32, No. 5 (October 1962), pp. 894–200.

[24] Thelma DuVinage, "Casework with Negro Clients," *Smith College Studies in Social Work*, Vol. 9, No. 2 (February 1938), pp. 181–182.

[25] Z. C. Hart, "Accommodation Attitudes of Negro Clients to Negro Caseworkers and Their Influences on Casework," *Smith College Studies in Social Work*, Vol. 10, No. 2 (February 1939), pp. 154–155.

[26] *See* Inabel B. Lindsay, "Race as a Factor in the Caseworker's Role," *Journal of Social Casework*, Vol. 28, No. 3 (March 1947), pp. 101–147;

Frequently mentioned is the white social worker's paternalistic and dependency-supporting behavior toward the Negro client.[27] Special treatment arising from guilt and discomfort does not enhance the developmental potentials of the client.[28] A lack of knowledge and understanding of the Negro client's subcultural patterns and general life circumstances is universally seen as a barrier to an effective helping relationship. Some are concerned that superficial understanding will lead to stereotyped behavior by the white social worker, confusing interaction and limiting the possibility of developing a meaningful plan of action.[29]

Integrated Groups

As part of a large natural experiment in two children's summer camps that were shifting from a policy of segregation to one of integration, the effects of a racial mixing of campers and counselors were observed with particular clarity.[30] Both camps served low-income children. The counselors were all positively motivated toward desegregation, although nearly all the Negro counselors showed some anxiety about their acceptance by the white children, and all of the counselors felt unsure of themselves in working out the new social relationships among the children in the newly integrated groups.

Decisions made on the basis of race dominated the initial operation, but lessened later. Control techniques tended to take a more extreme form in the integrated groups. Ambiguous situations quickly led to counselor intervention. The counselors verbalized feelings of greater social distance between themselves and the children in integrated groups. They found it more difficult to appraise objectively their successes and failures with the children. Not unexpectedly, the counselors tended to rank the children who were racially different from themselves more favorably than those of their own race, which was especially true of Negro counselors' evaluations of white children. This tendency also increased among white counselors as time went on. Yet it was reported that the counselors performed consistently well despite these difficulties. Their success illustrates the time-honored professional dictum that self-knowledge is one key to overcoming behavior that interferes with the helping process.

White Client, Negro Worker

It is interesting that most of the literature concerns the Negro client and the white social worker despite the fact that there is an increasingly large number of Negro social workers. It is likely that the Negro is most often thought of in terms of being a client and that this preconception therefore establishes this priority. Relatively little has been written about the problems of a Negro social worker with a white client. Some observers report that the Negro social worker's sense of adequacy is challenged by the white client's attitudes.[31] Others, while recognizing that white clients may feel prejudice and hostility toward Negro social workers, report

and Sol W. Ginsburg, "The Impact of the Social Worker's Cultural Structure on Social Therapy," *Journal of Social Casework*, Vol. 32, No. 8 (October 1951), pp. 319–325.

[27] Esther Fibush, "The White Worker and the Negro Client," *Journal of Social Casework*, Vol. 46, No. 5 (May 1965), pp. 271–277.

[28] Jean S. Gochros, "Recognition and Use of Anger in Negro Clients," *Social Work*, Vol. 11, No. 1 (January 1966), p. 33.

[29] See Ginsburg, *op. cit.*; Fibush, *op. cit.*; and Manning, *op. cit.*

[30] Leon J. Yarrow and Marion R. Yarrow, "Leadership and Interpersonal Change," *Journal of Social Issues*, Vol. 14, No. 1 (Winter 1958), pp. 47–59.

[31] Luna B. Brown, "Race as a Factor in Establishing a Casework Relationship," *Journal of Social Casework*, Vol. 31, No. 3 (March 1950), pp. 91–97.

that these do not necessarily serve as a deterrent to the treatment relationship.[32] It has also been noted that a Negro social worker may be unsympathetic or punitive toward a white client or may overidentify with the client's whiteness and be too permissive to be of help to him.[33]

Recognizing that the casework relationship is a product of mutual perceptions and expectations based on the life experience, Curry documented the variety of possibilities in such a relationship.[34] Frequently the white client has difficulty recognizing and accepting the Negro social worker's authority and professional ability. Curry noted that some clients, while able to accept the social worker as giving service, found it necessary to screen out the authoritarian aspect of the role. He stressed the fact that emotional distance as well as social distance between worker and client are powerful forces that must be recognized. In some instances the white client's reactions are influenced by the countertransference of the Negro worker as well as by his conscious reactions to a white client. If the Negro social worker is uncertain about his own identity, considerable anxiety is stimulated in the relationship. The author warned against using the white client as an audience before whom the Negro social worker plays out his own needs.

Hostility

It is interesting to note that while hostility is not generally considered a barrier

to treatment, it is thought of in these terms when the hostility reflects interracial antagonisms.[35] Indeed, hostility is one of the expected responses to deprivation, especially when the deprivation is associated with discrimination. What would be grist for the casework mill in other circumstances here becomes a barrier to effective service.

Gochros has recognized and attempted to use anger in working with Negro clients, from experience indicating that it is essential to explore racial attitudes quickly and directly as a general rule rather than as an exception.[36] White social workers were seen as either blind to the suspicions and hostility of Negroes or fearful of bringing them out into the open.

Rather than encouraging expressions of anger, social workers' total efforts have been perhaps unconsciously directed toward clamping down lids, irrationally forgetting their usual convictions about expressing hostility.[37]

Noted also is a double-bind communication in which the social worker may first encourage expressions of hostility and then point out that the client is overgeneralizing unfairly to whites. At times even honest discussion is inhibited, let alone attempts to resolve underlying psychosocial problems.

Empirical Studies

Special mention needs to be made of the Luna Brown study, inasmuch as it is one of the few empirical efforts to describe the effects of race as a factor in establishing a casework relationship.[38] Questionnaires were sent to forty agencies in thirteen states to inquire about the difficulties encountered in mixed racial client-worker

---

[32] Eric Layne, "Experience of a Negro Psychiatric Social Worker in a Veterans Administration Mental Hygiene Clinic," *Journal of Psychiatric Social Work*, Vol. 19, No. 2 (Autumn 1949), p. 69.

[33] Leonard C. Simmons, " 'Crow Jim': Implications for Social Work," *Social Work*, Vol. 8, No. 3 (July 1963), p. 26.

[34] Andrew E. Curry, "The Negro Worker and the White Client," *Social Casework*, Vol. 45, No. 3 (March 1964), pp. 131–136.

[35] Olga Verin, "Manifestations of Racial Conflict in Negro Clients of a Child Guidance Clinic," *Smith College Studies in Social Work*, Vol. 16, No. 1 (October 1945), pp. 1–25.

[36] Gochros, *op. cit.*, pp. 28–34.

[37] *Ibid.*, p. 31.

[38] *Op. cit.*

relationships. Of the twenty-five agencies returning the questionnaires, twenty reported few difficulties, while five reported a number of problems. Only one agency thought that the difficulties were serious enough to contraindicate undifferentiated case loads for Negro workers (e.g., resistance of white clients to home visits by Negro workers). Difficulties stemming from racial differences alone were infrequent and transfer of cases on this basis was not generally necessary. Nevertheless, a number of interesting observations were reported in the questionnaires. A number of agencies reported a lack of understanding of cultural forces that served to make the white social worker seem either naïve or offensive to the Negro client. In terms of client attitudes it was noted that

some special problems were observed in Negro clients who had a great deal of feeling about their race. While some Negro clients express appreciation when a Negro caseworker is assigned, feeling this constitutes recognition of professional ability found in their own race, others feel insecure with a Negro worker or think of the Negro worker in the same inferior position as themselves and thus too enfeebled to be of help. . . . Another Negro client, who could not accept herself as a Negro, completely rejected a Negro worker . . . also, . . . a stereotyped dependent relationship with a white worker was mentioned as an adverse factor. . . . A feeling of white superiority on the part of white clients might account for difficulty in assigning Negro workers to them. . . . A white client might feel that a Negro worker would be more attentive to his material needs, presuming the worker's pleasure at serving him. . . . A white client may show resistance to a Negro worker based upon the client's belief that the Negro worker is inadequate or that he is vulnerable to intimidation.[39]

It was observed that social workers, like clients, may project onto racial factors the difficulty they are having in a casework relationship. The key word used by agencies in describing the basis for the Negro social worker's difficulties was "insecurity." It was suggested that these feelings

[39] *Ibid.*, p. 93.

may lead to aggressiveness, hostility, and a domineering manner with white clients. A number of agencies made the observation that Negro social workers were more likely to be punitive toward Negro clients. Deviations from accepted standards would be seen as a reflection on the race itself. Feelings of superiority on the part of white social workers as well as denial of any feelings about race hampered effectiveness in interracial contacts. With denial or guilt frequently came the granting of material requests.[40] In concluding, Brown suggested:

The assumption that racial differences form an invisible barrier interfering with the development of a constructive casework relationship is not proved by the data submitted by the twenty-five agencies based on an analysis of actual experience. . . . The most important conclusion of the study was that much of the difficulty attributed to the factor of racial difference appeared to be based upon various difficulties in the client-worker relationship of a kind that may be found in any casework relationship and, as a rule, can be overcome through the experience, skill, and professional security of the worker. Racial differences may be used by a client as one of the many rationalizations of his resistance. The participating agencies were in general agreement that the personal adjustment and professional skill of the worker were more important than race.[41]

One recent experimental study has produced some evidence about the expectations with which a relationship across social lines may be approached. Meeks found that the aspirations of Negro and white boys were differentially responsive to the race of an examiner. Specifically, the lower-class Negro and white boys set significantly lower aspirations for themselves when dealt with by a Negro rather than a white adult. And while the performance of white middle-class boys was uninfluenced by the race of the examiner, Negro middle-class boys tended to overaspire in their encounter with a white adult.[42] These data describe

[40] *Ibid.*
[41] *Ibid.*, p. 97.
[42] Donald E. Meeks, "The White Ego Ideal:

divergent predisposing orientations toward a Negro-white relationship. Only for the middle-class white subject was the issue of race irrelevant; for other class and race combinations, race influenced behavior.

Directions for Further Research

Race as a social category is not only difficult to study because of the uncertain "race" concept, but because a great many other characteristics mediate identity and behavior. The Negro has been used as a case in point. It is clear that income, education, religion, and location affect the meaning of the referent for the label Negro. It is somewhat like the American Indian, who found himself an *Indian* only after he was so defined by the European adventurer who discovered the Americas. Before that he was a Crow, Onondaga, Cherokee, or any of dozens of other tribal groups. It is within these subgroups that similar behavior is found. The differences among the subgroups are considerable. Pan-Indianism prevails only as a result of mutual concerns in the face of prejudice and discrimination, not as a condition of basic identity affiliation. Social workers talk mostly about the Negro poor, but even among this group it is necessary to differentiate with other subclassifications. It will be increasingly important to understand the nature of those subclassifications as they mediate behavior. While it is true that a disproportionate number of Negroes in our society share the status of "poor," there are increasing numbers of stable working-class and middle-class Negroes. It will be necessary to learn more than is now known about their responses to prejudice and discrimination.

Twenty years ago Frazier discussed the issue of vested interest on the part of some

Negroes in maintaining segregation.[43] These attitudes are increasing today for many reasons. In addition to the Black Nationalist movement, which views the possibility of temporary, self-inflicted segregation (as opposed to outside-imposed segregation), there are those in the ghetto who have reaped considerable profit for their services and are reluctant to relinquish it.[44] Research is needed to understand the conditions under which progressive social programs can be fielded successfully in the communities having the greatest need.

Central to our purpose should be an increase in research devoted to understanding the conditions under which social distance between client and social worker can be reduced. What combination of characteristics, what structural conditions of agency service, what educational efforts and training programs can be established to reduce the strangeness between helper and client?[45] The variation among professional social workers and the conditions under which they engage in their work offer a wealth of possibilities in studying the combinations that affect social distance. Further, experimental studies are becoming increasingly possible as research is built into many government-funded demonstration projects and development programs.

There are several major ways to reduce prejudice toward a specific social category. One way is to destroy the category. An-

---

Implications for the Bi-Racial Treatment Relationship," *Smith College Studies in Social Work*, Vol. 37, No. 2 (February 1967), pp. 1–93.

[43] E. Franklin Frazier, "Human, All Too Human: The Negro's Vested Interest in Segregation," *Survey Graphic*, Vol. 36, No. 1 (January 1947), pp. 74–75.

[44] For example, a new comprehensive community health service in the Watts area of Los Angeles was bitterly fought by Negro members of the medical profession practicing in that area.

[45] *See* Jona M. Rosenfeld, "Strangeness Between Helper and Client: A Possible Explanation of Non-Use of Available Professional Help," *Social Service Review*, Vol. 38, No. 1 (March 1964), pp. 17–25; and Charles Kadushin, "Social Distance Between Client and Professional," *American Journal of Sociology*, Vol. 67, No. 5 (March 1962), pp. 517–531.

other is to make an equivalent value of that social category. The latter condition is more likely to prevail in our society. Additional research is needed to discover the conditions under which subcultural identity can be promoted and enhanced. The melting pot mythology served a purpose under conditions of extensive immigration that existed earlier in our history. We may now look toward a unity-in-diversity theme in society. Can we experiment with strengthening secondary ethnic and racial identities without the evils of invidious comparison and discriminatory consequences? Can a strong secondary identity be developed without the necessity of hating the outgroup? These are concerns directly related to the purposes of the social work community.

Continued attention must also be directed toward the conditions under which "passive discrimination" exists. What are the conditions of service set by social service agencies? Are these related to the needs of the client, to the technical methodology, or to the conditions of service defined by social workers? These are questions about which we do not have clear answers. Yet accusations are hurled back and forth, both within and outside the social work profession, as if the answers were self-evident and conclusive.

Research in this highly charged area needs to find a balance between color blindness and meaningful awareness of cultural and social differences. Only as we articulate a set of values about our common goals in the race relations area will we be able comfortably to engage in the necessary research that such a commitment demands. Only then will we be able to devote ourselves to the task of joining one another in shedding some light on the dark problem of our time.

Discussion

Social work in a racist society was the subject of the four papers grouped under the heading "Perspectives on Practice, Program, and Change." Discussion of these papers ranged from the practical aspects of interracial adoptions to policy-making and the role of social work in social change.

The Billingsley and Giovannoni paper, describing perhaps the boldest and most direct professional effort to penetrate racial barriers in the sensitive area of familial relationships, revealed the depth of racial division in society and the constraint imposed by racial barriers on practice. Conspicuous from the presentation and confirmed by the experience of the discussants was the caution, even trepidation, with which interracial adoption has been approached by social agencies. None of the evidence suggested that the goal of social reform figured prominently in the decisions of a few agencies to explore this avenue toward service; instead, these efforts seemed to have been motivated by a growing sense of responsibility toward an underserved client group and the need to find solutions for pressing individual problems.

The participants accepted the authors' conclusion that interracial adoption fails to constitute a viable resource for the substitute care of Negro children today. The important and immediate needs of specific children were differentiated from the broader issue of opening up society in a way that would make it more comfortable for interracial families or those who want to adopt children of other racial groups. The discussion centered initially on the practical service problems.

While the institute participants agreed with the authors' belief that the Negro community contains unrealized resources for the provision of substitute care for children, doubt was expressed about the importance of agency requirements in creating this circumstance. When inappropriate agency requirements such as infertility, age, income levels, and the presence of adopted

children or own children in the home have
been relaxed, the difficulty in finding adoptive homes has not been overcome. For
adoption to become a more realistic possibility it may be necessary to help the prospective adoptive family with some of its
other problems, including financial ones.

Questioned too was the viability of legal
guardianship as an alternative to adoption;
this seemed to offer little protection to the
child. The suggestion was made that institutional and group living arrangements
potentially offer attractive alternatives to
adoption, and that earlier research that
demonstrated the limitations of institutions
may have interfered with the development
of better institutional arrangements.

A host of research questions emerged
from the discussion. Interest was expressed in establishing the extent to which
agencies continue to ignore the needs of
Negro children and refuse to involve themselves in the search for appropriate forms
of substitute care, the influence of prejudice
on the part of staff as a factor in adoption
planning, the true capacity of the Negro
and white communities to accommodate
the needs of Negro children, the effectiveness of alternative recruitment and selection programs, and the constraints imposed
by the legal requirements now governing
adoptions. Finally, studies of adoption in
areas of cultural diversity such as Hawaii,
Alaska, Puerto Rico, and the Virgin Islands
were expected to reveal something about
the conditions necessary to develop cross-
cultural families.

BLUMER. [The interracial adoption] paper
brings to the surface a matter of the ut-
most theoretical importance for the study
of race relations. . . . Theoretical literature—which influences research work, by
the way—is pretty well shaped by the two
key concepts of prejudice and discrimination. It is these above all other concepts
that are lodged in the center when efforts
are made analytically to deal with the
area of race relations. . . . [I believe] that
there are many, many white people who in
no sense have any feeling of prejudice in

the form, let us say, of hostility or even . . .
of dislike toward Negroes and who have
no interest whatsoever in engaging in discrimination, who, nevertheless, as all these
facts indicate, just refuse to adopt a Negro
child. Now I put the matter this way to
indicate what seems to me to be the inadequacy and fruitlessness of trying to use
the concepts of prejudice and discrimination to account for the relations [that
exist] between whites and Negroes in the
United States. I think we need an entirely
different set of basic theoretical concepts
and a different theoretical point of view.

Dissatisfaction with the concepts of prejudice and discrimination—shared by several participants—failed to produce an
entirely new conceptual scheme. Instead,
efforts were made to examine and extend
these conceptions. For example, some assumptions intrinsic to our professional
culture were identified:

SCHWARTZ. There is an underlying psycho-
analytically oriented prejudice here that
relates to attitudes toward intermarriage—
namely, that to cross racial lines represents
an unhealthy kind of rebellion against authority. And I think that this is carried
over into the adoption field. The assumption is commonly made that people who go
out of their way to adopt across racial lines
must be sick.

Exclusionary Social Work Practice

The Eaton-Gilbert paper elaborated the
idea of discrimination by advancing the
concepts of discrimination, diagnostic differentiation, preferential treatment, and
discrimination in reverse. Criticized during
the discussion was the adequacy of this
formulation for capturing the important
elements in the diverse exclusionary practices found in society generally and in social work in particular. While the principle
of accurate diagnostic differentiation was
endorsed as critical for action, this conception seemed to describe only the intent
of the actor and not its effect on the subject.
Even in the description of intent, diagnostic differentiation was seen to blur into

discrimination, since the rationale for decision-making often includes assumptions about the effects of race.

More important, it was observed that diagnostic differentiation occurs at a late point in the time sequence under which exclusionary arrangements are sustained. It is not possible to hire a Negro carpenter, for example, because Negroes have been denied entry into that career line. Thus diagnostic differentiation in the employment of a carpenter would inevitably constitute an act of discrimination.

This observation raised question about the point in an action system at which preferential treatment is needed and where in society responsibility for preferential treatment can be lodged. Schools of social work, for example, have begun to take more responsibility for reaching out and recruiting Negro students and, if necessary, planning programs that last three years instead of two and providing tutorial programs and other supports. Even this progressive approach was seen as occurring late in the course of events that handicap the Negro applicant. The complexity of organizing earlier and wholesale preferential treatment was recognized, bringing with it the risk of a kick-back from the majority group and possibly the exigencies of a quota system.

Attention was called by O'Reilly and Jerome Cohen to the prevalence in practice of various deliberate or unintended exclusionary forces. Together the presentations suggested the inescapability of our involvement with prejudice and discrimination. While a course of action seemed clear and compelling in the case of actively discriminatory arrangements, other forms of discrimination, enmeshed in our entire culture, were seen as less accessible to preventive or corrective social work action.

There was little basis for satisfaction in the rather limited leverage achieved by social work for shifting the culture and in the limited goal of finding accommodations in social work practice to existing realities. Discomfort about these points may have accounted for the attack leveled at Jerome Cohen's rather mild suggestion about the merits of supporting the construction of a positive secondary identity for Negro clients. Some participants expressed the fear that such a strategy would maintain the status quo or that training oriented toward supporting the client's secondary identity could foster prejudice in the worker. If translated into the message that a Negro is a Negro, such fears would be well founded; Jerome Cohen made clear, however, his concern with understanding and aiding the Negro's ongoing effort to locate and define himself in the social world. He asked what alternatives the Negro has to feeling comfortable about being a Negro, and none was identified.

O'Reilly's paper also elicited a rather argumentative discussion. His major thesis, that discriminatory practice occurs, was confirmed by the experience and research alluded to by discussants. Disputed, however, were a number of the implications drawn from his data. One participant believed that the data describing the percentage of Negroes employed in social welfare were meaningless, since the positions occupied by Negroes within the administrative structure were unknown. More sweepingly, objection was taken to such analysis on the basis that the race of the worker or the client is unimportant in comparison with other forces affecting the work. The chairman pointed out that staff recruited from lower income areas on the premise that they would do the best job in these areas have been found to use their positions in social work for upward mobility and to migrate toward middle-class settings. Even the obvious suggestion that Negro representation on boards be increased failed to elicit any enthusiasm. While clearly a desirable step, this was seen as relatively unimportant in comparison with issues such as achieving a redistribution of economic resources, finding a role for the social agency, solving the problems of manpower and training, and achieving a different means of service delivery.

Finally, a call for further research met only qualified acceptance. For implementing a program to contravene discrimination, no further research into the presence of discrimination was regarded as necessary. One case of discrimination was seen to be sufficient to motivate the implementation of a value assumption.

Social Work and Public Social Policy

Although the inability of social work to determine major policies was acknowledged early in the conference, concern with broad policy issues was sustained throughout the discussions. As might be expected, frank dissatisfaction was expressed toward the policies that have shaped current welfare arrangements; both traditional and innovative service programs were criticized. Traditional services were seen by some as institutionalized around antiquated bodies of knowledge and beliefs and to present structural barriers to meeting current needs. The strategy of the poverty programs, which express an individually focused, future-oriented welfare construction of the problem rather than an economic viewpoint, was also criticized.

ORSHANSKY. [In our antipoverty programs] we will do anything but spend money.

Distinctions were drawn, however, between the commitments of the social welfare Establishment and those of social workers. While the Establishment may of necessity be oriented to maintenance of the status quo, it was asserted that the worker is not wedded to the existence of the current social welfare approach.

Evident in the discussion of policy issues was an attempt to find a vantage point for viewing broadly the nature of current programs in order to look beyond the concerns with immediate and practical problems. Expressed by one participant was the need to operate on both the ideal and the real level, without letting either perspective distort the picture.

LAUE. What are the implications for the social work profession of growing separatism and the possibilities of developing separatist institutions? Underlying this are the questions: Can social work as a profession, based on the research findings it already has and the research it is capable of doing, predict what is going to be happening in the whole area of intergroup relations broadly over the next couple of years? And can it then be ready in advance with policy statements and possibly implementation activities for what is going to happen? How does the profession get ready to respond? Can concern for the discriminatory practice of an individual worker continue to be a major focus?

The inability to advance affirmative and clear answers to these questions probably helps to explain the concern vested in policy problems. For it was observed that the profession is not now ready to deal with these problems. Indeed, the possibility of answering these questions during a period of rapid change was itself questioned:

NATHAN COHEN. One projection from concurrent race relations reaches something that looks like *apartheid*. I would have to go on the notion that the present development is a stage in something that may take one form or another. I have a strong feeling that a good deal of the decision-making on this question of segregation, separation, or whatever it is belongs to the Negro. I think that too long, and too often, we have sat and tried to find solutions for the Negroes. I think that they're going to have something to say about what it is they want to do. And we sit here almost as if they don't know enough to do this. I would have a hard time planning, at this time, for a separate Negro community with the notion that I was going to train people for this particular purpose. So my reaction is this: I think that we're going through a stage—a very serious process of change, the determination of which will be affected by responses both ways.

Attention was given to the conditions under which policy change can occur. One observer reported experience in promoting policy change by simply bringing to light the unwitting and unrecognized kind of exclusion that takes place. When, for example, federal judges learned that Negro felons were four times more likely to be sent to the penitentiary than were their white counterparts found guilty of the same offense, they instituted corrective measures. A number of participants quickly pointed out, however, that knowledge does not always bring change.

SCHWARTZ. The deficiencies, the inequities of the present federal-state public assistance programs have been spelled out ad nauseam. No one even wants to hear it any more. Practically everyone agrees with the fact that the system is inefficient as well as inadequate and inhumane—and the fact is that we still have it.

The federal judge was seen as a much more autonomous actor, with authority to introduce an incremental change in contrast to a step change that involves other authorities and must therefore take place in the political arena. A change from segregated housing, for example, involves the complex and intermeshed interests in real estate, insurance, mortgage finance, and legal practices.

It was suggested that there are three conditions under which remedial public policy changes occur in response to new information:

SCOBLE. One of these is when there are no apparent costs for whites. This is illustrated by efforts to integrate a police force and a fire department. The latter issue is much more touchy. When you integrate a police force, what it really means is that you are hiring Negro cops to police Negro residential areas, and there is only contact during working hours. In the fire station, members are on duty for twenty-four-hour periods. They live in close, intimate contact. Integration of fire departments has been much more difficult to achieve.

A second condition is when the demand can be phrased as a simple, straightforward, clear appeal to justice, equality, and fairness—to the basic norms of society. The struggle for suffrage is identified as achieving manhood and equality. It is much easier to appeal to the American white conscience here than it is, say, for a benign quota in preferential treatment.

Third is a condition of combined power and authority to institute changes. In the case of demonstrations, historically it has been easy to achieve some concrete policy results if it was clear that the mayor alone, or the mayor and the city council together, had both power and authority to produce some kind of change. In contrast is the situation in segregated housing, supported by all of the interlocking institutions existing there.

Directions for Social Work

Recurrent reference was made during the institute to the idea of a guaranteed minimum income as a matter of national interest. Acknowledged in the discussion of adoption problems, one-parent families, and service delivery efforts generally was the economic vulnerability of disadvantaged groups. The maintenance of adequate income was thus regarded as a necessary, if not sufficient, condition for the management of social problems. Contained in the emphasis on an economic foundation for service was a viewpoint about social welfare.

LEWIS. There is a disposition to think of social welfare more and more as a set of institutions designed to maximize choice, to increase options for people, rather than a set of institutions designed to parcel out in a reluctant fashion money and services as aid to the poor—particularly the deserving poor. We are coming to the position too that income has to be maintained by jobs if possible and, if not by jobs, by other means. This is a new agenda as far as social welfare is concerned.

Because civil rights groups have adopted the guaranteed minimum income as an action goal, a general political issue appeared to have become a racial issue. Nathan Cohen observed that in every generation an issue belonging to the whole society has been fought through a specific group. The racial displacement in viewpoints about the proposed program was seen as an effort to deny the existence of the basic problem of poverty and, by defining it as a Negro problem, justify inaction. Lewis advanced the opinion that the designation of a political issue as a Negro issue no longer assures its defeat. Increasingly, support can be mustered for a Negro issue, both at the polls and at other political leverage points. Whatever the political costs and gains, it appeared that the realization of a fundamental change in the direction of social welfare will depend to some extent on sentiments attached to race. In the forthcoming test of the responsiveness of the American social system to human need, organized social welfare will share a common destiny with the Negro.

Part III

Issues and Opportunities

Intergroup Relations at the Neighborhood Level

ST. CLAIR DRAKE

The dominant value judgment implicit in most studies of intergroup relations in the United States is that it is desirable to reduce tensions and to encourage harmonious relations among ethnic, racial, religious, and class groups. Wherever a functional view of the process of social change or a conflict model of analysis may lead, those in the mainstream of the social work profession accept this value premise as the rationale for their organized activity.[1]

The specific topic of this paper is set within the general frame of reference of approval of "intervention and ameliorative techniques seeking *to reduce alienation, separation, and economic and social problems of racial and ethnic minorities.*" The focus is on neighborhood organization and community patterns "seeking *to increase mutual respect, acceptance and transaction between people of different racial and ethnic origins.*"[2] It should be noted at the outset that pursuit of these goals may combine an equilibrium model and a conflict model for social action in which tension reduction is viewed as a long-term goal, but with some forms of conflict sanctioned as part of an ongoing process—even if accepted reluctantly as inevitable.

A growing number of social workers adhere to Martin Luther King's philosophy

St. Clair Drake, Ph.D., is Professor of Sociology, Roosevelt University, Chicago, Illinois.

[1] There has always been a minority in the academic subculture who have been interested in the sociology of conflict, some of whom view conflict not only as natural, necessary, or inevitable, but even as desirable or constructive in the process of social change. During the 1930's there was a tendency for this point of view to be represented by various varieties of Marxist scholars, but during the past decade a nonideological sociology of conflict has assumed increasing prominence. *See,* for example, Lewis Coser, *The Functions of Social Conflict* (Glencoe, Ill.: Free Press, 1956).

[2] These quotations are from the statement of objectives of the Institute on Research Toward Improving Race Relations.

of the utility and moral acceptability of nonviolently induced "creative tension" and have been involved in activities of the Congress of Racial Equality, Student Nonviolent Co-ordinating Committee, Southern Christian Leadership Conference, or similar organizations. Some, too, have been supporters of open occupancy measures or of school desegregation, and such activity has been likely to increase tension and conflict temporarily, rather than to reduce it. Saul Alinsky's pressure tactics are not rejected by all social workers, and a few (especially among Negroes) support one or another varieties of the exercise of Black Power. Involvement in federally supported Community Action Programs has probably increased the number of social workers who have found themselves organizing groups that eventually become involved in some types of conflict action. But *after* conflict, the problem of compromise and reconciliation remains. It is this aspect of the process of change that receives high priority among social workers as compared with full-time militant leaders.[3]

The literature on intergroup relations produced prior to 1959 gives little attention to the conflict aspects of racial and ethnic relations at the neighborhood level, although problems posed by attempts to desegregate the schools in southern states stimulated a considerable number of research projects on that subject.[4] Some were concerned with the "readiness" of population samples to accept desegregation; others were evaluative studies made after desegregation occurred. The bulk

of the published literature, with one significant exception—Herbert A. Thelen's *Dynamics of Groups at Work*—does not use the neighborhood as the unit for intergroup relations research at all.[5] Emphasis was on theory-building based either on experimental situations or on consideration of structure and process in large-scale organizational structures.

Research in Intergroup Relations, 1945–58

The caste-class hypothesis dominated the field of race relations research in the United States between 1935 and 1945, but the units for research were entire communities (Davis *et al.*'s *Deep South* and Dollard's *Caste and Class in a Southern Town*, for instance) or the entire United States, as in the case of Myrdal's *An American Dilemma*.[6] Immediately after the war, municipalities began to organize human relations commissions, the Rosenwald Fund sponsored organization of the American Council on Race Relations, and various governmental agencies became concerned with civil rights and housing and job opportunities for Negroes. The literature produced by such groups is voluminous, but most of it is policy related rather than theoretical and does not deal with neighborhood problems per se. This does not mean that no research at this level was done, but what was done tended to remain unpublished. On the other hand, basic theoretical research carried out during this period had far-reaching implications for neighborhood action programs. For this reason it will be discussed briefly.

The concern for grounding intergroup relations practice on a sound theoretical

---

[3] The author has discussed the relationship between social workers and militant social movements in the introductory chapter and the chapter on guidelines in his *Race Relations in a Time of Rapid Social Change* (New York: National Federation of Settlements and Neighborhood Centers, 1966).

[4] *See* E. A. Suchman, J. P. Dean, and Robin M. Williams, Jr., *Desegregation: Some Propositions and Research Suggestions* (New York: Anti-Defamation League, 1958).

[5] Chicago: University of Chicago Press, 1954.
[6] Allison Davis *et al.*, *Deep South* (Chicago: University of Chicago Press, 1965) ; John Dollard, *Caste and Class in a Southern Town* (Garden City, N.Y.: Doubleday & Co., 1957) ; Gunnar Myrdal, *An American Dilemma* (rev. ed.; New York: Harper & Row, 1962).

basis during the postwar period was expressed in the willingness of a number of foundations and voluntary associations, as well as some governmental agencies, to provide the financial resources needed for research.[7] The pioneering publication, and perhaps the most influential single contribution of the period, was *The Reduction of Intergroup Tensions* by Robin M. Williams, Jr.[8] During the same year Arnold Rose's *Studies in the Reduction of Prejudice* was published.[9]

The decade after the publication of Williams' monograph was one during which an integrated frame of reference for the study of intergroup relations crystallized, a small group of basic hypotheses was standardized, and a number of significant research projects were carried out in relation to the theory-building process. The results of some of this research were not published until well into the next decade (see Table 1 for a listing of the major publications). These studies all contributed to the acceptance of certain principles that became the basis for intervention and ameliorative action at the neighborhood level as well as in other areas of national life. The cardinal principles were these:

1. Harmonious intergroup relations and the correction of stereotypes are facilitated by the fostering of "equal-status contacts" across racial and ethnic lines.

2. Task-oriented activity focused on shared common goals cements relations across ethnic and racial lines and reduces conflict and tension among groups. Some reduction in prejudice and stereotyped conceptualization accompanies this process.

3. Most acts of discrimination result from conformity reactions or pursuit of economic interests and prestige, *not* from a psychological "need" to discriminate rooted in a personality type.[10]

4. Strategies for inducing social change should concentrate on eliminating discrimination rather than on changing individual prejudices.

5. The manipulation of "power structures" in order to set new contact situations involving different ethnic and racial groups is not only theoretically sound, but also ethically defensible.

6. The use of small group situations for fostering equal-status contacts results in the creation of new social norms that reinforce friendly attitudes and nondiscriminatory behavior.

During this period a number of manuals and various types of educational aids were prepared for use by governmental agencies and voluntary associations that attempted to popularize the findings of some of the research or to provide guides to action. Among these were *The Police and Minority Groups* and *Neighbors in Action: A Manual for Leaders in Intergroup Relations.*[11]

---

[7] Municipal commissions on human relations usually had their research units as did some state commissions. The American Jewish Committee, the Anti-Defamation League, the National Conference of Christians and Jews, as well as the major foundations gave generous support to research in this field. The role of the American Jewish Committee has been discussed in John Slawson, *The Role of Science in Intergroup Relations* (Chicago: Institute of Human Relations Press, 1962).

[8] Bulletin No. 57 (New York: Social Science Research Council, 1947).

[9] Chicago: American Council on Race Relations, 1947. The volume of community studies such as St. Clair Drake and H. R. Cayton's *Black Metropolis* (New York: Harper & Bros., 1945) began to diminish as did national syntheses such as Robert C. Weaver's *The Negro Ghetto* (New York: Russell & Russell, 1948). Emphasis shifted to more tightly structured research on specific race relations problems.

---

[10] During the five years after the publication of T. W. Adorno *et al.*'s *The Authoritarian Personality* (New York: Harper & Bros., 1950), the findings of that important work were placed in sociological perspective, with this general proposition being widely accepted.

[11] J. D. Lohman, *The Police and Minority Groups* (1947); Rachel Davis-Dubois, *Neighbors in Action: A Manual for Leaders in Intergroup Relations* (New York: Harper & Bros., 1950).

TABLE 1. A SAMPLING OF LITERATURE AND RESEARCH PROJECTS, 1945–58

Basic Theoretical Contributions	Research Reports and Research in Process
Kurt Lewin, *Resolving Social Conflicts* (New York: Harper & Bros., 1948), *see* especially chap. 13, "Action Research and Minority Problems."	T. W. Adorno *et al.*, *The Authoritarian Personality* (New York: Harper & Bros., 1950).
J. D. Lohman and D. C. Reitzes, "Notes on Race Relations in Mass Society," *American Journal of Sociology*, Vol. 58, No. 3 (November 1952), pp. 240–246.	Morton Deutsch and Mary Evans Collins, *Interracial Housing: A Psychological Evaluation of a Social Experiment* (Minneapolis: University of Minnesota Press, 1951).
D. C. Reitzes, "The Role of Organization Structures," *Journal of Social Issues*, Vol. 9, No. 1 (January 1953), pp. 37–44.	Leon Festinger and Harold H. Kelley, *Changing Attitudes Through Social Contact* (Ann Arbor: Research Center for Group Dynamics, University of Michigan, 1951) (a housing project study sponsored by the Research Center for Group Dynamics).
Robin M. Williams, Jr., "Review and Assessment of Research on Race and Culture Conflict." Paper presented at the Conference on Research in Human Relations, Rockefeller Foundation, New York, 1953.	
J. D. Lohman and D. C. Reitzes, "Deliberately Organized Groups and Racial Behavior," *American Sociological Review*, Vol. 19, No. 3 (June 1954), pp. 342–344.	Daniel M. Wilner, Rosabelle B. Walkley, and Stuart W. Cook, "Residential Proximity and Intergroup Relations in Public Housing Projects," *Journal of Social Issues*, Vol. 8, No. 1 (January 1952), pp. 45–69.
Herbert A. Thelen, *Dynamics of Groups at Work* (Chicago: University of Chicago Press, 1954).	
Arnold M. Rose, "Intergroup Relations vs. Prejudice: Pertinent Theory for the Study of Social Change," *Social Problems*, Vol. 4, No. 2 (October 1956), pp. 173–176.	Arnold M. Rose *et al.*, "Neighborhood Reactions to Isolated Negro Residents," *American Sociological Review*, Vol. 18, No. 5 (October 1953), pp. 497–507 (a neighborhood study).
R. E. Murphy, "Intergroup Hostility and Social Cohesion," *American Anthropologist*, Vol. 59, No. 6 (December 1957), p. 1033.	Irwin Katz, *Conflict and Harmony in an Adolescent Interracial Group* (New York: New York University Press, 1955) (a camp).
Leon A. Festinger, *A Theory of Cognitive Dissonance* (Evanston, Ill.: Row, Peterson, 1957).	Morton Deutsch and Mary Evans Collins, *Human Relations in Interracial Housing*, 1955.
Muzafer Sherif, "Superordinate Goals in the Reduction of Intergroup Conflict," *American Journal of Sociology*, Vol. 63, No. 4 (January 1958), pp. 354–356.	Judith T. Shuvall, "Class and Ethnic Correlates of Casual Neighboring," *American Sociological Review*, Vol. 21, No. 4 (August 1956), pp. 453–458 (a neighborhood study).
Edward A. Suchman, J. P. Dean, and Robin M. Williams, Jr., *Desegregation: Some Propositions and Research Suggestions* (New York: Anti-Defamation League, 1958).	M. L. Kohn and Robin M. Williams, Jr., "Situational Patterning in Intergroup Relations," *American Sociological Review*, Vol. 21, No. 2 (April 1956), pp. 164–174 (a public accommodations situation).
Ronald Lippitt *et al.*, *The Dynamics of Planned Change* (New York: Harcourt, Brace, 1958).	

One social psychologist summed up the manner in which the body of theory elaborated in the works listed in Table 1 was applied, commenting:

In the past, measures to combat the problem of intergroup conflicts, proposed by social scientists as well as by such people as administrators, policy makers, municipal officials and educators, have included the following: introduction of legal sanctions; creation of opportunities for social and other contacts among members of conflicting groups; dissemination of information to break down false prejudices and unfavorable stereotypes; appeals to the moral ideals of fair play and brotherhood; and even the introduction of rigorous physical activity to produce catharsis by releasing pent-up frustrations and aggressive complexes in the unconscious. Other methods proposed include the encouragement of cooperative habits in one's own community, and bringing together in the cozy atmosphere of a meeting room the leaders of antagonistic groups.[12]

After this faintly sarcastic statement, he presented the results of a research project of his own. His evaluation of current theory and practice was not wholly negative, however, and he stated:

Many of these measures may have some value in the reduction of intergroup conflicts but to date very few generalizations have been established concerning the circumstances and kinds of intergroup conflict in which these measures are effective. Today measures are applied in a somewhat trial and error fashion. Finding measures that have wide validity can in practice come only through clarification of the nature of intergroup conflict and analysis of the factors conducive to harmony and conflict between groups under given conditions.[13]

The empirical research on which theorizing in the field of intergroup relations was based during this period included a variety of situations—housing projects, summer camps, business enterprises, factories, trade union halls, places of public accommodation. It also included population samples to which various types of attitude tests were administered. One of the most significant projects going on in the latter part of the period was the evaluation of the effect of the Encampment for Citizenship by Herbert Hyman, but the results did not appear in print until 1962.[14] The Cornell Studies in Intergroup Relations were also begun and several articles were published, but the definitive volume did not appear until 1964.[15] The latter research did involve investigations at the neighborhood level, as did two other items on the list. But virtually none of the published research involved the study of deliberately induced change within neighborhoods or even evaluative or ex post facto studies of intervention by various social agencies into the free flow of social processes within the neighborhood. The one significant exception—studies of the Hyde Park–Kenwood neighborhood in Chicago—will be discussed in some detail.

Two highly significant events occurred at the federal government level during this period that had repercussions in local communities throughout the United States—a Supreme Court decision in 1948 that declared restrictive covenants unenforceable in the courts and the 1954 decision which ruled that enforced segregation in the public schools was a violation of the constitutional rights of Negroes. The latter decision stimulated a series of well-financed and well-designed studies the results of which began to appear in print during the next decade, but few of these dealt with processes at the community level designed to

---

[12] Muzafer Sherif, "Superordinate Goals in the Reduction of Intergroup Conflict," *American Journal of Sociology*, Vol. 63, No. 4 (January 1958), pp. 349–350.

[13] *Ibid.*, p. 349.

[14] Herbert H. Hyman, Charles R. Wright, and Terence K. Hopkins, *Applications of Methods of Evaluation: Four Studies of the Encampment for Citizenship* (Berkeley: University of California Press, 1962).

[15] Robin M. Williams, Jr., *Strangers Next Door: Ethnic Relations in American Communities* (Englewood Cliffs, N.J.: Prentice-Hall, 1964).

foster acceptance of the Supreme Court decision.[16]

It is possible that considerable data on social change at the neighborhood level involving race relations are available in the files of settlement houses and neighborhood centers, the minute books of churches and associations, the records of real estate offices, and the pages of neighborhood newspapers. The records, too, of such agencies as the National Urban League and city human relations commissions undoubtedly contain rich material on processes within neighborhoods that might be studied with reference to the general body of theory in the field or that could be subjected to evaluative research procedures. Such studies if done now would have greater theoretical than practical value, however. Robin Williams' volume on the Cornell Studies, *Strangers Next Door,* which reports on research carried out during the 1950's, is one of the most significant contributions to the study of racial and ethnic relations in the United States. It does not, however, report on "intervention" studies, although such research was done in one city as part of a larger study:

1949–1950: First trials of active intervention in intergroup situations for purposes of diagnosing process.
1950–1951: Continuation of detailed study of the inception and functioning of local interracial and intercultural organizations. In particular, the research staff worked closely with the Hometown Mayor's Committee on Human Relations.
1951–1952: Continuation of the intensive study of the Mayor's Committee on Human Relations in Hometown. The data provide materials for a detailed study of processes of involvement and redefinition of problems in a group attempting to deal with intergroup relations at a local level. (A special

questionnaire was administered to meetings of intergroup relations practitioners in five cities including Chicago.) [17]

Williams was asked by this writer if the Cornell group ever intended to publish the results of these studies. He replied:

The data from the Cornell "intervention" studies probably never will be published—most of them now seem "dated" because the total situation is so different.

It is unlikely that this material could make any new contribution at the theoretical level although it might contain case material that would be valuable for those facing action problems in similar situations. An inventory of unpublished data of this nature, as well as of unpublished master's theses and doctoral dissertations, might be useful to practitioners in the field of intergroup relations, who could then make their own contacts with sources that have material of use to them.

The type of neighborhood of most concern during this period was the so-called transitional neighborhood adjacent to heavy concentrations of Negroes. Two factors set off massive population movements out of the ghettos: (1) possibilities opened by the Supreme Court decision of 1954 and (2) land clearance owing to urban renewal and redevelopment projects. Throughout the United States white neighborhoods close to Black Belt areas were forced to adopt some attitude toward Negroes wishing to rent or buy or toward brokers wishing to obtain property for Negro occupancy. Unable to stem the tide any longer by injunctions, some such neighborhoods resorted to violence. Others began to organize associations to prevent panic selling or to co-operate with incoming Negroes in preserving middle-class values in the neighborhood. The only major works of the period dealing with neighborhood action in transitional communities are about Chi-

---

[16] *See,* for example, Melvin Tumin *et al., Desegregation: Resistance and Readiness* (Princeton: Princeton University Press, 1958).

[17] Williams, *op. cit.,* Appendix.

cago, although there are numerous articles on other areas.

Studies of white neighborhoods remote from Negro concentrations but with a few Negro residents, either of long standing or newcomers, are rare. Those involving multi-ethnic neighborhoods are rarer. Studies of race relations within the ghetto, important as that subject is, are few and far between, too. First examined will be the literature on the Chicago situation during the 1950's, for research carried out there had important theoretical implications.

The Chicago Experience

Several of the works listed in Table 1 represent reflection on and conclusions drawn from what might be called "the Chicago experience." After the Detroit race riot of 1943, the city of Chicago moved swiftly to set up a Mayor's Committee on Race Relations (which evolved into the Chicago Commission on Human Relations). Its basic aim was riot prevention, so a program of training was set up immediately for the Park District police and a sociologist, Joseph D. Lohman, prepared a teaching aid.[18]

Implicit in this operation were assumptions, based on role theory and the concept of the mass society, about how policemen could be expected to act and how races could be expected to relate to each other. Five years later these assumptions were made explicit in articles published in academic journals by Lohman and his colleague Reitzes.[19] They were not concerned

primarily with the problem of neighborhood organization and community patterns as these operate to increase mutual respect, acceptance, and transaction among people of different racial and ethnic origins. Their focus was on the larger bureaucratic structures—federal and municipal agencies, industry and labor unions. Insofar as they worked with the concept "mass society" they did not place emphasis on the *networks* of voluntary associations, although specific associations were studied, nor was tension reduction a primary concern. Prevention and control of overt violence were, for them, the most urgent problems. Attention was given to the possibilities of changing interracial behavior by the deliberate action of those in what C. Wright Mills called "the command posts" of the power structures. However, their demonstration that white individuals structure their personal behavior toward Negroes through varied role situations had profound implications for neighborhood organization.

The Lohman-Reitzes theorizing was going on at a time when massive changes were taking place in Chicago at the neighborhood level. The 1948 Supreme Court decision resulted in accelerated block-by-block movement out of the ghetto and generated tension areas all around the Black Belt. Neighborhoods-in-transition, as a type, were defined as a social problem by everyone concerned with civic welfare. For three years after the decision some of these neighborhoods were battlegrounds where Negroes fought for every inch gained in the face of arson and bombing.[20] In one area of the city, however, a group of leaders—Unitarians, Quakers, and Reformed Jews—decided to try to mobilize the community in order to prevent violence,

---

[18] *The Police and Minority Groups.*

[19] Joseph D. Lohman and D. C. Reitzes, "Notes on Race Relations in Mass Society," *American Journal of Sociology*, Vol. 58, No. 3 (November 1952), pp. 240–246; Reitzes, "The Role of Organization Structures," *Journal of Social Issues*, Vol. 9, No. 1 (January 1953), pp. 37–44; and Lohman and Reitzes, "Deliberately Organized Groups and Racial Behavior," *American Sociological Review*, Vol. 19, No. 3 (June 1954), pp. 342–344.

---

[20] Maps of areas where arson and bombing occurred are presented as part of a discussion of this process in the appendix to St. Clair Drake and Horace Cayton, *Black Metropolis*, Vol. I (New York: Harper & Row, Harper Torchbook, 1962).

stem the precipitate flight of white families from the city, and organize the whites who remained and the incoming Negroes in an effort to maintain high standards of property use and improve the total environment. The story of the formation of the Hyde Park–Kenwood Community Conference has been told in detail by one of the founders.[21]

Despite the zeal of the leaders and the favorable response of many of the residents of the area, it was impossible for a voluntary association to shape and control a fluid situation such as this one was, although their activities played a major role in keeping it free of violence. Ultimately the Hyde Park–Kenwood Community Conference found it necessary to ally itself with a powerful neighborhood institution —the University of Chicago—which had set up its own organization, the Southeast Chicago Commission, with emphasis on controlling crime in the area. The latter organization broadened its interests through interaction with the conference, and the university ultimately threw its weight behind a program of planning that involved both private and federal funds.

The goal of the program was to transform the neighborhood into a predominantly middle-class one by astute use of the bulldozer, various forms of legal and social pressure, and the building of high-income, high-rise apartments and town houses. Open occupancy was the stated goal and what might be called "controlled integration" was the means. Tensions arose and conflict broke out in the neighborhood between the university and some of the residents, who felt that they were being displaced, and some of the members of the conference felt that the original goals of that organization were perverted by the alliance with the university.

This situation has been analyzed within the broader city-wide context by two Uni-

versity of Chicago social scientists.[22] Their work is one of the few studies that consider the problem of the relationships between a neighborhood organization started by "liberals" to preserve open occupancy and middle-class standards and the larger urban social structures. The inescapable conclusion is that in such an alliance the neighborhood organizations may have their freedom of action drastically curbed but manage to see some of their goals realized, although by means that leave many of them feeling guilty. This type of situation exists in a number of American cities, and the findings of Rossi and Dentler have a generality beyond the Chicago situation.

The Hyde Park–Kenwood Community Conference was fortunate in the early stages of its growth to have a number of social scientists who lived in the neighborhood available for counsel and advice as well as for supervision of some of the necessary research.[23] Among them was a social psychologist—Herbert A. Thelen—who used the conference to train students in group dynamics. Out of his association with the conference has come the most careful analysis of its activities and an attempt to relate its work to a broader body of theory. Portions of his book, *Dynamics of Groups at Work,* are devoted to a discussion of conference activities.

Chapter 1 of Thelen's book considers "Rebuilding the Community Through Citizen Action," and another chapter, "The Context of Group Operation," is specifically concerned with the problem of inter-

---

[21] Julia Abrahamson, *A Neighborhood Finds Itself* (New York: Harper & Bros., 1959).

[22] Peter H. Rossi and R. A. Dentler, *The Politics of Urban Renewal* (New York: Free Press of Glencoe, 1961).

[23] This writer and Dr. Everett Cherrington Hughes were, for a time, cochairmen of the research committee of the organization, which involved its members in gathering data for a number of surveys. Later the conference commissioned a group of planners to draw up a model plan for redeveloping the area, which, incidentally, was rejected by the University of Chicago.

racial and interethnic co-operation. It was his view that "events in the Hyde Park–Kenwood community have amply demonstrated the importance for community betterment of massive, creative participation by the citizenry," and he set as his aim "to transfer to more general terms and for use in other areas, some of the experience gained in the Hyde Park–Kenwood Community Conference program in Chicago." [24] The emphasis is on block organization with a task-oriented program ("Membership is based on willingness to work, not on ideology"), a subject discussed at one point as follows:

In general, it is assumed that people will hold different opinions about Negroes, city offices, liberals, real estate agents, etc. These differences can be accepted as differences of opinion rather than as the start of a battle. . . . Whatever one's opinions, attitudes or ideology, he is pretty likely to join with his neighbors to get a wrecked jalopy off the street, a rat colony discouraged, or a new landlord indoctrinated.[25]

Each block club and the conference as a whole are defined by Thelen as "bridging groups," that is, they incorporate members from many other diverse groups, bringing them together around a task that forces them constantly to reappraise their attitudes toward each other. There is, then, some feedback into the other groups to which they belong. In a section on "Resolving Intergroup Conflict: A Model," what Thelen calls "the salient features of the operation" are stated:

1. Bringing about communication between members of the opposing groups under conditions such that neither has to "defend" his group.
2. Developing the bridging group itself into a strong one with its own culture and appeal to members.
3. Operating the bridging group as a training situation in which the members can learn the experimental method of group problem-solving.
4. Facilitating acceptance by members of each other and of the groups they represent.
5. Influencing the members of the home groups toward gradual change of their ways of operating, toward a more problem-reality-oriented approach.[26]

Thelen's analysis does not deal adequately with the initial stages of the formation of a "bridging group" within a transitional area. In the stage of trying to prevent the flight of white residents or panic selling, quite different problems are posed from those that come later when Negroes and whites are working together to maintain high community standards. He has not dealt, either, with the dilemmas faced by Negroes who may be caught in the conflict between racial group loyalty and social class group loyalty. He has, however, come to grips with the problem of how such neighborhood groups must work out their relations with larger structures and includes in his model "Basic Principles for Groups in Relation to the Larger Community":

1. Community problem-solving is put ahead of organizational power as the objective.
2. Anyone who can help with the problem-solving is welcome, regardless of professed belief or our theories about his personality.
3. Efforts are made to seek out and reach working agreement with other groups working for the same objectives.
4. The group serves as a bridging group to reduce conflict among the other groups to which the members are loyal.
5. The group adopts an experimental methodology, determining action at each step on the basis of evaluation of results of preceding steps.
6. The group pays attention to self-training and to its own development so that leadership is strengthened, goals are kept realistic, individuals make satisfying contributions, and workable solutions to problems can be formulated explicitly and passed on to other groups and communities.

---

[24] *Op. cit.,* p. 13.
[25] *Ibid.,* p. 16.

[26] *Ibid.,* p. 335.

7. The group collects adequate data about the problem. . . .

8. The group realistically appraises its own resources and skills and gets professional help when needed.

9. Throughout all action, the group defines its "enemy" as *objectively defined conditions in need of change* rather than in terms of individuals or groups to be demolished. [Italics added.] [27]

These generalizations were made before the alliance between the neighborhood organization and the university and, therefore, before serious crises arose within the organization and between it and the university. For these crises Rossi and Dentler are the analysts. It is interesting to note, however, that Thelen conceived of the possibility of the original group *not* becoming an arm of the larger bureaucratic structure, stating:

The original groups continuously redefining specific goals would have—and will always have—a place. It is that of the active social conscience, the prophet of change, the formulator of new values. And it is only through such groups that individual insight, sensitivity and creativity can be utilized for the development of the "humane community" toward which man's nature (including the processes described so far) is driving him.[28]

The conference lost this "prophetic" role, although it still exists. The executive director of the Chicago Commission on Human Relations stated that by 1962 fifteen neighborhood groups existed in the city, all of which had profited from what he called the frankly admitted mistakes of the pioneer organization as they were outlined in Abrahamson's book, *A Neighborhood Finds Itself*. He summed up the principles that the conference arrived at by trial and error:

1. Do not appeal to people in neighborhoods on the basis of any kind of ideological principles.

2. Always appeal in terms of enlightened self-interest.

3. Action should be task-oriented.

4. Make alliances with groups that have power and influence.[29]

The work of the Hyde Park–Kenwood Community Conference received national (and even international) publicity. It must have influenced, to some extent, the work of similar groups in other cities.

A detailed comparison of the fifteen groups alluded to by the director of the Chicago Commission on Human Relations would be illuminating if it were available. There is only *one* Hyde Park–Kenwood with its heavy concentration of liberally oriented university types! Middle-class white neighborhoods made up of first- and second-generation European immigrants have been violently resistant to suggestions that they absorb even a token number of Negroes. No accounts of attempts to organize such communities in relation to "invasion" by Negroes exist in print. They are needed, both to test theoretical formulations and as a guide to action in similar communities elsewhere.

There is also a body of "Chicago experience" with respect to neighborhood organization in predominantly Negro neighborhoods of several social class types. The problem of racial and ethnic relations in the ghetto is a specialized one that will be discussed in some detail later in this paper, and it takes on urgent significance today. At this point, one Chicago case might be mentioned—that of Woodlawn, an area adjacent to the University of Chicago. This apartment house area has gradually become nearly all-Negro, is seriously overcrowded, and crime and delinquency rates are high. Within its boundaries is the Hyde Park High School, once the elite

---

[27] *Ibid.*, pp. 365–366.
[28] *Ibid.*, p. 364.

[29] Edward Marciniak, review of Julia Abrahamson's *A Neighborhood Finds Itself*, *Journal of Intergroup Relations*, Vol. 2, No. 1 (Winter 1960–61), pp. 369–372.

high school of the city, but now operating under conditions that cause its alumni to wince. When the university planners decided to give this neighborhood the same redevelopment treatment to which parts of Hyde Park were subjected, Saul Alinsky's Industrial Areas Foundation set up the Temporary Woodlawn Organization (TWO) to resist the university's pressure. Alinsky's theory of organization is far removed from that of Thelen. Select an "enemy"—the university—and rub the sores raw. TWO won, and Silberman extols it as one of the most significant projects of community action in the country.[30] What its implications are for intergroup relations will be discussed later.

Literature on Intergroup Relations, 1959–67

Except for one contribution by Robin Williams, the past decade has seen no significant new contributions to the theory of intergroup relations, even in those studies summing up large-scale research projects begun in the previous period.[31] Herbert Blumer has suggested that it is unlikely that any new theoretical developments will occur in the field of race relations.[32] New problem areas have been defined, however, and more refined research procedures have been designed to test propositions elaborated earlier. Emphasis on the study of neighborhoods-in-transition has continued, but there is also growing concern with preparing residents in white neighborhoods to accept positively the possibility that in the future Negroes may appear on the scene as their neighbors—and this involves suburban areas as well as neighborhoods within the city. The most significant shift in focus has been the attention given to intergroup relations within the ghetto itself since the outburst of riots in 1964 and the rise of the Black Power concept, although little such research has been published. In all of these situations two types of research are prominent: (1) the study of how larger organizational structures influence neighborhood situations and (2) the evaluation of specific types of action techniques.[33] While significant new contributions during this period at the theoretical level have been few, some questions have been raised about the adequacy of some of the existing formulations, accompanied by suggestions for research designed to test generalizations now taken for granted. For instance, one student of intergroup relations has called for a reexamination of what he names the "equal-status contact hypothesis," noting that it may apply in only some conditions. For example, the questions might be asked: "Does contact among those of an equally *deprived* status have the same results as among the equally *privileged?*" and "Does equal-status contact lead those who have

---

[30] Charles S. Silberman, *Crisis in Black and White* (New York: Random House, 1964); and Saul Alinsky, *Citizen Participation and Community Organization in Planning and Urban Renewal* (Chicago: Industrial Areas Foundation, 1962).

[31] Note the final report on the Cornell studies, Williams, *Strangers Next Door.* Another of these studies is discussed in Saul D. Lesser and Charles Warrick, "Direction, Salience, and Intensity of the Effects of an Intergroup Education Experience," *Journal of Intergroup Relations,* Vol. 2, No. 1 (Winter 1960–61). This is a favorable review of the Encampment for Citizenship Study referred to in Table 1, which was published as Hyman, Wright, and Hopkins, *op. cit.* The section on "Principles of Evaluation" is a definitive statement and a model for such research.

[32] His view is that contributions are more likely in the field of applied sociology. Herbert Blumer, "Recent Research on Race Relations in the United States of America," *International Social Science Bulletin,* UNESCO, Vol. 10 (1958), pp. 403–447.

[33] Note for (1) Williams, *op. cit.,* pp. 379–382. For (2), *see,* for example, *The Management of Neighborhood Change* (Chicago: Chicago Commission on Human Relations, 1959), and various studies summarized in this paper.

been prejudiced to conclude that 'these are exceptions that prove the rule'?" [34]

Robin Williams, in summing up two decades of research and his own Cornell studies, presents an important chapter on "Structures and Processes in Multigroup Society" combining a modified Parsonian analysis with a more general sociological frame of reference. He stresses the likelihood of a culturally and structurally pluralistic society persisting in America. Williams also re-emphasizes, in his own words, the basic findings of Thelen:

. . . it was interaction with awareness of a congruent community of interest that minimized ethnic prejudice and encouraged the reduction of discrimination. . . .[35]

He states further:

It is a genuine tragedy that we have so little objective, systematic study of school desegregation or of the massive social change in group relations now under way in the central cities of the large northern metropolitan areas.[36]

Northwood has emphasized the same point, stating that "the accounts of stabilization by fair housing committees are for the most part anecdotal rather than systematic" and "the meager empirical research on neighborhood change needs to be drastically supplemented in the near future." [37]

In reviewing the few contributions available, research in two cities—Detroit and Philadelphia—involving several different types of neighborhoods will be discussed,

after which a miscellaneous group of studies carried out in various northern cities will be considered briefly. The South will be dealt with separately, and the need for new types of studies of all-Negro communities is suggested.

Detroit Studies

During the late 1950's and early 1960's, some of the most significant research at the neighborhood level was sponsored by the Merrill-Palmer Institute of Human Development and Family Life in Detroit. The Russell Woods area of Detroit was placed "under sociological surveillance" in 1955.[38] By the end of 1957, this middle-class Jewish neighborhood had become 20 percent Negro; by 1959, 50 percent. There was no violence during the transition period, but the research does not make clear whether an interracial civic association that replaced the old restrictive neighborhood improvement association was a factor in preserving the racial peace or in preventing panic selling, which did not occur. There was a steady white movement outward, however. During 1959 members of 234 white households out of 670 were interviewed in order to ascertain the factors involved in decisions to move away from the neighborhood. Neither "prejudice" nor the presence of young children in the home seemed to be crucial factors. There was a greater tendency for the higher income, self-employed renters to move than for those not so well off who owned their own homes. Attitudes toward Negroes improved during this period, but this did not alter the decision of white individuals to move when they could.

Another Detroit area, Highland Park, was studied with regard to the possibility of developing a stable interracial neighbor-

[34] J. Milton Yinger, "Sociological Guidelines for Research in Intergroup Relations Education," *Journal of Intergroup Relations*, Vol. 4, No. 3 (Summer 1965). *See also* Allen D. Grimshaw, "Relationships Among Prejudice, Discrimination, Social Tension, and Social Violence," *Journal of Intergroup Relations*, Vol. 2, No. 4 (Autumn 1961), pp. 302–310.

[35] *Op. cit.*, p. 390.

[36] *Ibid.*, p. 391.

[37] Lawrence K. Northwood and Louise H. Klein, "The 'Tipping Point'—A Questionable Quality of Neighborhoods," *Journal of Intergroup Relations*, Vol. 4, No. 4 (Autumn 1965), pp. 226–239.

[38] Eleanor P. Wolf, "Racial Transition in a Middle Class Area," *Journal of Intergroup Relations*, Vol. 1, No. 3 (Summer 1960).

hood.[39] The population of 46,393 in this attractive three-square-mile area was 8 percent Negro in 1950. Then it began to get the overspill from the effects of urban renewal in a nearby Negro neighborhood that was being redeveloped. By 1960 the population had decreased to 38,000 but more than one in five residents were now Negro. It was assumed that neighborhood stabilization demanded block organization and that extreme differences in attitudes and values would make the task more difficult. The goal was eventually to study "neighborhood formation" and "the effect of reference group orientation on neighborhood cohesion. . . ." [40] Interviews were conducted with a random sample of residents. The Negroes turned out to be somewhat lower in socioeconomic status than the whites and more inclined to be involved in social club membership. Negroes did not perceive the situation as one presenting "social problems" to the extent the whites did. Yet 53 percent of the Negroes as compared with only 29 percent of the whites thought that block clubs were needed. Some of the whites who felt the need for such clubs also felt that it was impossible to form them in a mixed community. Seventy-five percent of the whites felt that in any event there would be an increasing drift toward an all-Negro neighborhood. Conclusions relevant to practice were drawn:

. . . in making plans for community organization, it would seem to be very important to have cognizance of differing attitudes and values within a group of newcomers before launching any program designed to further their integration in the total community.[41]

The Merrill-Palmer group carried out a program in one Detroit mixed middle-class neighborhood in which there was no tension, although change was taking place slowly. An eleven-day workshop under the direction of a sociologist was organized around the theme "Rearing Children in the Racially Changing Neighborhood." Twenty families—twelve white, seven Negro, and one interracial—including thirty-eight children participated. Experts conducted workshops for parents, and children were organized into play groups. A one-way glass screen made possible observation of the children. Questionnaires were administered at the end to try to elicit self-assessment and opinions of the effect of the workshop on spouses. Judges were asked to study tape recordings of discussions at the beginning and the end of the period. The authors state:

. . . the educational offering was most successful in helping these families analyze and understand their own racial feelings better; fairly successful in suggesting to them eventual means of community organization to meet the challenge of racial change; less successful in providing new factual knowledge of direct use to them in their child rearing and community life.[42]

This study provides an example of an attempt to prepare a predominantly white neighborhood before it becomes an area in transition. The authors themselves felt they should test their program in an area just about to experience a change in racial composition. The crucial test comes, of course, when the pace of change quickens. There is as yet no report on that situation.

When the Detroit Highland Park Study was concluded, the researchers were convinced that the pull of old voluntary associations and preoccupation with child care both militated against the establishment of friendship ties between new resi-

[39] Kathryn P. Meadow, "Negro-White Differences Among Newcomers to a Transitional Urban Area," *Journal of Intergroup Relations*, Vol. 3, No. 4 (Autumn 1962).

[40] The theoretical framework for such a study was Eugene Litwak, "Reference Group Theory, Bureaucratic Career, and Neighborhood Primary Group Cohesion," *Sociometry*, Vol. 23, No. 1 (March 1960), pp. 72–84.

[41] Meadow, *op. cit.*, p. 330.

[42] Richard K. Kerckhoff and Flo Gould, "Education for Interracial Neighborhood Living," *Journal of Intergroup Relations*, Vol. 1, No. 1 (Winter 1959–60), pp. 76–79.

dents and older ones. As Negroes moved in, there was passive acceptance of them and no organized resistance or overt hostility. But there were also few evidences of friendly interaction. The researchers felt that an active effort to establish block clubs should be encouraged.

Philadelphia Studies

Some research has been reported from Philadelphia on attempts to "prepare" white residents for accepting Negroes as future neighbors. In 1959 four meetings were held in one neighborhood under the auspices of the Commission on Human Relations, using a "kit" that included a handbook titled "Your Home in a Changing City," a sound film strip on "The Good Neighbors," and a thirty-minute movie, "All The Way Home." The next year feelers were put out to three other neighborhoods. In one of these the leaders unanimously rejected the overtures; another responded favorably, but not enough staff members were available to carry out the program. In the third neighborhood a student intern worked three weeks to promote a program in a predominantly Jewish community of 10,000 households, twelve of which were Negro. Homes in the area ranged in price from $10,000 to $25,000. There was some hositlty toward the commission, so no attempt was made to "sell a line." Emphasis was placed on trying to state facts about what happens to property values in changing neighborhoods and what the aftermath of change is. A network of contacts was made through talks with leaders and visits to homes. The outcomes were assessed as favorable, with achievement of a better image of the commission and sensitization of the neighborhood group to the probable consequences of neighborhood change.[43]

The Commmission on Human Relations subsequently reported on a project in which parts of the kit were offered free to 2,488 families in a racially changing neighborhood. Eleven percent of those circularized (269 families) requested the material. Two staff members report:

In order to test the effectiveness of this method of distribution, a thirteen percent sample of those requesting the kit was interviewed, on an average of fourteen and one-half weeks after receiving it. While all twenty-eight persons interviewed remembered having received the kit, only three had read it in its entirety, fifteen had read parts of it, six had glanced through it, four had not even done that. Six of the fifteen who had read parts of it could not remember which parts. . . . Only two actually intended to make use of the materials in any way other than as reading matter. . . . Curiosity seemed to be the main reason, mentioned by eighty-two percent of the respondents.[44]

The research team concluded:

Simply offering. . . educational materials without personal contact by professional staff and continued efforts at community organization accomplished very little.[45]

When staff time became available "an increasingly effective community group" was organized and "has brought forth good block leaders."

Studies in Other Cities

A project was devised by the Greater Minneapolis Interfaith Fair Housing Program as a pilot action-research program, its aim being—in Tillman's words—"to conceive, use, and test methods for achieving residential dispersion for all citizens in the Greater Minneapolis area" and "to activate and catalyze" the religious insti-

---

[43] Dennis Clark, "Leadership Education in an All-White Neighborhood," *Journal of Intergroup Relations*, Vol. 3, No. 1 (Winter 1961–62), pp. 38–44.

[44] Martha Lavell and Dennis Clark, "Curiosity is Not Enough: A Report of Work with a Leadership Training Kit," *Journal of Intergroup Relations*, Vol. 3, No. 4 (Autumn 1962), pp. 360–363.
[45] *Ibid.*

tutions, as well as "to evaluate, systematize and codify principles derived from experience." A listing service was set up and participant-observers were assigned the task of carrying out educational programs in "previously closed neighborhoods." The assumption was that most people were "unprejudiced discriminators." From observation of the neighborhoods a "life cycle of resistance" was formulated that included the following consecutive stages:

1. Incipient resistance by a hostile group.
2. Organization of resistance by the "committed."
3. Competition between the "committed" and the hostile group, a crisis stage in which by a series of public meetings the hostile group is placed on the defensive.
4. Accommodation of the hostile group to the change.
5. Incipient integration.

The author's attempt at generalizing is valuable, but he does not indicate what happens if in Stage 3 the hostile group is not "outgeneraled" by the committed. The "desegregation process" (Stages 1–4) involves from one to six weeks. The integration process covers a much more extended period. A theory of "compartmentalization" was used that did not involve an expected total change in racial attitudes. It was concluded:

. . . it is possible to construct programs of action which can accelerate the creation of open communities when there is a clear recognition that resistance to such neighborhoods serves a precise function for personalities of majority groups who foment and sustain the resistance.[46]

A research report on Kalamazoo, Michigan, which in 1961 had a Negro population of 5,000 and a total population of 160,000, indicated that the majority of whites were indifferent about movement of Negroes into their neighborhoods, with the older residents seeming to be more favorable than newer residents. Yet the city was experiencing increasing ghettoization.[47]

Open Housing Action: Special Problems

Weaver speaks of the large number of "fair play in housing" committees organized in northern suburban areas. A small proportion of the upper middle and upper classes in these areas has committed itself to token integration.[48] As early as 1960 an attempt was made to evaluate the effectiveness of action-education programs being used by a group of such organizations in the Philadelphia area.[49] Films, workshops, seminars, and discussion groups were used in areas far removed from the ghettos in an effort to get individuals to sign a statement committing themselves to a program of open occupancy. Few Negroes moved into such areas, but when they did there was little friction and no evidence of panic selling—expected reactions on the basis of theory and previous experience in such neighborhoods. The author felt that simply presenting such neighborhoods with the *fait accompli* of a Negro move-in justified the effort, but that basic research was needed because

[46] James A. Tillman, Jr., "Morningtown, U.S.A. —A Composite Case History of Neighborhood Change," *Journal of Intergroup Relations*, Vol. 2, No. 2 (Spring 1961), pp. 156-167.

[47] W. E. Upjohn, *Research Report on Integrated Housing in Kalamazoo* (Kalamazoo: Western Michigan University, 1959) ; and Chester L. Hunt, "Private Integrated Housing in a Medium-Sized Northern City," *Social Problems*, Vol. 8, No. 3 (Winter 1959–60), pp. 196–209.

[48] Robert C. Weaver, *Dilemmas of Urban America* (Cambridge, Mass.: Harvard University Press, 1965).

[49] Thelma W. Babbitt, "Fair Housing Practices Committees—Bringing Willing Buyers and Sellers Together," *Journal of Intergroup Relations*, Vol. 1, No. 1 (Winter 1959–60), pp. 62–67. Such groups, usually sponsored by churches or professional action agencies, were existing in Philadelphia, Boston, Chicago, San Francisco, Hartford, Princeton, Cleveland, Des Moines, and Pasadena.

few data are available so far to indicate whether movement of minority members into a formerly closed neighborhood actually has been effective in creating in the larger community a climate of tolerance receptive to the principle of open occupancy housing. . . . [But equally important is the need for knowing something about] the degree of actual acceptance of the [Negro] family into the total life of the community. . . .[50]

Fair housing committees express some disappointment at what seems like lack of enthusiasm for "pioneering" on the part of Negroes. Some research has been done on factors inhibiting Negroes from moving into white neighborhoods, but more extensive investigation in this area is necessary.[51] A study in Seattle that dealt with the attitudes of both whites and Negroes in mixed neighborhoods gives some clues about optimum conditions for residential integration, and a study in Roxbury, Massachusetts, throws some light on factors that make Negroes feel "more comfortable" in Negro areas.[52]

Full understanding of prospects for open

occupancy in America demands study of Negroes' attitudes and behavior as well as those of whites. Seattle, which had a Negro population of 4,500 in 1940, 16,500 in 1950, and 27,000 in 1960, has been expanding on a block-by-block basis. Research in two middle-class white neighborhoods revealed that where "For Sale" signs were up, most sellers claimed willingness to offer their property for sale to Negroes, but most realtors were opposed, and Negroes generally did not know of the willingness of the owners. Research and publicity were suggested as first steps in breaking down "barriers to the flow of information."[53]

Problems in the South

There is a paucity of published literature on neighborhood programs in the South. This may be due to the fact that in cities like Atlanta and New Orleans, where unstable transitional neighborhoods have come into being during the last fifteen years—sometimes with violence—no attempts have been made to organize programs for stabilization on an interracial basis. (At least, discussion of such action does not appear in the literature.) Southern church-related liberals pioneered during the 1920's in the organization of committees for interracial co-operation within the framework of a "separate-but-equal" philosophy. More recently, groups like the Southern Regional Council and a variety of church committees have been working for acceptance of desegregation.[54]

The crucial issue as defined by white southerners has not been residential integration, but school integration. Because the impact of the 1954 Supreme Court de-

[50] *Ibid.*, p. 66.

[51] Note documentation for Syracuse, N.Y., in Imogene Smith and Robert L. Hale, Jr., *Survey of Negro Families Living Outside of the 15th Ward Area in Syracuse, N.Y., and Surrounding Areas* (Syracuse: Syracuse Fair Housing Committee, 1955). *See also* Eunice S. Grier, "Factors Hindering Integration in America's Urban Areas," *Journal of Intergroup Relations*, Vol. 2, No. 4 (Autumn 1961), pp. 293–301.

[52] Lawrence K. Northwood and Ernest A. T. Barth, *Urban Desegregation: Negro Pioneers and Their White Neighbors* (Seattle: University of Washington Press, 1965); and Howard A. Freeman, *The Middle Income Negro Family Faces Urban Renewal* (Waltham, Mass.: Brandeis University Research Center, 1964). *See also* Rubin Morton, "The Negro Wish to Move: The Boston Case," *Journal of Social Issues*, Vol. 15, No. 4 (October 1959); Helen Hughes and L. G. Watts, "Portrait of the Self-Integrator," *Journal of Social Issues*, Vol. 20, No. 2 (April 1964), pp. 103–115; and Marc Fried and Peggy Gleicher, "Some Sources of Residential Satisfaction in an Urban Negro Slum," *Journal of the American Institute of Planners* (November 1961).

[53] Ernest A. T. Barth and Susan March, "A Research Note on the Subject of Minority Housing," *Journal of Intergroup Relations*, Vol. 3, No. 4 (Autumn 1962).

[54] *Problem Solving Through Race Relations Committees* (Atlanta: Southern Regional Council, 1960).

cision has been felt at the neighborhood level, full documentation of this process would be of both theoretical and practical import. It has not been possible for the writer to explore the sources thoroughly, but it is significant that a southern city that achieved notoriety from an attempt to resist school desegregation—Little Rock, Arkansas—has been the locale for a city-wide attempt at "reconciliation."

Experiences in Little Rock during 1960 suggest that a conference can be a useful resource for fostering interrelationships and establishing a kind of communication from which informed, responsible, and dedicated leadership may develop. Four conferences on community unity were held over a period of several months after three months of quiet work by a representative of a national church-related organization, the American Friends Service Committee. The organizers of this project report outcomes that they believe had feedback into neighborhood churches and associations.[55]

Negroes and whites live in close residential proximity in numerous southern towns, and under a caste system have sustained harmonious relations. How such relations are restructured during a period when caste no longer operates as a controlling principle should receive high research priority.

Intergroup Relations Within the Ghetto

Over two decades ago, when the writer first published material on the ghetto, he and his colleague pointed out that one of the most obvious consequences of residential segregation was to reduce drastically the chances that an individual would have any equal-status contacts with whites until he entered the labor market.[56] Today the

North has more ghettoization, not less, and we are witnessing one of its inevitable consequences—the insistent cry of "Black Power," coupled with the "soul brother's" command to "Get whitey"—his stores, his automobiles, and his person, especially if it is clothed in a policeman's uniform. The harshness, the vindictiveness, the hatred that suffuse the new ghetto mood are as disquieting as they are startling. What we are witnessing may turn out, in the long run, to be what Sartre calls "antiracist racism," but at the moment, and in the aftermath of the arson, looting, and vandalism of the big city riots of 1967, it can only be defined as tragic from the standpoint of those who have devoted themselves to the goal of achieving integration.

The demand for Black Power within the ghetto inevitably takes on overtones of anti-Semitism in situations when Jewish merchants are doing business in the Black Belts. White schoolteachers often become the targets of hostility and are under continuous pressure to contribute toward developing "black consciousness." Many of them have already had stereotypes reinforced or have developed them if they did not have them previously, and the Negro slum generates negative attitudes among white teachers.[57] Demands are sometimes made to replace white school principals with Negroes. All of the following occupational types are "vulnerable" if they are white: policemen, firemen, bus drivers, taxi drivers, bill collectors, apartment building service employees, nurses, and hospital employees. Social workers find themselves in the same anomalous position as they try to work in the ghetto.

Little research has been published about the impact of the new militant mood on relations between superordinate whites and varied segments of the Negro community. Two avenues of investigation merit immediate attention: study is needed of (1)

[55] Thelma W. Babbitt and Arthur W. Chickering, "The Conference as a Resource," *Journal of Intergroup Relations*, Vol. 3, No. 1 (Winter 1961-62), pp. 12–20.

[56] Drake and Cayton, *op. cit.*

[57] Kenneth B. Clark, *Dark Ghetto* (New York: Harper & Row, 1965), chap. 6.

the possibilities of developing "bridging groups," if it is assumed that the ghetto is by no means likely to disappear within the foreseeable future and that Black Nationalism will probably become stronger (e.g., interracial adolescent groups that function on a city-wide basis articulated to major institutions might serve in this capacity), and (2) the extent to which certain Black Belt institutions can devise programs that will both channel Black Nationalism constructively and provide opportunities for equal-status interracial contacts (e.g., local businessmen's associations, service clubs, PTA, YM-YWCA, settlement houses, and churches).[58] A synthesis and critical analysis of articles appearing in journals is a first step to be followed by carefully designed action-research projects.[59] Postmortem surveys of riots are not enough.

Research Priorities and Functions

During 1960 a long-time student of the housing problem and of race relations gave a list of areas "most urgently in need of fact-finding, analysis, and research, based on the replies of twelve leading intergroup relations practitioners.[60] Among the topics listed were studies of the following:

1. *The racially stable neighborhood,* because "a truly searching analysis of the factors which promote racial stability in some neighborhoods could, by inference,

reveal much of value about the conditions which encourage change in others."

2. *The "tipping point" hypothesis:* "an elusive creature when one tries to pin it down."

3. *Factors related to tension situations in neighborhood change,* because "up to this point . . . it has not been possible to predict with reasonable assurance where outbreaks are likely to occur."

4. ". . . analysis and evaluation of neighborhood centered efforts to smooth transition of neighborhoods from all-white to racially mixed and to prevent their further transition to all-Negro."

Need for More Evaluative Research

Review of the literature has revealed a considerable amount of material describing various programs and projects at the neighborhood level, usually by those involved in planning and action. Little of the activity has been subjected to critical evaluation of its effectiveness, however, or the evaluative research has not been published. In presenting his own efforts at carrying out such research, Robbins commented:

While social scientists have written abundantly on general strategies to curb prejudice and discrimination, they have not examined as closely the claims for effectiveness entered by the intergroup relations organizations devoted exclusively to combatting intolerance.[61]

This criticism seems as valid today as when it was made seven years ago. There are few such published studies. This may be due, in part, to a loss of interest in this specific kind of problem on the part of social scientists. Yet the files of commissions on human relations, the American Friends Service Committee, numerous fair

---

[58] Some of these problems are discussed in St. Clair Drake, *Race Relations in a Time of Rapid Social Change* (New York: National Federation of Settlements, 1966).

[59] *See,* for example, Celia S. Heller and Alphonso Pinkney, "The Attitudes of Negroes Toward Jews," *Social Forces,* Vol. 43, No. 3 (March 1965), p. 364; G. Franklin Edwards, "The Changing Status and Self-Image of Negroes in the District of Columbia," *Journal of Intergroup Relations,* Vol. 4, No. 1 (Winter 1962–63).

[60] Eunice S. Grier, "Research Needs in the Field of Housing and Race," *Journal of Intergroup Relations,* Vol. 1, No. 3 (Summer 1960), pp. 21–31.

[61] Richard Robbins, "Local Strategy in Race Relations: The Illinois Experience with Community Human Relations Commissions and Councils," *Journal of Intergroup Relations,* Vol. 2, No. 3 (Summer 1961).

housing committees, and local neighborhood associations must be bulging with raw data available for evaluative studies. At least one plea for the use of such material has been voiced:

The pressing needs of the public agencies have dictated that what their researchers most frequently do is better described as data gathering and statistical analysis than as research. Ironically, nowhere else is more raw data being assembled about the dynamics and patterns of discrimination, and yet public agency researchers lack the time to extract the more significant of the information they fondly gaze upon in their files. . . . Why could not public and private research team up . . .? . . . Is this not the time for the public and private agencies to ask for multi-faceted research programs? . . .[62]

One of the few published accounts of well-designed evaluative research is Robbins' own, carried out at the request of the governor of Illinois—a study of the network of action groups in the field of intergroup relations in Illinois. Among conclusions covering the full range of organizational structures, the following comment was made about neighborhood associations:

. . . the community voluntary associations in Illinois make a modest but meaningful contribution to the reduction of racial problems in the state.[63]

A system of scaling was used and the effectiveness of such associations was said to be "cyclical," being at the peak during crises.

No *ex post facto* research can substitute, however, for scientifically designed action-research with built-in evaluative procedures. It has been pointed out that such research often becomes a part of the process of change itself, for it may concretize issues and problems for local residents and co-operating sponsoring agencies.[64]

Another attempt to apply rigorous evaluative procedures was also made in Illinois, this time in a local situation—the university town of Champaign.[65] A human relations commission had been established by the mayor in 1958, and by 1960 a social problem had been defined—fights between teen-agers after high school games. A decision was made to convene a group of young people to discuss this problem, suggest organization of a youth council, and to use this as an instrument for trying to change racial attitudes. A survey was made of youth clubs in Champaign, and it was found that of thirty-three such clubs, twenty-three were church affiliated. All clubs were invited to join the council, which proceeded to sponsor a prekindergarten group, a "Pal Program," a "Hire-a-Teen" campaign, recorded program sessions, home discussions, and a film series on race relations. There was no marked change within groups from which council members came.

Implications for Social Work

Some social work agencies have been concerned with intergroup relations as a normal part of their routine activities, such as, for instance, settlement house workers. Community organization and group work in the inner city have produced a rich body of experience and some theory on which workers in the emerging field of intergroup relations have drawn.

---

[62] Robert J. Greene, "Some Proposals Looking Toward Cooperation Among Public and Private Intergroup Relations Agencies," *Journal of Intergroup Relations*, Vol. 3, No. 1 (Winter 1961–62), pp. 21–27.

[63] Robbins, *op. cit.*

[64] This point has been made in a report on a project in Newton, Mass., sponsored by the American Friends Service Committee. Morton Rubin, "The Function of Social Research for a Fair Housing Practices Committee," *Journal of Intergroup Relations*, Vol. 2, No. 4 (Autumn 1961), pp. 325–331.

[65] Frank Costin, "An Intergroup Activity for Youth Evaluated from Two Viewpoints," *Journal of Intergroup Relations*, Vol. 5, No. 4 (Autumn 1966).

Serious discussion has gone on from time to time about relations between the two fields. More is needed.

One significant discussion of this relationship at the neighborhood level appeared in 1962 in an article by Iskander.[66] He pointed out that the urban renewal and redevelopment process had resulted in a proliferation of organizations in many urban areas, variously referred to as community councils, neighborhood improvement associations, citizens' renewal councils, block clubs, civic improvement leagues, and so on. He discerned a pattern in the process—"spontaneous" problem-oriented group formation at the neighborhood level and then "the local settlement or neighborhood center may provide part-time or full-time staff assistance, or the city-wide federation of social agencies may offer a well-trained 'area worker.'" (No one seems to have discussed this body of social work experience within a single volume or even a single article.) Iskander refers to the activities of these local groups, often functioning with social worker guidance, as "neighborhood development" designed "to prevent or stem physical blight and social breakdown. . . ."

The article was based on a study of organizations in Pittsburgh, where the local Human Relations Commission states that one of its objectives is *"to help people of equal status to work together across lines of difference on matters of common concern."* A neighborhood section of the Human Relations Commission (also called the Tension Control Section) had as one of its functions sponsorship and assistance to neighborhood associations. A priority list of activities was set up:

1. Dealing with tensions and complaints of discrimination.

2. Working in changing neighborhoods.
3. Working in mixed, established neighborhoods (prevention).

The program began with two full-time workers and three students from a school of social work. Although there was some resentment on the part of the commission's already existing staff over the decision to use social workers, Iskander suggests that "intergroup relations workers would do well to take a good look at this new and vital source of personnel . . . social workers with specialization in community organization." He did concede the point that "social workers have no monopoly . . . in doing effective community work."

During the early 1960's there was considerable discussion about the status and training of intergroup relations workers. There were those who felt that the community organization field in social work provided both an action model and a source for recruiting personnel for public and private agencies. The director of the North Central Area of the American Jewish Committee, Walter Zand, defended his view that community organization training in a school of social work was ". . . relevant, valid and applicable to the field of intergroup relations."[67] He reports on an experiment in providing nine months of field work for a social work student from the University of Chicago. Listing ten principles of "the community organization process," he concluded that "the conceptualization of process is needed to make the practice of community relations move from that of an occupation to a profession." As to whether modifications of social work theory and practice were necessary, he suggested that "basic research and further evaluative experimentation" were needed to determine if such a thing as an "intergroup relations process" is something quite

---

[66] Michel L. Iskander, "The Neighborhood Approach in Intergroup Relations," *Journal of Intergroup Relations*, Vol. 3, No. 1 (Winter 1961–62), *see* especially p. 80.

[67] Walter Zand, "Training for Intergroup Relations," *Journal of Intergroup Relations*, Vol. 3, No. 1 (Winter 1961–62), pp. 45–54.

distinct from "the community organization process."

Another intergroup relations official in the Midwest insists that at the neighborhood level "social work may help because there is a considerable volume of published and accessible knowledge in the field of social work pertinent to intergroup relations." Also: "Many schools of social work include content on the field and process of working in intergroup relations. . . ." [68]

Social work training has been criticized on the ground that most of the products of the process know neither how to utilize

the theory of race relations research nor how to design and carry out research itself. If this is still (or ever was) true, it suggests that curriculum revision should take high priority. As an "outsider" the writer would raise two questions: (1) To what extent are social work students being made aware of work such as that of Thelen or the occasional relevant reports that appear in the *Journal of Intergroup Relations*? (2) To what extent is there any interest in research on interracial and interethnic relations among administrators, schools of social work, or professional organizations in the social work field? Collaboration in *action* that has occurred might well be expanded into collaboration in action-research and evaluative studies.

---

[68] John C. Kidneigh, "Intergroup Relations and Social Work," *Journal of Intergroup Relations,* Vol. 2, No. 2 (Spring 1961), pp. 167–170.

Family Structure and Composition: Research Considerations

ELIZABETH HERZOG AND CECELIA E. SUDIA

There is every reason to believe that the family is the oldest of human social institutions and that it will survive, in one form or another, as long as our species exists. . . .[1]

. . . . .

All the evidence points to the infinite capacity of the family to change—to change its composition, to redefine the way it shares the care of children with other social institutions—and yet to retain its over-all responsibility for them.[2]

It is generally conceded that the stereotype is the enemy of good race relations and that accurate, comprehensive information about the members of any group is the enemy of the stereotype. Seen in this context, an obvious function of research is to provide the intimate, detailed information that can defeat the stereotype. It is there-fore startling to discover the extent to which we as social scientists have managed to promote a number of stereotypes.

This paradox is not the main theme of the present discussion, but is, rather, an insistent obligato weaving in and out of the following pages and demanding brief prominence in the coda. At this point, however, it is only fair to remark that some research-fostered stereotypes have resulted from a respectable effort to inquire into the evidence concerning older, more noxious ones. The neo-stereotype is sometimes an inadvertent product, representing what careless readers do with careful research. Nevertheless, when a new insight

Elizabeth Herzog is Chief, and Cecelia E. Sudia, MA, is Research Specialist, Child Life Studies Branch, Division of Research, Children's Bureau, Social and Rehabilitation Service, U.S. Department of Health, Education, and Welfare, Washington, D.C.

[1] Ralph Linton, "The Natural History of the Family," in Ruth N. Anshen, ed., *The Family: Its Function and Destiny* (New York: Harper & Bros., 1949), p. 18.

[2] Helen Witmer and Ruth Kotinsky, eds., *Personality in the Making: The Fact-Finding Report of the Midcentury White House Conference on Children and Youth* (New York: Harper & Bros., 1952), p. 209.

degenerates into a neo-stereotype it becomes a threat to mutual understanding and respect.[3] It should be recognized also that many stereotypes contain a kernel of truth that is inflated and distorted by overgeneralization, underqualification, and confused attribution of cause and effect.

The curious role of research in the contest between stereotyping and accurate descriptive analysis is evident in current formulations about the family in general and fatherless families in particular. For present purposes, it is appropriate to focus chiefly on Negro families and, among them, chiefly on families that are fatherless and poor, since such families command a large share of attention in research, practice, and general discussion involving race relations. The low-income fatherless Negro family also attracts a substantial share of current stereotypes and neo-stereotypes, even though the majority of Negro families are not fatherless and the majority of the poor are not Negroes.

It is sometimes hard to remember or believe that the majority of poor families are white, when one considers the high proportion of Negro families who are poor and the high proportion of Negroes among the poor in some of the largest cities and among the population to which the poverty programs are chiefly directed. Yet national statistics tell us that this is the case, if the country as a whole is considered.[4]

Nevertheless, although a majority of the poor are not Negroes, a sobering proportion of nonwhite families are poor—about 48 percent of those with children under 18 (compared with 12 percent of white families), according to the poverty index of the Social Security Administration.[5] We rehearse, again and again, figures about poverty and Negroes (or, as the census records, "nonwhites," over 90 percent of whom are Negroes). We keep finding different ways to group and present the facts, trying to sharpen the bite of their meaning. We say, for example, "nonwhite children run a risk of poverty four times that of the white." [6] And then we say that, according to the SSA poverty index, 60 percent of nonwhite children are poor, as compared with 16 percent of white children, and that, of nonwhite children in female-headed families, 86 percent are poor.[7]

From being cited so often and in so many ways, the figures themselves are tired—but not nearly as tired as some of the women they represent. For example, the mother of a child enrolled in a preschool enrichment program explained to a visiting staff member why she had not been able to attend a parents' meeting:

Her hours of work are 6:00 P.M. to 12:00 P.M. "I worked for one week during the day while we were getting settled. . . . It's just too hard to get someone to look after your children when you work during the day. That week I worked, I was getting different relatives to come by to sit with the baby. . . . The only thing is I get so tired because I work here so hard in the house during the day and then I am on the go every minute on the job." The house and hall had clothing drying which she had probably washed earlier in the day.[8]

Confounded Variables

Clearly, when we are talking about Negro children in fatherless homes, we are talking mainly about children who are poor. A conspicuously unsolved research problem

[3] Elizabeth Herzog and Hylan Lewis, "Priorities in Research on Unmarried Mothers," in *Research Perspectives on the Unmarried Mother* (New York: Child Welfare League of America, 1962), pp. 32–39.

[4] Mollie Orshansky, "Who's Who Among the Poor: A Demographic View of Poverty," *Social Security Bulletin*, Vol. 28, No. 7 (July 1965), pp. 3–32.

[5] Mollie Orshansky, "Recounting the Poor—A Five-Year Review," *Social Security Bulletin*, Vol. 29, No. 4 (April 1966), pp. 20–37.

[6] *Ibid.*, p. 34.

[7] Orshansky, "Who's Who Among the Poor."

[8] Staff Notes, Howard University, 1965.

TABLE 1. INCOME DISTRIBUTION FOR ALL FAMILIES BY SEX AND COLOR OF HEAD, 1964 (PERCENTAGE)

Total Money Income	White		Nonwhite	
	Male Headed (N=39,200,000)	Female Headed (N=3,881,000)	Male Headed (N=3,629,000)	Female Headed (N=1,126,000)
Under $3,000	13	38	29	65
$3,000–$5,999	25	33	37	27
$6,000–$9,999	36	20	24	6
$10,000 and over	26	10	10	2

SOURCE: Special tabulation by U.S. Bureau of the Census of data from March 1965 Current Population Survey for the Social Security Administration.

is to differentiate between the effects of fatherlessness and the effects of poverty.

It is a problem not specific to the nonwhite members of the population. Although concern here is primarily with Negro families, low income is also related to the sex of the family head in white families. The figures in Table 1 bring home both the male-female and the white-nonwhite differential in all families, with or without children. The pattern becomes stronger in families with children under 18. However, recent figures are not available for that breakdown.

Another research problem, also to a large extent unsolved, is the problem of differentiating between the consequences of poverty and of color. Solution of that problem has been postponed by the frequent reporting of differences in terms of color rather than of socioeconomic status. The reasons are obvious, since it is extremely difficult to construct and apply dependable indexes of socioeconomic status.

Lefcowitz has demonstrated roughly (as have a good many others) that color differences on a number of variables (e.g., family composition, education of children, relative education of wife and husband) are dwarfed by differences in income level.[9] Even this kind of demonstration, however, hardly does justice to the potency of the economic factor, especially in the low-income brackets. Often the attempt to control for socioeconomic status rests on a three-way breakdown into high-, middle-, and low-income level. But Negroes tend to cluster at the lower layers of each level, so that this kind of control does not obviate substantial differences within levels. Some studies, in fact, explicitly report such within-level difference when describing the sample, but do not take it into account in formulating final conclusions.

The usual three-way breakdown suffers especially from the fact that the lower one goes on the income ladder, the more important rather small dollar differences become. Here is where E. H. Weber's law operates: the significance or perceptibility of a difference is determined by the size *relative* to the quantities compared. According to his findings, if one candle is added to ten candles, the difference is clearly perceptible, whereas if one candle is added to a hundred candles, the difference is barely perceptible.[10] Similarly, the difference between $1,500 and $2,000 in yearly incomes is associated with perceptible differences in effective economic status. The difference between $15,000 and $15,500 as a yearly income has far less impact on

[9] Myron J. Lefcowitz, "Poverty and Negro-White Family Structures." Background paper for White House Conference "To Fulfill These Rights," Washington, D.C., November 1965.

[10] As reported in Robert S. Woodworth, *Experimental Psychology* (New York: Henry Holt, 1938), p. 430.

effective economic status. The importance of small dollar differences in low incomes was evident in a recent Children's Bureau study of a preschool enrichment program, which shows interesting relations between dollar income per child and the pattern of gain in IQ score as measured by the Stanford-Binet test, within a low-income group.[11]

Families and Nonfamilies

The fatherless low-income Negro family is perceived and reacted to against a background of various assumptions and beliefs about prevailing family norms. The accepted norm is the monogamous, two-parent, father-headed family. Almost 90 percent of this country's children live in this kind of family.[12] Whatever may be the norm for other societies, any radical overt departure from this norm carries penalties, some of which are the direct result of the departure and some of which result from prevailing attitudes and assumptions concerning it.

The most familiar departure from this norm is the one-parent mother-headed family, which for convenience will be referred to here as the fatherless family. Not quite 10 percent of children in the U.S.A. live in homes of this kind, but that relatively small proportion represents some six million children.

It is the authors' strong impression that there is a widespread tendency to regard the one-parent family as a sick family, a nonfamily, or an unfamily. This tendency is reflected in the absence of mention of the one-parent family from textbooks and

college courses on family life education, in the formulation of research questions about family life, and in the early—and to some extent persisting—absence from many programs of Aid to Families with Dependent Children of built-in day care and homemaker services. The question may be raised, however, whether a form that includes so many children and has produced many effective and apparently happy adults deserves a less negative status. It might be useful to give clearer recognition to the one-parent family as a family form in its own right—not a preferred form, but nevertheless one that exists and functions and represents something other than mere absence of true "familyness."

Among reasons for reassessment of the one-parent family as a family form in its own right are the following:

1. Through time and space the family has evolved a vast array of different forms and still has continued to function as the family.

2. The fatherless family is with us and shows no sign of evaporating.

3. The modal American family may not be as functionally two-parent or as "patriarchal" as is sometimes assumed.

4. There is reason to believe that children in fatherless families are adversely affected by the negative assumptions clustering around that kind of family.

5. Many fatherless families possess strengths that tend to be overlooked.

Different Family Forms

It is a piquant and enjoyable exercise to review the myriad forms the family has assumed, especially the (to us) more exotic forms, and to remember that each in its time and place has been viewed by those born into the specific society as a simple reflection of human nature. However, for present purposes such a review is unnecessary. It is enough to recognize

[11] Jean C. Fuschillo, "The Preschool Experience of Children from Age 3. II. The Evaluation," *Children*, Vol. 15, No. 4 (July-August 1968), pp. 140–143.

[12] U.S. Bureau of the Census, "Household and Family Characteristics, March 1966," *Current Population Reports*, Series P-20, No. 164, April 12, 1967 (Washington, D.C.: U.S. Government Printing Office, 1967).

that no society has existed without some kind of family structure; that an amazing variety of family structures have appeared to function adequately in various societies; that each has been regarded by members of the society as natural, adequate, and inevitable; and that, amid wails about the weakening and degeneration of the family in our own society, a good deal of evidence points to its continuing viability.[13]

Most societies recognize the importance of the parent-child relationship. The majority assume a continuing relationship between sexmates. The majority, however, do not require the intense one-to-one relationship fostered by our norms and ideals.[14] It is worth recognizing both the variety of family patterns and the constants or near-constants that cut across these patterns. It would, of course, be folly to assume that our culture could swallow whole and assimilate patterns native to another culture. At the same time, recognition of the variations that exist and the amount of modification that has been tolerated in the course of history may serve as an antidote to what Linton calls the "calm ethnocentrism" that places our own norm "at the apex of all lines of development." [15]

Concern about the imminent demise of the family appears to be diminishing, at least among social scientists. Vincent maintains that its "adaptive function has been and continues to be overlooked" and suggests that its alleged loss of functions is a myth:

... one can argue that, in each case of a traditional function supposedly lost to the family as a social institution, the loss has in reality been but a *change in content and form.* While it is true, for example, that the family in the United States is no longer the *economic producing unit* that it was several generations ago, it is now an *economic consuming unit.* . . . Similar arguments can be advanced concerning the purported loss of the educational, religious and protective functions. . . . If the family has lost its educational and religious functions, why do the majority of children hold religious, political, and social-class beliefs similar to those of their parents? Why are the asocial attitudes and immoral practices of the delinquent and the criminal traced to the family and not to the school or church? Why is it that the family in general and the parents in particular are considered to be key variables in determining how well and how far the child progresses in school? [16]

A good many others support Vincent's views about the continuing vitality of the family as an institution, the importance of its adaptive capacity, and the indications that family patterns are changing faster than what Goode called our "misleading stereotype" of "the classical family of western nostalgia." [17] Some emphasize the continuing vitality not only of the nuclear but also of the extended family, for which dirges have been sung in recent years.[18]

---

[13] *See,* for example, William J. Goode, *World Revolution and Patterns* (New York: Free Press of Glencoe, 1963) ; Eugene Litwak, "Occupational Mobility and Extended Family Cohesion," *American Sociological Review,* Vol. 25, No. 1 (February 1960), pp. 9–21; Otto Pollak, "The Outlook for the American Family," *Journal of Marriage and the Family,* Vol. 29, No. 1 (February 1967), pp. 193–205; Clark E. Vincent, "Mental Health and the Family," *Journal of Marriage and the Family,* Vol. 29, No. 1 (February 1967), pp. 18–39.

[14] Linton, *op. cit.*

[15] *Ibid.,* p. 19.

[16] *Op. cit.,* p. 26.

[17] *Op. cit.,* p. 6.

[18] *See,* for example, Sydney E. Bernard, "Fatherless Families: Their Economic and Social Adjustment," Paper in Social Welfare No. 7 (Waltham, Mass.: Florence Heller Graduate School for Advanced Studies in Social Welfare, Brandeis University, 1964) ; Albert K. Cohen and Harold M. Hodges, "Lower Blue-Collar Class Characteristics," *Social Problems,* Vol. 10, No. 4 (Spring 1963), pp. 303–333; Reuben Hill, "The American Family of the Future," *Journal of Marriage and the Family,* Vol. 26, No. 1 (February 1964), pp. 20–28; Hope Jensen Leichter and William E. Mitchell, *Kinship and Casework* (New York: Russell Sage Foundation, 1967) ; Marvin B. Sussman and Lee Burchinal, "Kin Family Network: Unheralded Structure in Current Conceptualizations of Family Functioning," *Marriage and Family Living,* Vol. 24, No. 3 (August 1962), pp. 231–240; Clark E. Vincent, "Family Spongia: The

Frequency of Fatherless Families

As has been mentioned, some six million of this country's children live in fatherless families.[19] This figure includes over one-fourth of nonwhite children, according to Orshansky.[20]

The frequency of fatherless families is far higher among Negroes than among whites, and has been far higher for many years. The reasons for the difference are much, and sometimes hotly, debated—as is the question of whether the over-all proportion of female-headed families has risen dramatically since 1959.[21] However, the present point is merely that there are likely to be large numbers of fatherless families for some time to come, and that a larger proportion of Negro than of white families will fall into this category. Even if, as many hope, improved economic status for Negro men and greater availability of family planning should contribute to family stability and so eventually reduce the proportion of fatherless families, the number is unlikely to diminish while the number of women in their child-bearing years continues to increase.[22]

Adaptive Function," *Journal of Marriage and the Family*, Vol. 28, No. 1 (February 1966), pp. 29–36; J. Milton Yinger, "The Changing Family in a Changing Society," *Social Casework*, Vol. 40, No. 8 (October 1959), pp. 419–428.

[19] U.S. Bureau of the Census, *op. cit.*

[20] Orshansky, "Who's Who Among the Poor."

[21] *See*, for example, Goode, *op. cit.*; Elizabeth Herzog, "Is There a 'Breakdown' of the Negro Family?" *Social Work*, Vol. 11, No. 1 (January 1966), pp. 3–10; Lefcowitz, *op. cit.*; Hylan Lewis, "Culture, Class, and Family Life Among Low-Income Urban Negroes," in Arthur Ross, ed., *Employment, Race, and Poverty* (New York: Harcourt, Brace & World, 1967); Lee Rainwater and William L. Yancey, *The Moynihan Report and the Politics of Controversy* (Cambridge, Mass.: MIT Press, 1967); Hyman Rodman, "On Understanding Lower-Class Behavior," *Social and Economic Studies*, Vol. 8, No. 4 (December 1959), pp. 441–450.

[22] James E. Cowhig, "Marital Instability Among Women in the United States," *Welfare in Review*, Vol. 3, No. 7 (July 1965), pp. 12–14.

Modal American Family

Some purists object to calling the modal American family structure patriarchal. The extent to which children in two-parent families are reared by women at home and taught by women at school has been the subject of extensive comment. "Momism" has been lampooned and denounced, especially on the middle-class intact-home level.[23] A good deal of "father absence" occurs in so-called intact homes when the father commutes to work or travels frequently on business. Many fathers, of course, devote thought, time, and energy to making up for unavoidable absences by spending time with their children when possible. Nevertheless, the lives of most children are rather strongly pervaded by women.

The occasional absence of a father from an intact home is certainly different from permanent or greatly protracted father absence. At the same time, the prevalence of partial father absence and the prominence of women in the lives of most children may reduce to some extent the contrast between children in homes classified as "father absent" and "father present."

Effects of Negative Assumptions

An important reason for second thoughts about relegating one-parent families to the nonfamily category is the effect on children who grow up in such families. They are subject to the disadvantages of fatherlessness and, in addition, suffer from constant reminders of their disadvantage and its assumed consequences.

The effects on children of life in a fatherless home are influenced by their perception of their family status as conforming to or diverging from a norm. To the ex-

---

[23] David M. Levy, *Maternal Overprotection* (New York: Columbia University Press, 1943); Edward A. Strecker, *Their Mothers' Sons* (Philadelphia: J. B. Lippincott & Co., 1946).

tent that this is so, the impact of a one-parent home may vary in different social, economic, and ethnic groups. The effects of feeling "different" also, obviously, vary with individual children and are mediated by the attitudes, behavior, and circumstances of the one parent within the home as well as by the attitudes and behavior of others. Since the parent without a partner is likely to be besieged by a cluster of social, economic, and psychological problems, it is exceedingly difficult to isolate the effects of family composition per se.

Although there has been little systematic investigation of children's ideas about fatherlessness, there is abundant anecdotal testimony that children are alert to the classifications implicit in questions at school about father's occupation, in social differences between mothers with and without spouses, in the activities of children who do not have a father to take them places and do things with them.

A father's absence is a stubborn fact; the subtle or overt responses to that fact on the part of adults and other children are responsive to popular assumptions and are capable of change if those assumptions change. Accordingly, those who feed generalizations into the professional literature and the mass media are under special obligation to be sure that they do not magnify the indirect disadvantages of growing up without a father or underplay any limitations or qualifications that exist in our knowledge about those disadvantages, their universality, and their irreversibility. To suppress information because it might hurt someone is a dubious and probably fatuous undertaking. But it is doubly important to be sure that generalizations are soundly based, if those generalizations in themselves can aggravate the disadvantages of growing up fatherless.

No doubt middle-class children are more conscious of their "broken home" status and of prevailing attitudes toward it than are children in extremely poor homes. For one thing, they are more in the minority and therefore feel more "different." Nevertheless, probably no child in a fatherless home escapes consciousness of being disadvantaged and different. Dick Gregory tells of a poignant incident in which a teacher scolded him for talking about his father along with the other children, scornfully reminding him: "We know you don't have a Daddy." [24]

Research concerning placebo effects and recent studies of school achievement suggest the potency of the self-fulfilling prophecy. There is a good deal of evidence to support Clark's thesis that deprived inner-city children fail to learn because their teachers are convinced that they cannot or will not learn.[25] If the principle of the self-fulfilling prophecy represents a threat to children in fatherless homes, there is more reason to be especially scrupulous about the accuracy and qualifications, when appropriate, of generalizations about such homes, especially if such generalizations carry the status label "research shows. . . ."

Strengths of Fatherless Families

It is often easier to document negatives than positives, partly perhaps because we

---

[24] Dick Gregory, *Nigger* (New York: E. P. Dutton & Co., 1964), p. 45.

[25] Kenneth B. Clark, *Dark Ghetto: Dilemmas of Social Power* (New York: Harper & Row, 1965). *See also* Robert Rosenthal and Lenore Jacobson, "Self-Fulfilling Prophecies in the Classroom: Teachers' Expectations as Unintended Determinants," paper presented at the meeting of the American Psychological Association, Washington, D.C., September 1967. (Mimeographed.) This paper is a condensation of a fuller report prepared as a chapter of Martin Deutsch, Irwin Katz, and Arthur R. Jensen, eds., *Social Class, Race, and Psychological Development* (New York: Holt, Rinehart & Winston, 1968). *See also* Alvin Shapiro, "Influence of Emotional Variables in Evaluation of Hypotensive Agents," *Psychosomatic Medicine*, Vol. 17, No. 4 (July–August 1955), pp. 291–305.

know more about them. Nevertheless, a small but increasing number of social scientists and psychiatrists call attention to some strengths in fatherless families and to the function of this family form in a situation that greatly depresses the economic, social, and psychological status of the low-income male. Those who emphasize the positives have for the most part been discussing the low-income fatherless Negro family. Riessman maintains that because of the functions it serves, "the so-called broken family . . . deserves re-examination.' . . ." [26] Granted that it represents a response to highly undesirable economic and social conditions, some investigators still maintain that until such conditions are improved the female-headed family is a functional form and one that, because of the low and unstable earning power of many Negro men and the regulations of some welfare departments, "is economically advantageous for some women at a poverty level," as compared with having a man in the house. [27]

Others speak of the strong family ties that manage to survive in many of these families, the high degree of mothering that some women are able to show under the most adverse circumstances, the mutual support, aid, and acceptance often evident within and between such families. Erikson, among others, refers to the magnificent strength of Negro mothers who have enabled the family to survive at all. [28] Wickenden refers to mothers in one state who risked starvation by withdrawing their ap-

plications for AFDC rather than risk losing their children under the "suitable homes" ruling. [29] Studies in depth reveal abundant examples of family cohesiveness under stress.

The authors have found no recommendation that one-parent families should replace the two-parent norm. On the contrary, Riessman speculates (somewhat optimistically) that

as poverty disappears, this family form will undoubtedly fall away. . . . But this should not prevent the perception that under special undesirable environmental conditions, the female-led, extended family is a powerful coping device for dealing with the problems of the poor. [30]

Generalizations About Fatherless Families

The authors are engaged at present in a review of research relating to fatherless families and the effects on children of growing up in them. Since the analysis is still under way, we are not in a position to report its final results. If present impressions are supported by further analysis, we shall probably be left with a number of inconclusive conclusions, even when analysis is completed. However, our exploration so far does afford grounds for accepting a few familiar generalizations about fatherless families, rejecting a few, and recommending considerable qualification or suspended judgment about others. Space, time, and human limitations prevent a comprehensive listing of generalizations in any of these three groups. However, a sampling of each can be offered.

---

[26] Frank Riessman, "Low-Income Culture: The Strengths of the Poor," *Journal of Marriage and the Family*, Vol. 26, No. 4 (November 1964), pp. 417–421.

[27] Arthur Besner, "Economic Deprivation and Family Patterns," *Welfare in Review*, Vol. 3, No. 9 (September 1965), pp. 20–28.

[28] Erik H. Erikson, "The Concept of Identity," *Daedalus*, Vol. 95, No. 1 (Winter 1966), pp. 145–171.

[29] Elizabeth Wickenden, "Poverty and the Law—the Constitutional Rights of Assistance Recipients" (New York: National Social Welfare Assembly, March 25, 1963). (Mimeographed).

[30] *Op. cit.*, p. 418.

Generalizations Supported by Evidence

1. A really "good" two-parent home (stable, harmonious, warm, supportive, responsive to individual needs and characteristics) is likely to be more favorable to a child's happiness and development than a one-parent home.

2. Aside from other advantages of the two-parent home, it is better for children to have an adequate resident male model than to lack one.

3. The frequency of one-parent homes is inversely related to socioeconomic status—as income and education decrease, the proportion of broken homes increases.

4. The disadvantaged economic position of the Negro male contributes to family instability.

5. Increasing availability of information about and resources for effective family planning is likely to increase family stability among low-income Negroes, especially if it is concomitant with improved economic status of Negro men—including better job opportunities and job training, better remuneration, and more stable employment.[31]

6. The lower one goes on the socioeconomic ladder, the more bitter and overt becomes the war between the sexes. Accordingly, it is a reasonable hope that improvement in the socioeconomic position of the Negro male is likely to enhance the happiness as well as the stability of low-income homes.[32]

7. Children are likely to fare better in a favorable one-parent home than in an unfavorable two-parent home.

These generalizations have been widely discussed. Moreover, by now most of them are so widely accepted among researchers that there seems little need to buttress them with discussion or even with a great number of references, although many could be cited. It is difficult to refrain, however, from a word about two of them: the first, even though it is probably the one that commands widest support, and the last, which sometimes seems to be forgotten.

A "good" two-parent home. Research studies have identified a number of reasons for wishing that every child could grow up in a good two-parent home. One of the chief reasons, however, is supported by observation, experience, and conviction more directly than by systematic investigation. That reason is happiness. A good many studies attempt to measure the presumed resultants of unhappiness, but relatively few have defined, captured, and rated the elusive quality itself. For obvious and respectable reasons, the full impact of a child's grief and longing for an absent father is more likely to be conveyed through fiction, biography, observation, and experience than through a neat and bloodless empirical study. Dick Gregory evokes it in his simple account of how as a child he used to sidle up to a grown man on the street, hoping that the man would tousle his hair and call him "son." [33]

---

[31] *See*, for example, in *Journal of Marriage and the Family*, Vol. 26, No. 4 (November 1964), Frederick S. Jaffe, "Family Planning and Poverty," pp. 467–470; E. James Lieberman, "Preventive Psychiatry and Family Planning," pp. 471–477; and Elizabeth C. Corkey, "A Family Planning Program for the Low-Income Family," pp. 478–480. *See also* Lee Rainwater, *Family Design* (Chicago: Aldine Press, 1965) ; and Rainwater and Karol Kane Weinstein, *And the Poor Get Children* (Chicago: Quadrangle Books, 1960).

[32] *See* Elizabeth Herzog, "Some Assumptions

About the Poor," *Social Service Review*, Vol. 37, No. 4 (December 1963), pp. 389–402; Hylan Lewis, *op. cit.*; Elliot Liebow, *Tally's Corner* (Boston: Little, Brown & Co., 1967) ; Lee Rainwater, "Crucible of Identity: The Negro Lower-Class Family," *Daedalus*, Vol. 95, No. 1 (Winter 1966), pp. 172–216; Hyman Rodman, *op. cit.*; John H. Rohrer and Munro S. Edmonson, *The Eighth Generation: Cultures and Personalities of New Orleans Negroes* (New York: Harper & Bros., 1960).

[33] *Op. cit.,* p. 38.

It may be that for some children grief and longing can lead to strengthening and growth. Yet for many this kind of deprivation has the opposite effect. And few adults would recommend so stern a prescription even if it seemed more generally beneficial. Aside from proved or unproved assumptions about the effects of a broken home on children's egos, identification processes, aggression, school achievement, or the many other variables and characteristics that have been investigated, most of us cherish a naïve wish for children to be happy. The authors' investigation so far has revealed no challenge to the proposition that for most children the best prospect for a happy childhood is offered by a good two-parent home.

A "good" one-parent home. Available evidence supports the proposition that children are likely to be better off in a good one-parent home than in an intact home that is burdened by instability, marital conflict, destructive parental inadequacy, and other characteristics that, according to child development theory and research, are damaging to children.[34] The finding is not at all surprising if the range of two-parent

---

[34] *See* Ruth E. Hartley, "The Child in the One-Parent Family," unpublished manuscript, College of the City of New York, 1960; Lois W. Hoffman and Ronald Lippitt, "The Measurement of Family Life Variables as Related to Child Behavior and Development" (Ann Arbor: Research Center for Group Dynamics, University of Michigan, 1959) (mimeographed) ; Judson T. Landis, "A Re-examination of the Role of the Father as an Index of Family Integration," *Marriage and Family Living*, Vol. 24, No. 2 (May 1962), pp. 122–128; Joan McCord, William McCord, and Emily Thurber, "Some Effects of Paternal Absence on Male Children," *Journal of Abnormal and Social Psychology*, Vol. 64, No. 5 (March 1962), pp. 361–369; Oliver C. Moles, Jr., "Child Training Practices Among Low-Income Families," *Welfare in Review*, Vol. 3, No. 12 (December 1965), pp. 1–19; Jerome K. Myers and Bertram H. Roberts, *Family and Class Dynamics in Mental Illness* (New York: John Wiley & Sons, 1959) ; F. Ivan Nye, "Child Adjustment in Broken and in Unhappy Unbroken Homes," *Marriage and Family Living*, Vol. 19, No. 4 (November 1957), pp. 356–361.

homes is taken into account. The alternative to a one-parent home, unfortunately, is not necessarily a warm, stable, adequate two-parent home. No one would hesitate to prefer that for an American child. When the counts against one-parent homes are marshaled, it often appears to be with the assumption that all two-parent homes are warm, stable, and adequate. The familiar terms broken and intact seem to embody such an assumption.

Yet the most casual consideration of intact homes is a reminder that a resident father and mother do not necessarily insure an intactness that goes beyond census definition. In a recent conversation, a research investigator reported glowing results from a program that provided "substitute fathers" to boys who had shown delinquent tendencies. At the end, as an afterthought, he remarked that "of course almost all of these boys come from intact homes," but for various reasons (alcoholism, mental or emotional instability, marital conflict, and the like) their fathers were not fulfilling the paternal function. The homes, in other words, were not functionally intact.

Such an anecdote does not impugn the value of an adequate father, but it does serve as a warning against an unqualified assumption that the technical intactness or brokenness of the home is in itself the variable that determines whether a child will reach his full potential. As in so many cases, it is an extremely important variable, the net effect of which depends on a number of other important variables. And, as in so many cases, the net effect can be helped or hindered by community supports and attitudes.

Generalizations Challenged by Evidence

1. The frequency of female-headed families among Negroes is primarily a legacy

from slavery and derives more from cultural than from economic factors.

2. Because of the cultural history and context, low-income Negroes do not place a high value on marriage and no stigma is attached to out-of-wedlock births.

3. The low-income female-headed Negro home is matriarchal.

The first and second generalizations have been challenged so often by one of the present authors that it would be unbearably repetitious to belabor them again.[35] The third is by far the least important, yet it clusters so cozily with more important pronouncements that it merits a passing objection. A matriarchal society typically is one that provides accepted roles for its males and masculine role models that are viewed as adequate by the society of which they are a part. A matriarchal society accepts the ascribed roles of its men and women and does not view the women as arrogating to themselves functions that should belong to men or as stepping into the breach caused by the inadequacy or perfidy of the men. It also provides a tenable economic situation for a family that is viewed as a "real" family, functioning in accordance with the norms of the society.

These statements do not hold true for the female-headed family among low-income Negroes. There is abundant evidence that, despite variations and exceptions, on the whole the alleged matriarchs do not accept their role as correct and desirable, and that they bitterly resent what they view as the weakness and perfidy of their men in imposing such a role on them.[36]

The term matriarchal as applied to low-income Negro families is often associated with references to the favored economic situation of the female, and this too needs qualification. It is not true that the Negro woman is less likely than the man to be involuntarily unemployed. It is true, however, that when the man has a job it is likely to pay better than the woman's. In 1964 nonwhite women's incomes were about three-fifths those of nonwhite men, according to the Bureau of Labor Statistics.[37] It might be added that the same ratio held true for white men and women.[38]

If the Negro mother heading a one-parent family in the inner-city slums is a matriarch, she usually does not know it. And if her position is more favorable than the man's, she usually does not know that either, and neither does he. As one unwitting matriarch put it: "I've often heard a woman wish she was a man, but I never heard a man wish he was a woman." A Negro male in an allegedly matriarchal household said: "I ain't got no education but I do have a lot of mother wit and I know that there ain't nothing no more important to a woman than a man." [39] Apparently some low-income people think money is not all, even when one has little of it.

Because of its connotations of social sanction and individual role acceptance, the term matriarchy seems ill suited to describe the kind of family with which we are here mainly concerned. Granted that usage with regard to these families has made the term nearly synonymous with

---

[35] Elizabeth Herzog, *About the Poor: Some Facts and Some Fictions* (Washington, D.C.: Children's Bureau, U.S. Department of Health, Education, and Welfare, 1968) ; and Herzog and Hylan Lewis, *op. cit.*

[36] Without implicating others in these generalizations, it should be noted that they draw heavily on the child-rearing study directed by Hylan Lewis as well as on the writings of Rohrer and Edmondson, Rainwater, Miller, Riessman, and other investigators who have given depth accounts, including verbatim transcriptions of interviews with extremely low-income Negroes.

[37] Bureau of Labor Statistics, U.S. Department of Labor, *The Negroes in the United States— Their Economic and Social Situation*, Bulletin No. 1511 (Washington, D.C.: U.S. Government Printing Office, June 1966).

[38] *Ibid.*, p. 4.

[39] Camille Jeffers, *Three Generations* (Washington, D.C.: CROSS-TELL, October 1966).

"matrifocal," it would still seem desirable to reserve it for societies in which matriarchy is accepted as natural, adequate, and "right." Although the one-parent family deserves to be recognized as one form of family, its social setting and the attitudes held toward it, even by its members, do not qualify it to be termed a matriarchy. And although quibbling over words is often windmill-tilting, there may be a value in avoiding terms that carry deceptive connotations.

Generalizations Still in Question

1. Boys in fatherless homes suffer more than girls from the lack of a resident male model.

2. Children in fatherless homes are more likely than others to engage in socially disapproved behavior, e.g., to become juvenile delinquents, to bear children out of wedlock, to achieve poorly in school.

3. Children in fatherless homes are more likely than others to suffer from emotional and psychological inadequacies, e.g., excessive immaturity, dependency, anxiety, feelings of inferiority (i.e., problems of sex role and identification).

The authors' analysis has not yet reached the point at which we can report even tentatively on the extent to which the research findings reviewed support or challenge each of the correlations implied in these generalizations. We can, however, report some impressions. Moreover, although further analysis may modify the impressions with regard to specific variables, certain observations about content and method already have firm support in the evidence reviewed.

Boys in fatherless homes. Research findings consistently show a differential impact of father absence on boys and on girls. The need for qualification concerns not the fact of differential impact, but the measures used and the conclusions based on them—including the nature of the impact and the differences. For example, it is proverbial that girls do better in grade school than boys, so that special care must be taken to separate expected difference from additional difference caused by father absence.

One of the most deplored effects on children of the broken home is the absence of a male model for the boy. Specialists in child development generally agree that the optimum situation for a child is the presence in the home of adequate male and female models, to provide opportunities both for identification and imitation.

Disagreement concerns not the desirability of the optimum model, but rather the nature, degree, and inevitability of the toll exacted by absence of a male model. Usually this is considered only in relation to boys, but it can by no means be assumed that absence of the cross-sex parent fails to affect either sex. The girl's relation to her father is no more to be minimized than the boy's relation to his mother.[40]

A question is raised occasionally as to whether the presence of a blatantly inadequate male model is better for a boy than no resident male at all. If the father is a confirmed alcoholic, suffers from psychosis, beats his wife unmercifully, gambles away all his wife's earnings—is the son better off than he might be in a one-parent home? The answer is not at all a foregone conclusion, and the question must be recognized as pertinent to consideration of homes at any income level in any ethnic group.

It is one thing to say that presence in the home of an adequate male model is a good fortune for children and that it may be especially important for male children. It is another to say just how damaging the lack of such a model is, whether substitute models are feasible, and, if so, what kind and how much they are likely to help.

---

[40] Ruth E. Hartley, "Sex Roles and Urban Youth: Some Developmental Perspectives," *Bulletin on Family Development*, Vol. 2, No. 1 (January 1961), pp. 1–12.

Among the many unanswered questions are: How important is residence? How much can substitute models not resident in the home make up for the deficit?

Big Brothers and some other organizations operate on the belief that surrogate male models can help to some extent. Claims are made for the effectiveness of such efforts, and counterclaims raise question about the evidence on which the claims are based. Much that has been written on the subject of positive and negative identification puts a heavy burden of proof on those who claim efficacy for the surrogate model. On the other hand, much that has been claimed for attempts to supply surrogate models demands attention and analysis. At this point it can be stated merely that the need for a resident male model would repay further study and that effects attributed to the absence of a resident model at times are claimed to be the effects of other factors.

Some investigators ask whether absence of a resident father necessarily implies absence of an adequate resident male model. An anthropologist suggests that in Puerto Rico many "fatherless" boys do have resident male models—but that these happen to be related to the mother by ties other than marriage.[41] Another anthropologist has commented, in informal discussion, on the adroitness of small Puerto Rican boys in annexing an adult male "friend" who serves them as surrogate father figure. To what extent such patterns are relevant to problems of Negroes in the United States is another question worth looking into.

Socially disapproved behavior and psychological problems. Concerning the second and third generalizations, research studies present a mixed picture. Some report that a fatherless home is conducive to various forms of socially disapproved behavior; some report the opposite finding. This is the case, for example, with regard to juvenile delinquency. One of the most frequent comments about fatherless homes is that "research has shown" they produce juvenile delinquency, and beyond doubt many studies have so reported—too many to require documentation at this point. On the other hand, a number of studies have exonerated fatherless homes in this respect—a fact that should be recognized, since such a finding runs counter to popular assumptions.[42] (Eisner reported that juvenile delinquency was correlated with living in a fatherless home for white boys and for some middle-class Negroes, but not for extremely low-income Negroes, a finding analogous to some reported in relation to probationers.[43])

Reports also differ about birth out of wedlock, poor school performance, and school dropouts. Prevailing assumptions and repetitive findings are on the side of holding fatherless homes responsible for this kind of deviance, so that it is expedient

---

[41] Hazel du Bois, "Working Mothers and Absent Fathers—Family Organization in the Caribbean." Paper presented at the annual meeting, American Anthropological Association, Detroit, Mich., November 1964.

[42] *See* F. Ivan Nye, *Family Relationships and Delinquent Behavior* (New York: John Wiley & Sons, 1958); Edwin Powers and Helen Witmer, "An Experiment in the Prevention of Delinquency," *The Cambridge-Somerville Youth Study* (New York: Columbia University Press, 1951); Aaron L. Rutledge, "Marriage Problems and Divorce," *Survey Papers*, 1960 White House Conference on Children and Youth (Washington, D.C.: U.S. Government Printing Office, 1960), pp. 219–241; Richard S. Sterne, *Delinquent Conduct and Broken Homes* (New Haven, Conn.: College and University Press, 1964); William W. Wattenberg and John B. Moir, "A Phenomenon in Search of a Cause," *Journal of Criminal Law and Criminology*, Vol. 48, No. 1 (May-June 1957), pp. 54–58; Margaret Wynn, *Fatherless Families* (London, Eng.: Michael Joseph, 1964).

[43] Victor Eisner, "Effect of Parents in the Home on Juvenile Delinquency," *Public Health Reports*, Vol. 81, No. 10 (October 1966), pp. 905–910; Albert J. Reiss, Jr., "The Accuracy, Efficiency, and Validity of a Prediction Instrument," *American Journal of Sociology*, Vol. 56, No. 6 (May 1951), pp. 552–561.

to note that some studies report the opposite finding.[44]

Similarly, many studies report that a broken home is directly related to psychological problems, including defective sex identification, aggression, passivity, low self-esteem, low achievement motivation, inability to delay gratification. Some report that they are not, and again only a few examples that run counter to prevailing assumptions will be cited here.[45]

It is too early in the authors' analysis to report the extent to which one kind of finding correlates with given characteristics of sampling, criterion variables and measures, or data analysis, although judging from experience some such correlations may be forthcoming. In reviewing research about working mothers, for example, it was observed that the majority of the studies reviewed were likely to report adverse effects associated with maternal employment, but that the relatively few studies with adequate sampling and carefully matched controls were likely not to find adverse effects directly associated with maternal employment. A related observation was that findings varied according to whether the study was focused on the effects of maternal employment or on some other subject area, with the working mother correlation a by-product.

The sketchy report just given about the "score" on specific variables is not intended to indicate a conclusion that the generalizations involving them fail to stand up when evidence is analyzed. It indicates, rather, that further analysis is required before one can accept or reject the generalizations as stated. It indicates, further, an undeniable hunch that, whatever the final conclusion, it will stipulate qualification—a commodity rare in these generalizations as usually made.

Recurrent Questions

When doctors disagree, one chooses an expert, basing one's choice on the criteria that seem most relevant to the situation. In attempting to apply our own criteria, we have been plagued by some nagging questions about research in this area and about summary discussions or interpretations of research findings. Further analysis may elaborate or add to these questions, but it is unlikely to eliminate any of them. They can be subsumed under three headings:

1. The nature of the research methods used.

2. The tendency of investigators and commentators to stretch or lump study findings.

[44] *See*, for example, Jean W. Butman and Jane A. Kamm, *The Social, Psychological and Behavioral World of the Teen-Age Girl* (Ann Arbor: University of Michigan Press, June 1965); James S. Coleman *et al.*, *Equality of Educational Opportunity* (Washington, D.C.: Office of Education, U.S. Department of Health, Education, and Welfare, 1966); Wyatt Jones, "What Are Unmarried Mothers *Really* Like?" paper presented at the National Conference on Social Welfare, Atlantic City, N.J., June 1960; Bernard Mackler and Morsley G. Giddlings, "Cultural Deprivation: A Study in Mythology," *Teachers College Record*, Vol. 66, No. 7 (April 1965), pp. 608–613; Erdman Palmore, "Factors Associated with School Dropouts and Juvenile Delinquency Among Lower-Class Children," *Social Security Bulletin*, Vol. 26, No. 10 (October 1963), pp. 4–9; Clark E. Vincent, *Unmarried Mothers* (New York: Free Press of Glencoe, 1961).

[45] Lee G. Burchinal, "Characteristics of Adolescents from Unbroken, Broken and Reconstituted Families," *Journal of Marriage and the Family*, Vol. 26, No. 1 (February 1964), pp. 44–51; Thomas Langner and Stanley Michaels, *Life Stress and Mental Health*, Vol. 2 of the Midtown Manhattan Study (New York: Free Press of Glencoe, 1963); P. H. Mussen and J. J. Conger, *Child Development and Personality* (New York: Harper & Bros., 1956); Frank A. Pederson, "Relationships Between Father-Absence and Emotional Disturbance in Male Military Dependents," *Merrill-Palmer Quarterly*, Vol. 12, No. 4 (October 1966), pp. 321–322.

3. The readiness to base conclusions, interpretations, and recommendations on research that has not been adequately reviewed and assessed.

Research Methods

Without going into detail, questions about research methods often relate to the nature of the sampling, the criterion measures used, and the presence or adequacy of control or comparison groups. Such questions are especially insistent in relation to studies of socially unsanctioned behavior, which often use client, patient, inmate, or school populations without reporting relevant information about the population outside these limited groups and without adequate controls.

In studies focused on the correlation between fatherless homes and social adjustment or psychological difficulties, methodological misgivings often center on the criterion measures. In some cases these are ingenious and impressive—and still leave room for doubt whether they measure what they are supposed to measure. This kind of question is intensified with regard to measures for determining the adequacy of a child's sex identity, a subject prominent in efforts to assess the psychological effects of growing up in a fatherless home. A number of commentators have challenged the validity of certain items designed to determine adequacy of sex identification. Erikson, for example, asks whether it makes sense to score a low-income Negro boy as feminine because he says he would like to be a singer when he grows up, pointing out that this has been one of the few roads open to Negroes for achieving high status and that male singers have been numbered among the current culture heroes.[46]

Endless questions can be and have been asked about specific items used. It is relevant here only that study findings tend to be accepted without question and without examining the items.

A different kind of question about ratings of adequate or inadequate masculine or feminine identification has to do with the definition of what is adequately masculine or feminine. Are the item-constructors clear about the optimum? What norms or ideals would we like little boys to emulate? Is there a continuum from All-American Boy to All-American Girl? Or is it possible that the apotheosis of womanhood and of manhood are not as far from each other as downright defect in either is from both? If so, this posits a model different from the one implied by the nature of some masculinity-femininity test items. Possibly the constellation of traits represented by either ideal norm does not lend itself to adequate testing by a handful of items. Possibly also, the tolerable variation in trait clusters, trait intensity, and amount of overlap between masculine and feminine is so extensive that clear lines cannot be drawn between adequate and inadequate.

Still another kind of question is being raised in connection with social changes that may have gotten ahead of some paper-and-pencil self-reports.[47] Pollak commented a few years ago that we seem to be working "with yardsticks of masculinity and femininity which in the middle of the twentieth century are obsolete."[48] Vincent more recently observed:

The items in many M-F tests and scales were selected initially, because they discriminated significantly between the responses of the sexes *at the time the tests were constructed.* To the degree that these items reflect the concept of a traditional, male-dominant family and society; to the degree that male-female

---

[46] *Op. cit.,* p. 157.

---

[47] Paper-and-pencil self-reports in themselves raise some questions that will not be considered here.

[48] Otto Pollak, "Interrelationships Between Economic Institutions and the Family," *Social Security Bulletin,* Vol. 23, No. 10 (October 1960).

role expectations are becoming more *equalitarian;* and to the degree that the role expectations *effect socialization;* it would appear to follow that M-F items need to be revised and M-F scores reinterpreted within the context of current male-female role expectations.[49]

Tendency To Stretch or Lump Findings

It is always possible to quarrel with research methods, and obviously our own criteria for assessing evidence and qualifications will include characteristics of the research methods on which contradictory findings are based. A different kind of problem is represented by readiness to stretch or overgeneralize reported findings. Sometimes this is done by the investigator in the research report. Sometimes it is done by other social scientists in reviewing research results or using them as a basis for program recommendations.

Among the more interesting targets of this readiness is a study of father absence conducted in Norway that is among the studies most frequently cited as evidence of the deleterious effects of father absence.[50] Part of the interest lies in the high quality of the research and the care with which its focus and its limitations are set forth. As described by Grønseth, the purpose of the

study was to investigate the effects of frequent, prolonged, but temporary father absence in the setting of a closely knit puritanical village community. The fathers were sailors of the officer class and the control group consisted of children of men in managerial positions. It was hypothesized that, among other factors, the rigid rectitude of the mothers would complicate the effects of father absence on their children.

Among the findings was the problem the sailors' sons had in establishing adequate masculine identity. This finding was based partly on interviews with the mothers and partly on a structured doll-play test with the children, all of whom were 8 or 9 years old. The evidence from this test was, in effect, an inference based on such clues as the frequent selection of the father over the mother, in contrast with the selection made by the sailors' daughters and the control group boys and girls. The inference is supported by psychoanalytic theory. Nevertheless, in this instance a question remains as to whether the boys might have missed their fathers more than their sisters did.

It is not necessary to debate the interpretations, however, in order to wonder about citing this specific study as evidence that low-income Negro boys in fatherless New York homes suffer from feminization. Granted that they may. It is even possible that the situations are analogous enough to justify applying the Norwegian study findings to inner-city ghettos not noted for a rigid religious repression of sexual impulses, for closely knit village life, or for father absence that is temporary, planned, and socially sanctioned. The striking thing is that the study is cited repeatedly as established proof, without any effort to show that the application is valid or why it is, and apparently without any assumption that such effort would be appropriate. Yet children are affected by community norms as well as by family characteristics, and on both grounds direct

---

[49] Clark E. Vincent, "Implications of Changes in Male-Female Role Expectations for Interpreting M-F Scores," *Journal of Marriage and the Family*, Vol. 28, No. 2 (May 1966), p. 199.

[50] Erik Grønseth and Per Olav Tiller, "Father Absence in Sailor Families and Its Impact Upon the Personality Development and Later Local Adjustment of the Children," *Studies of the Family*, Vol. II (Göttingen, Norway: Vandenhoeck & Ruprecht, 1957), pp. 95–114; David B. Lynn and William L. Sawrey, "The Effects of Father-Absence on Norwegian Boys and Girls," *Journal of Abnormal and Social Psychology*, Vol. 59, No. 2 (September 1959), pp. 258–262; and Tiller, "Father Absence and Personality Development in Children of Sailor Families," *Nord. Psychological Monograph*, Serial No. 9 (1958).

applicability can hardly be taken for granted.

Related to, yet not identical with, the leap from culture to culture or from one socioeconomic level to another is the leap from a statistically significant difference to an assumption that the trait or difference observed embraces all members of the population under investigation, or at least a large proportion of them. This is a familiar stretch that requires little comment here.[51] A problem in lumping rather than stretching concerns the qualifications about intact homes already referred to: What kind of two-parent home? Is it psychologically intact? If not, are its disadvantages for the child greater or less than those of a one-parent home? And again, what kind of one-parent home?

The last question involves an array of kinds of father absence. What is the reason for father absence—death, divorce, separation, desertion, prison, military service, business obligations? How does the child perceive the reasons and how does this perception affect his reactions? Does it incline him to overidealize the absent father, and with what results on his self-concept? Does it incline him to despise or resent the absent father, and again with what results?

Other questions relate to the age of the child at the time of separation and still others to his age at the time of the study. Relatively few studies are able to report long-term effects as manifested in adults who experienced father absence as children. And the few long-term reports provide relatively insubstantial evidence with regard to the facets investigated. But if a child of 8 shows perceptible effects of father absence, how much does this tell about its effects on his ultimate development? A few studies grapple with this point, espe-

cially studies of low-income Negro families. Often, however, it is assumed as self-evident that limited test findings in preadolescence predict characteristics in adulthood. It may be so, but the existence of the question needs to be recognized, and a number of longitudinal studies raise doubts about the answer.[52]

Inadequate Review

The tendency to expand or overgeneralize relates in turn to a fascinating readiness on the part of researchers (present authors not excepted) to seize on research findings that support a relevant point and to accept them as evidence without inquiring too closely about how solid the evidence is. One of the most frequent generalizations about fatherless homes, for example, is that they are conducive to juvenile delinquency. As noted, we are not in a position to support or challenge that generalization. It is interesting and relevant, however, that in a later effort to apply the well-known Glueck Social Prediction Table, ratings involving the father were eliminated because so large a proportion of the homes were fatherless in the low-income group under study, and also because the investigators concluded that fatherless homes could be "cohesive." In England, Leslie Wilkins eventually dropped the broken home element from the scale used in his borstal studies because it did not add enough to prediction about juvenile delinquency.[53]

---

[51] Catherine S. Chilman, "Some Differences Between People and Statistics," *Children*, Vol. 13, No. 3 (May-June 1955), pp. 99–103.

[52] Jerome Kogan and Howard A. Moss, *Birth to Maturity* (New York: John Wiley & Sons, 1962); and Jean Walker MacFarland, "From Infancy to Adulthood," *Childhood Education* (March 1963), pp. 83–89.

[53] *See* Maude M. Craig and Selma J. Glick, "Ten Years' Experience with the Glueck Social Prediction Scale," *Crime and Delinquency*, Vol. 9, No. 1 (July 1963), pp. 249–261; Elizabeth Herzog, "Identifying Potential Delinquents," *Ju-*

One reason for indiscriminate generalization and application of findings is suggested by a statement about sociologists that applies equally to other social scientists:

A careful examination of the sociological literature shows that many of the most widely acclaimed works have large and demonstrable errors of interpretation. One reason for the prevalence of such errors is that sociologists do not learn to read critically—to compare the author's facts with what he says about them.[54]

Often the reading may be uncritical. But often, apparently, social scientists do not read the reports they cite, depending instead on summary abstracts of findings or on reference to them in the work of some other social scientist.[55] An informal "survey" of reactions to the voluminous Coleman report revealed a surprising number of social scientists ready to express an opinion about its accuracy and what it "really" said, but also ready to admit that they had not read it. This may be one reason why such diverse conclusions are attributed to it and cited as reasons for recommending divergent courses of action.[56]

The research explosion is likely to increase this kind of problem. Who can read carefully and critically every study that pertains to his area of specialization? There is no easy answer. There is, however, a critical need for some professional invention to meet the problem. And even before that, there is a critical need to recognize that the problem exists. It not only exists, but it is a potent contributor to the promulgation of stereotypes.

Implications for Research

The readiness of laymen and professionals to convert correlations into generalizations and generalizations into stereotypes places a heavy responsibility on research investigators and reporters, especially at a time when significant action is more possible than in the past and more attention is paid to research findings. In the process of seeking needed answers to complex questions, research investigators are liable to become makers and breakers of stereotypes. The purpose of the foregoing pages has not been to complain about research or researchers, but rather to present some evidence and some problems with regard to research concerning the effects on children of growing up in one-parent homes.

Review of such research points up, even before the review is completed, a need for restraint in formulating conclusions and perhaps even more in citing the conclusions of others. Some of us, in our eagerness to demonstrate the need for sound and constructive programs, have "pushed the panic button" harder and sooner than the evidence may warrant. The objective is worthy but the side effects can prove destructive. And there is enough sound evidence of the need for such programs to eliminate the need for promoting them in this way. If the objective is to convince legislators, reliable statistical facts and figures buttressed by anecdotal accounts are as likely to be convincing as

venile Delinquency Facts and Facets, No. 5 (Washington, D.C.: Children's Bureau, U.S. Department of Health, Education, and Welfare, 1966); Alfred J. Kahn, "The Case of the Premature Claims," *Crime and Delinquency*, Vol. 11, No. 3 (July 1965), pp. 217–228; Richard S. Sterne, *op. cit.*; Leslie T. Wilkins, "What Is Prediction and Is It Necessary in Evaluation Treatment?" in *Research and Potential Application of Research in Probation, Parole, Delinquency Prediction* (New York: Research Center, Columbia University School of Social Work, July 1961).

[54] Hanan C. Selvin, "Implications of the Sibley Report for the Undergraduate Curriculum in Sociology," *American Sociologist*, Vol. 2, No. 2 (May 1967), p. 79.

[55] William Lee Miller, "Moynihan Revisited," *The Reporter*, August 10, 1967, pp. 46–48.

[56] Coleman *et al., op. cit.*

recourse to insufficiently tested research findings that risk destructive side effects. (Sufficient testing includes replication, among other things.)

In university statistics courses, much is made of Type I and Type II errors and how to avoid them. Perhaps more needs to be made of what might be called the Type III error: the erroneous belief that available evidence justifies a firm conclusion.

Another kind of implication for research concerns the topics or areas to be studied if research is undertaken with a view to applying its results toward improvement in social conditions. It is possible to differentiate between research that is or is not likely to be fruitful. The authors' review has already raised a question about the fruitfulness of the dichotomy of broken versus intact homes, and in fact a question whether the dichotomy itself is false.

Once more, the history of research about maternal employment may suggest the probable course of research about fatherless homes. Not so many years ago, conferences were discussing the effects on children of having a mother work outside the home. Distressed mothers, alarmed at the publicizing of one research study, were writing to the Children's Bureau to ask: "Am I making my child into a juvenile delinquent because I have to work?" At present the main focus of discussion is, rather, what factors mediate the effects on children of having their mothers work outside the home and what kinds of daytime care or other supervision should be established to help the working mother fulfill her demanding dual role.

Today there is remarkable consensus among research investigators that whether the mother works is not in itself the determining variable, but that the impact on a child of her employment depends on a number of other variables, such as her attitude toward working or not working; the attitudes of other family members; the

marital relationship (if any); the age, sex, and special needs of the child; and so on.[57]

The possible parallel lies in the shift of focus from a single variable, assumed to be *the* determining factor, to a cluster of interacting factors that, on the one hand, mediate its effect and, on the other, provide clues to methods of diminishing the adverse elements in its effects.

Although research has moved away from pointing to maternal employment as the crucial variable, the public at large still cherishes a number of stereotypes about employed mothers. Research did not initiate these stereotypes, but it has contributed a share to the present situation in which many mothers feel guilty if they do work and many feel guilty if they do not. (Unfortunately, research also suggests that a mother's sense of guilt is likely to be worse for the child than her working or not working.)

The working mother parallel suggests another consideration concerning whether research is likely to be fruitful. Whether a home does or does not remain intact is even less responsive to recommendation or edict than whether a mother should or should not work. As suggested earlier, the number of fatherless homes is unlikely to decrease in the near future. Two points are relevant here: (1) There is solid research grounding for the proposition that the mother's personality and behavior are among the strongest influences affecting children and that both are affected by her

---

[57] *See*, for example, Elizabeth Herzog, *Children of Working Mothers* (Washington, D.C.: Children's Bureau, U.S. Department of Health, Education, and Welfare, 1960); F. Ivan Nye and Lois W. Hoffman, *The Employed Mother in America* (Chicago: Rand McNally & Co., 1963); Alberta Engvall Siegal and Miriam Bushkoff Haas, "The Working Mother: A Review of Research," *Child Development*, Vol. 34, No. 3 (September 1963), pp. 513–542; Lois Meek Stolz, "Effects of Maternal Employment on Children: Evidence from Research," *Child Development*, Vol. 31, No. 4 (December 1960), pp. 749–782.

situation. (2) The situation of the mother in a one-parent family is difficult and demanding in the extreme. The second point holds for mothers at any socioeconomic level, but is intensified and compounded for the extremely low-income Negro mother in a fatherless home. Her situation is likely to include the dual role of homemaker and wage earner, complicated by the lack of a partner to give support in both aspects. The demands of the dual role are likely to be compounded by loneliness. Rainwater found a large majority of female respondents saying that a separated woman will miss most companionship, love, or sex, or simply that she will be lonesome.[58] It is likely to be still further compounded by a number of other factors, including concern about the physical and social welfare of her children, loss of self-esteem because she is left alone, grinding fatigue, malnutrition, physical ailments, and the baying of the wolf at the door.

It seems reasonable to speculate that research on the effects of growing up in a fatherless home may follow a course analogous to that of research on the effects of maternal employment. It may be that a period of struggle with a presumably critical variable and a presumably clearcut dichotomy has prepared the way for a shift of focus to more promising, although more complex, constellations of interacting variables. This would mean a shift away from efforts to measure to what degree and in what ways fatherless homes are unfavorable to children's development. At this point it may prove more fruitful to focus on clues to (1) helping the mother in a fatherless home fulfill her difficult role and (2) helping children to develop their full potential in homes that, structurally or psychologically, are not intact.

The first direction may call for action rather than research. The second includes

---

[58] Lee Rainwater, "The Problem of Lower-Class Culture." Unpublished paper, September 23, 1966. (Mimeographed.)

programs that do require heavy research efforts to evaluate and to innovate. It is only fair to add that the authors would include, under the second, devices for providing adequate male models, even though belief that they are needed is not based primarily on the studies of father absence that have been reviewed. It is only fair to admit also a belief that improved education, job training, jobs, income maintenance, and family planning are likely ultimately to reduce the frequency of fatherless homes among low-income Negroes, and that this would be a good thing.

Closing Comment

We would like to close, not with a formal summary, but by pulling together five points that we have tried to communicate:

1. The fatherless family merits recognition and study as a family form in its own right.

2. It is a vulnerable type of family and needs the support of community services to help the mother fulfill her crucial and demanding dual role.

3. Some familiar generalizations about the adverse effects on children of growing up in fatherless homes are subject to qualification and possibly to challenge. Relevant research is plagued by the difficulty of separating the effects of poverty, color, and fatherlessness, as well as by questions about measures used for determining and predicting psychological attributes.

4. It is all the more desirable that any generalizations made about fatherless families should be accurate and—when appropriate—qualified, since stereotyping of such homes can set in play the mechanism of the self-fulfilling prophecy.

5. Social scientists are in a position to support or to combat stereotypes. To combat them requires eternal vigilance that becomes more difficult and more imperative as research findings proliferate.

An Agenda for Research About Race and Social Work

L. K. NORTHWOOD AND ROBERT L. REED

Social work research should be used to obtain knowledge that will implement the institutional values of the profession. Such research becomes race related because social work in the United States continually is confronted by the imperative for change in the racial status quo. Negroes and other minorities are heavy consumers of social services. The disengagement of social work from the poor has occurred regularly only in limited sectors of private social welfare such as family counseling and leisure-time activities for youth. In contrast, there is continued overrepresentation of Negroes in the public assistance programs, correctional agencies, schools and neighborhood centers in ghettos and interracial areas, and so forth.[1]

The social worker is supposed to understand the background and social environment of the clients he serves in order to provide more adequate services. Thus, the norms of proper professional practice push the worker to acquire knowledge of the machinery of racial prejudice, discrimination, and segregation—a knowledge that frequently is lacking.

Even without this overrepresentation of Negro clients, the social worker would be confronted with the need to understand

L. K. Northwood, Ph.D., is Professor, School of Social Work, University of Washington, Seattle, Washington. Robert L. Reed, MSW, is Director, Holly Park Branch of Neighborhood House, Seattle, Washington.

[1] Richard A. Cloward and Irwin Epstein, "Private Social Welfare's Disengagement from the Poor; the Case of Family Adjustment Agencies" (New York: Columbia University School for Social Work, April 1964). (Mimeographed.) *See also* S. M. Miller, "The Disengagement of Social Workers from the Poor," in R. E. Will and H. G. Vatter, eds., *Poverty and Affluence* (New York. Harcourt, Brace & World, 1965), pp. 241–243; Martin Rein, "Poverty, Social Services, and Social Change," in W. C. Kvaraceus, J. S. Gibson, and T. J. Curtin, eds., *Poverty, Education, and Race Relations: Studies and Proposals* (Boston: Allyn & Bacon, 1967), pp. 23–48; G. W. Steiner, *Social Insecurity: The Politics of Welfare* (Chicago: Rand-McNally, 1966).

prejudice, discrimination, and segregation. Racial policies and practices complicate almost every aspect of American life. They are involved in personal decisions about where one will live and work, where one will go to school, who will become one's friends or spouse. Broad social policies of urban development and foreign policy become explicitly and openly associated with racial prejudice and segregation. As the demand for changes in the discriminatory status quo becomes articulated in the form of organized resistance and spontaneous rioting, the confrontation is more urgent.

Organized social work traditionally has been the spokesman for the poor with the Establishment, and sometimes social workers have been organizers of the poor as well as advocates of ameliorative change. These traditional roles are being reactivated and reinforced by the antipoverty programs. The uprisings in Watts, Detroit, Newark, and other major cities underline the need for expanded programs of social services in the solution of the worsening urban conditions.

In short, there is no permanent escape for the social worker from racial issues, even when he is serving an all-white clientele and treatment of the client seems unrelated to prejudice and discrimination. The tiny white microcosm of the clinical dyad, isolated from the rest of the world, has been shattered by life in a multiracial society. The challenges race presents to social work also demand new efforts in research.

The intimate relationship between "appropriate" research and the social work value base clearly is mandated in the *Bylaws of the National Association of Social Workers* and in *Goals of Public Social policy:*

To further the broad objective of improving conditions of life in our democratic society through utilization of the professional knowledge and skills of social work, and to expand

through research the knowledge necessary to define and attain these goals.[2]

. . . . .

Social work is the profession which concerns itself with the facilitating and strengthening of basic social relationships between individuals, groups, and social institutions. It has, therefore, a social action responsibility which derives directly from its social function and professional knowledge. This responsibility lies in the following three areas: (a) the identification, analysis, and interpretation of specific unmet needs among individuals and groups of individuals, (b) advancing the standard of recognized social obligation between society and its individual members so that those needs will be met and a more satisfying environment for all achieved, and (c) the application of specific knowledge, experience, and inventiveness to those problems which can be solved through social welfare programs.[3]

General Functions of Research

Research in race relations, as used in this paper, refers to research that has specific relevance for social work practice, that will provide knowledge to help implement the basic social work philosophy, and that will help in establishing feasible and realizable change goals. Such research, of course, will need to meet at the same time sound criteria for reliability and validity. What can such research be expected to accomplish? It has three general functions:

1. *Research can serve to dispel myths and to describe reality.* Often social work practice is based on what may actually be little more than myth, whereas with proper research more reliable and valid guides for action can be set. For example, research should be directed at a number of assumptions that have been expressed about the concept of Black Power: (a) that it is

---

[2] *Bylaws of the National Association of Social Workers*, Article II—Purposes, p. 5.

[3] *Goals of Public Social Policy* (rev. ed.; New York: National Association of Social Workers, 1967), p. 10.

a mobilizing cry that helps build self-identity among Negroes and aids in involvement for self-help, (b) that it is a divisive slogan alienating civil rights supporters and opening the door for white backlash, (c) that it is a slogan approved by only a small minority of Negroes and condemned by most, and (d) that it finds wide support and tacit approval from large numbers of Negroes who do not express their views vocally. One might ask also if it is not a myth to say that white backlash is a response to Black Power.

The continued vitality of some racial myths and half-truths requires a periodic rebuttal via research. One such myth is that of the inevitability of property deterioration following the movement of Negroes into a neighborhood. This relationship between property values and race has been studied comprehensively by Luigi Laurenti and others, who substantially disprove it.[4] Yet the myth still persists in its original form, with some new variations involving the postulation of a racial "tipping point" of neighborhoods, the point after which no new white family will move in and the neighborhood gradually becomes more and more segregated.[5]

Some research therefore needs to be repeated again and again, both to enhance the validity of the original findings and to refocus attention on their action implications. Moreover, the persistence of mythology in itself is a proper subject for research.

Many myths have a kernel of truth that should be sifted out through the research process. Much has been done to sort the kernel of truth out of the myth of racial inferiority. The results have prime relevance for social welfare action. The "truth" in statements about the low motivation of Negro youths, the presence of high illegitimacy rates among Negro families, and so forth should lead to research that digs into the why of these conditions and what can be done to change them.

2. Appropriate research can better enable social workers to identify developing problem situations and to take appropriate countermeasures. The more the interrelation of any set of variables is known and understood, the better are our predictions and projections about the future. One might ask, for example, why riots have occurred in some cities and not in others; why they are sparked and develop with greater or lesser degrees of destructiveness. Only a limited number of studies have dealt with such conflicts despite the fact that they have a tremendous impact on social welfare services.[6]

3. Research can be an aid in evaluating the effectiveness of what social work is doing and thus make possible the selection of appropriate methods of intervention when alternative courses are possible. Social work values remain rather abstract and meaningless unless implemented with appropriate strategies for achieving specific change objectives. How does one aid in

---

[4] *See* Luigi Laurenti, *Property Values and Race, Studies in Seven Cities* (Berkeley: University of California Press, 1960); Erdman Palman and John Howe, "Residential Integration and Property Values," *Social Problems*, Vol. 10, No. 1 (Summer 1962), pp. 52–55.

[5] Lawrence K. Northwood and Louise H. Klein, "The 'Tipping Point'—A Questionable Quality of Neighborhoods," *Journal of Intergroup Relations*, Vol. 4, No. 4 (Autumn 1965), pp. 226–239.

---

[6] A recent study by Stanley Lieberson and Arnold R. Silverman, "The Precipitants and Underlying Conditions of Race Riots," *American Sociological Review*, Vol. 30, No. 6 (December 1965), pp. 887–898, examines seventy-six race riots in the United States between 1913 and 1963, using journalistic accounts and census data. The authors raise a number of points that deserve further research. In addition, the more recent conflicts, especially the one in Detroit, appear to have other factors that need examination. Integrated looting is quite different from jeering mobs harrassing Negro marchers; neither fits the older picture of white mobs invading and destroying Negro areas. "Riot" is an entirely inadequate word to describe a number of different kinds of conflict with some racial basis.

"improving the conditions of life" for Negroes? Within our framework of commitment to democratic ideals we need to be able to specify what we want to achieve and how we expect to achieve it. For example, a concept that has been more or less taken for granted—that of integration —is now being challenged by Black Nationalism. The concepts with which we work need to be researched and operationally defined. What is meant by integration, segregation, discrimination? Do these terms mean the same to the target population as they do to social workers?

At least three kinds of research are needed to implement social work values with respect to race relations: cultural-historical, organizational, and psychosocial. Some high-priority research questions that pertain to these levels of activity will be identified.

Cultural-Historical Research

One of the first priorities in research is for studies that are both concrete and historical.[7] Social workers continually are using historical and cultural data in their work for the better understanding of client and community and in order to develop programs for their agencies. Moreover, the demand for knowledge about Negroes and other minorities has been intensified during this period of growth of Black Nationalism, since there is a greater striving among Negroes and other minorities for a sense of identity and group consciousness-of-kind. The state of the knowledge is not

sufficient to meet this demand. In fact, cultural-historical research about Negroes and other minorities at best is fragmentary and incomplete, and at worst is biased and mistaken.[8] To some extent these deficiencies of the past are being overcome. The federal government in particular has compiled a series of excellent reports about statistical trends in employment, education, health, housing, and other aspects of the life of Negroes and other minorities.[9] The official government statistics occasionally are given sociological and historical perspective, and in some instances they are supplemented with a community and situational context. However, for the most part there is a dearth of concrete, empirical research that is relevant to both local action and comparative analysis.

This lack was clearly indicated by two short inventories the authors made in prep-

---

[7] There is no substitute for historical studies that are also concrete and empirical. This point of view is discussed cogently in C. W. Mills, *The Sociological Imagination* (New York: Oxford University Press, 1959), pp. 143–164. *See also* J. C. McKinney, *Constructive Typology and Social Theory* (New York: Appleton-Century-Crofts, 1966); and C. V. Good and D. E. Scates, *Methods of Research* (New York: Appleton-Century-Crofts, 1954), pp. 170–254.

[8] An excellent attempt to rectify this deficiency is Philip Durham and E. L. Jones, *The Negro Cowboys* (New York: Dodd Mead, 1965). Specific details about the distortions and omissions are presented in Lloyd Marcus, *The Treatment of Minorities in Secondary School Textbooks* (New York: Anti-Defamation League of B'nai B'rith, 1961).

[9] *See*, for example, *The Negroes in the United States, Their Economic and Social Situation* (Washington, D.C.: U.S. Department of Labor, 1966). The *Monthly Labor Review* periodically publishes illuminating reports on the subject. An illustration would be D. K. Newman, "The Negro's Journey to the City," which appeared in May and June 1965 and was then reprinted as Special Report 2466, U.S. Department of Labor, Bureau of Labor Statistics. Some governmental analyses receive broader publication, such as Mollie Orshansky, "Counting the Poor: Another Look at the Poverty Profile," *Social Security Bulletin*, Vol. 28, No. 1 (January 1965), pp. 3–29, which was reprinted in L. A. Ferman, J. L. Kornbluh, and Alan Haber, eds., *Poverty in America* (Ann Arbor: University of Michigan Press, 1965), pp. 42–81. Not so statistical but illuminating is Alvin L. Schorr's *Slums and Social Insecurity*, Research Report No. 1 (Washington, D.C.: Social Security Administration, U.S. Department of Health, Education, and Welfare, 1963). *See also* the reports of the U.S. Commission on Civil Rights.

aration for the Institute on Research Toward Improving Race Relations. In the first, a brief questionnaire was sent to persons invited to participate in the institute, requesting that they identify research studies that were especially good in race relations content relevant to social work and that also used excellent research techniques. Other questions asked for opinions about research techniques that were overused or underused in the study of prejudice, discrimination, or segregation.

Most of the nineteen replies (out of forty-five requests) contained disclaimers of expertise in the field of race relations research, despite the fact that this was the basis on which invitations to the institute were sent. Only four of the correspondents identified a recent "best" study of race relations. The studies cited were Williams' *Strangers Next Door*, Coleman's study with the Department of Education, the Moynihan report, and the 1967 U.S. Civil Rights Commission report, *Racial Isolation in the Public Schools*.[10] Three replies mentioned "excellent studies" in which specific research techniques were utilized. Four respondents answered the questions dealing with overused and underused research techniques. One person identified the overused techniques of

pen-and-paper self-reports concerning attitudes and behavior (despite evidence of low validity); overstructured questionnaires, sometimes with double-barreled questions and sometimes distorting complex attitudes by

forcing a uni-dimensional answer; and reliance on the one-variable hypotheses to "explain" complex social phenomena.

For underused techniques he listed participant observation, anthropological field studies, extended exploratory investigations, combinations of quantitative and qualitative data, and combinations of historical, legal, sociological, psychological, and anthropological approaches. Two other respondents mentioned participant observation as an underused technique and one noted the lack of longitudinal studies.

The meager response to this inventory was at least in part due to the limited time (ten days) given for replies to the questionnaire. However, responses such as these were common: "Sorry. Not acquainted with this area of research." "I would like to oblige, but must unhappily say that I am not well enough read in the current race-relations field for a reply to be meaningful." "Sorry, indeed, that I do not feel sufficiently familiar with the field currently to answer your questions."

A second inventory produced a similar finding. A survey was made of the race-related contents of eleven sociological and social work journals published from January 1965 through April 1967.[11] Seventy-four articles were found that were peripherally about research in race relations. The samples in seventy of these studies were of fewer than fifty persons. All seventy-four dealt with cases from a single time period.

The findings of these two inventories buttress the authors' conclusions that there is a great need for comprehensive, empirical studies of concrete situations involving race and social work that use diverse, reinforcing techniques: statistical, historical, and direct observation. One

---

[10] Robin M. Williams, Jr., *Strangers Next Door: Ethnic Relations in American Communities* (Englewood Cliffs, N.J.: Prentice-Hall, 1964); *The Negro Family, the Case for National Action* (Washington, D.C.: U.S. Department of Labor, March 1965) (the Moynihan report); *Racial Isolation in the Public Schools* (Washington, D.C.: U.S. Commission on Civil Rights, 1967); J. S. Coleman *et al.*, *Equality of Educational Opportunity* (Washington, D.C.: U.S. Department of Health, Education, and Welfare and the Office of Education, 1966).

[11] This survey was made by Ann Whitley on an assignment for a seminar in social work research at the School of Social Work, University of Washington, 1967.

might ask if this is the proper subject matter for social work researchers. Certainly in the past the great social welfare historical sociologists—researchers such as Frederic Le Play, Charles Booth, the Webbs, the Hammonds, Philip Klein, and others—were concerned with the lives of the poor.[12] It should also be remembered that the first great study of a Negro community, the study of Philadelphia Negroes by W. E. B. DuBois, was commissioned by a neighborhood social agency.

What kinds of cultural-historical studies are needed for the improvement of social work with Negroes and other minorities? Two areas will be dealt with, the Negro subculture and crosscultural relations.

Nature of the Negro Subculture

Are there, as some writers claim, certain characteristics that distinguish the life-styles of Negroes, especially lower-class Negroes, from the life-styles of Caucasians at a similar economic level? Are the problems of the Negro poor different from those of the Caucasian poor? Have historical factors resulted in the development of a Negro subculture that should be considered in working with Negro clients or in seeking to improve majority-minority relations? Significant cultural variations, if any, should be sorted out.

Myrdal, for example, says that American Negro culture "is a distorted development, or a pathological condition, of the general American culture." [13] Is a pathological condition really involved? Kenneth Clark also writes of the "pathology of the ghetto." [14]

What does this mean in cultural terms? Is it really pathology or meaningful adjustment to reality? Does the pathology refer to the conditions or to the residents' response to the conditions? This must be determined.

Some social work writers have rejected the idea of cultural uniqueness per se for Negroes. Allen, for example, says:

[The Negro group in America] has no distinctive culture and no peculiar social institutions. It knows only the culture of America, and the points at which behavior differs can be attributed to external influences such as the social and economic limitations which have been imposed upon it and the resultant and inevitable psychological effects of such limitations.[15]

Manning quotes him and adds:

The Negro's so-called racial characteristics are culturally determined ways of adapting to, or retreating from, or getting even with, a world that considers him and treats him as an inferior.[16]

We are, of course, starting from the premise that any cultural differences that may exist have absolutely no basis in genetics and are the result of man-made conditions. Milton Gordon explains ethnic group differences in terms of subculture and subsociety. Subculture, as he defines it, means

. . . the cultural patterns of a subsociety which contains both sexes, all ages and family groups, and which parallels the larger society in that it provides for a network of groups and institutions extending throughout the individual's entire life cycle.[17]

---

[12] A brief account of these studies appears in Pauline V. Young, *Scientific Social Surveys and Research* (3d ed.; Englewood Cliffs, N.J.: Prentice-Hall, 1956), pp. 3–40.

[13] Gunnar Myrdal, *An American Dilemma* (New York: Harper & Bros., 1944), p. 928.

[14] Kenneth B. Clark, *Dark Ghetto* (New York: Harper & Row, 1965).

[15] Alexander J. Allen, "A Commentary on Studies of Negro Adoptions," in David Fanshel, *A Study in Negro Adoption* (New York: Child Welfare League of America, 1957), p. 87.

[16] Seaton W. Manning, "Cultural and Value Factors Affecting the Negro's Use of Agency Services," *Social Work*, Vol. 5, No. 4 (October 1960), p. 5.

[17] *Assimilation in American Life* (New York: Oxford University Press, 1964), p. 36.

The preconditions for the development of this subculture, as Gordon sees it, are a set of relationships in which members of an ethnic group are interdependent with other members of the group and have closer ties within the group than with the larger society. He sees a subsociety (and the subculture that goes with it) existing when

within the ethnic group there develops a network of organizations with informal social relationships which permits and encourages the members of the ethnic group to remain within the confines of the group for all of their primary relationships and some of their secondary relationships throughout all the stages of the life-cycle.[18]

An area needing more comprehensive research would, therefore, appear to be comparison of life-styles and attitudes of lower-class Negroes with their counterparts in the white community or in mixed neighborhoods. Studies dealing with life-styles and their relationship to values held by segments of the population have tended to stress economic variables without making a distinction between Negroes and Caucasians. While intuitively we may sense that being a Negro in a racist society helps create a value structure significantly different from that of the general culture, more explicit information on the subject is still needed.

Most ghettos are not residentially uniracial and some whites have vested interests or other affiliations there. Should a ghetto be characterized as a community rather than a subculture? What is its cohesiveness or lack of it, its relationship to the rest of the metropolis, the functions it serves, its resistance or willingness to change, the resistance or willingness of the larger society to see it changed?

Crosscultural Relations

Although the social structure in the United States has no parallel elsewhere,

---

[18] *Ibid.*, p. 34.

much of recorded history has dealt with conflict between oppressor and oppressed, majority and minority populations, and the struggles of the minority for their place in the sun. Colonialism is being challenged in many parts of the world. In what way are there similarities to the struggle for equality in this country?

With new nations being established in Africa under Negro leadership, it is necessary to examine the impact of this development on Negro self-concept and action in this country. What bonds of sympathy exist with other movements for "liberation"? To what extent do Negroes "identify" with colonial movements for independence? What "solutions" to racial conflict may be discovered in other countries that would be adaptable to this one?[19]

Organizational Research

Another area with high research priority for social work deals with organizational change. Two basic premises underline the importance of organization theory for social work and social work research. First, social work should be viewed as a form of social organization, with stasis and change being inseparable parts of the organizational process. Furthermore, the everyday practice of social work should be viewed as directed toward bringing about benevolent changes in social organization.

---

[19] A good start in this direction is found in Immanuel Wallerstein, *Social Change: The Colonial Situation* (New York: John Wiley & Sons, 1966). *See* especially G. Balandier, "The Colonial Situation: A Theoretical Approach," pp. 34–61. R. A. Schermerhorn has developed theories of majority-minority relations that are useful in such an analysis. *See* his "Toward a General Theory of Minority Groups," *Phylon*, Vol. 25, No. 3 (Fall 1964), pp. 238–246. H. M. Blalock, Jr., also pursues this approach in *Toward a Theory of Minority Group Relations* (New York: John Wiley & Sons, 1967). G. K. Zollschan and Walter Hirsch provide a broad theoretical context for such an analysis in their book *Explorations in Social Change* (Boston: Houghton-Mifflin, 1964).

If these premises are valid, then to be effective the social worker must be a competent organization theorist and the social work researcher must be concerned with generating and testing organization theory.

For the purposes of this paper, social organization is defined as the process of applying constraints to human behavior in an environment in which options are available. The structural product of organization is a pattern of interactive relationships among persons defining the lines of authority, responsibility, and communication.[20] A broad view of social organization is adopted in this paper. The concept is not limited just to formal work establishments, but pertains to all recurrent patterns of interactive relationships.

At the beginning of the paper the writers asserted that activities and decisions in social work practice inevitably are affected by racial considerations in a race-conscious, multiracial society such as the United States. If this assertion is true, then racial considerations must affect the forms and activities of organization, even social work organization.

Social workers at times have appeared to avoid the issue of race by taking a "color-blind" stance, holding to the view that need for the service per se, regardless of race, should be the only criterion for guiding relations with clients. This may have been a progressive position in certain local situations when services were not previously offered to Negroes or were offered on a discriminatory basis. The Civil Rights Act of 1964, plus other legislation, court decisions, and administrative decrees by the federal government, however, have now largely confirmed "legal" rights to service on an equal basis. These measures have

not compensated for conditions that exist as a result of heritages from the past. They give support to professed democratic aims and they give social workers instruments with which to work. But the present condition of the Negro population was not created as a result of color-blindness. It is unrealistic to expect that real change can be effected without an equal consciousness of color in change efforts. Social work needs to be not only color-conscious but color-wise; Negroes are not just clients —they are *Negro* clients, and research efforts need to be directed at their special sets of problems and at finding appropriate ways of dealing with them. What kinds of organizational studies are needed for the improvement of social work with Negroes and other minorities?

Agency Segregation and Discrimination

Perhaps the first priority in organizational studies is one that answers the question: To what extent does improper discrimination against minorities actually exist in social welfare?[21] What steps might be taken to correct it where it does exist? In response to a query sent out by the writers in 1965 to the national offices of sixteen major welfare organizations, assurances were received from all of them that they have policies on a national level of nondiscrimination because of race.[22] It is, of course, quite expedient to have such a written policy in order to share in many of the federally financed programs. The

---

[20] Of course, much more is needed for an adequate definition of social organization. For this, *see* Lawrence K. Northwood and Robert L. Reed, "Organization and Change: Theoretical Guides" (Seattle: University of Washington School of Social Work, 1967). (Mimeographed.)

[21] Under certain circumstances compensatory services are provided to the disadvantaged group. Such compensatory services would be considered a "proper" form of discrimination.

[22] The results of this survey will be reported in full in a forthcoming book, Lawrence K. Northwood and Robert L. Reed, *Race and Social Welfare: A Manual for Social Workers*, which is being prepared with the assistance of a grant from the Anti-Defamation League of B'nai B'rith.

question is this: To what extent does a policy of nondiscrimination actually prevail in hiring of staff and service provision?

National organizations have varying degrees of control over their local affiliates. In another survey reported by the Seattle Urban League it was stated that (1) assistance and counseling of nearly half the health and welfare agencies in King County seldom if ever reach beyond a white clientele to the Negro members of the community, (2) employment of Negroes as professional or nonprofessional staff members is nonexistent in half the agencies in the country, and (3) there is a total lack of nonwhite representation on nearly half the policy-making boards of agencies throughout the country.[23] One would suspect that this is rather typical of other areas of the country. One national youth organization replied:

We have always operated on a philosophy of nondiscrimination, but since our program is locally applied, there are, of course, the differences occasioned by attitudes in different parts of the country.

This does not imply that welfare organizations are not concerned with the problem of race relations or that progress has not been made in recent years. The known facts, however, are far too limited, and it appears that few national organizations have made real studies of the situation among their own affiliates.[24] The authors do suggest that discrimination exists in social welfare and it is perfectly consistent with our professional role as social workers to be concerned with the facts. Again, the problem is not one of just cataloging

---

[23] *Social Welfare Agencies and the Negro* (Seattle: Seattle Urban League, 1967).

[24] One notable exception is the study by St. Clair Drake, *Race Relations in a Time of Rapid Social Change* (New York: National Federation of Settlements and Neighborhood Centers, 1966). The YWCA has also consistently published material showing the extent to which their facilities are integrated. There may have been other studies of which the writers are not aware.

percentages of Negro staff and clientele—although that is a good starting point—but of examining the availability of programs and services to Negroes and the extent to which they meet actual needs of this population segment.

Questions of the order just dealt with are essentially ethical and pragmatic. The research to determine the answers, thus, is appropriately called evaluative research. An ethical standard is required before the "improper" forms of discrimination can be identified. The results of the investigation pertain to the specific organization undergoing study; that is, the research is pragmatic. Scientifically based social work will need to be founded on knowledge of a more theoretically general order than that produced by evaluative research. In race relations, for example, this means that we must be able to state the organizational conditions that bring about and dissolve racial segregation. An executive order can proclaim an end to segregation in institutional facilities and to discriminatory practices in the employment of its personnel. But the executive order says little about the individual, social, and cultural factors that are required to achieve an enduring organizational change. For this, more basic study is required.

Organizational Strategies

One kind of much-needed basic study is of effective strategies for the formal organization of segments of the community. Some of the critical questions about strategies were raised during the civil rights revolution of the past five years. The attempt to achieve the goal of maximum feasible participation of the poor in the antipoverty programs has brought this issue to the attention of social workers even more forcibly. Such questions as these arise: What are the optimum forms of organization to achieve maximum feasible participation—those based on locality, such as a block club or neighborhood council, or those based on the mutual interests of a target population, such as a tenants' council or a group of welfare mothers? If the guiding strategy is locality, then how large a geographic area should be embraced? If the guiding strategy is mutual interest, then should there be just one program emphasis or many? When both forms of organization are found, the questions sometimes become these: What forms of organization are compatible? What mix of organizations creates or nourishes conflict? When the slogan of Black Power is raised, one asks: In what forms of organization can and should Negroes and whites work together? What are the enduring organizational effects of work through segregated structures? What organizational conditions contribute to ghetto formation? As the community is fragmented, knowledge about the forms of federation and coalition becomes essential.

Nonparticipation and Protest

Studies are needed about unwillingness to participate in formal organizations. It is customary to attribute such nonparticipation to individual apathy or anomie. Such propositions should be examined from an organization theory perspective. Perhaps the person who refuses to participate in groups and agencies organized by social workers is engaged fully elsewhere, in family, friendship, or kinship networks, in institutionalized patterns of the minority community, or in organized forms of the "illegitimate opportunity structure." In such a case it may be more correct to characterize nonparticipation as alienation rather than anomie. Examination of nonparticipation will probably bring the researcher into a direct consideration of the community conditions that result in protest, uprisings, and other forms of radical social

change. A high priority for research should be given to the study of social movements and the conditions under which these occur and are transformed. It is not sufficient to treat the current city riots and uprisings as a dramatic set of unique events. Historical, cultural, and organizational research are required for the proper understanding of their shape, form, and progression.

Psychosocial Research

Despite the recent push of the social worker into the mainstream of organizational change, much of his work will continue to be with individual clients for extended periods of time and in one-to-one or small group relationships. A variety of race-related research problems pertain to the nature of social work of this order. Perhaps the most important refers to how problems of racial prejudice affect social work practice and ways of coping with this professionally. What is needed is knowledge about the conditions that create problems for the client and block personal problem-solving, whether the client is Negro or Caucasian. To what extent is the individual social worker limited in his effectiveness because of prejudiced attitudes that may not even be recognized by him as such? Does the extent of prejudice among social workers differ significantly from that found among the general population? What barriers may exist between worker and client when one is Caucasian and the other Negro? How can the prejudiced person be changed? What methods of seeking change are effective? What are the damages to the prejudiced person if this "crutch" is removed? What can be substituted?

Can one speak of a "pathology of prejudice" in which the prejudiced individual thinks and acts in accordance with norms widely held by those with whom he associates, but when the whole group or section of the population has extreme racist views? The study of group norms and their relation to prejudice would seem to fall into the first category mentioned—the societal level. Beyond that, however, is the effect of prejudice on the individual. Jahoda and Berelson and Steiner stress the relationship of prejudice to personality disorder. Berelson and Steiner say:

The personality of a prejudiced person tends to be characterized by one or more of the following factors: high frustration and displaced aggression; neuroticism; conservatism, conventionalism and conformism, authoritarianism and orientation to power; projection of undesired impulses (notably sexual ones) and sexual repression; rigidity and intolerance of ambiguity; insecurity; cynicism; a "jungle philosophy of life." [25]

Jahoda says that, in one sense, prejudice is "an attitude toward out-groups which refrains from reality testing . . . because the attitude itself fulfills a specific irrational function for its bearer." [26] As such, it

would appear to be an inappropriate problem-solving mechanism that stands in the way of constructive solutions for individual problems. If prejudice is recognized as an obstacle hampering social work efforts, then clearly what is needed is more information on how to deal with it as a professional responsibility.

Summary

In this paper the authors have attempted to document the position that social work research must be concerned with race relations practices involving the profession because this is crucial to good work. Such research will help in the implementation of institutionalized values of the profession (1) by dispelling myths, (2) by identifying imminent problem situations and appropriate countermeasures, and (3) by evaluating the effectiveness of courses of ameliorative intervention. The need for theoretically general research in the investigation of social work practice has been stressed. Within the time limits of the paper and based on the writers' own personal preferences, an agenda for research has been suggested that will enhance knowledge of the subject at hand.

---

[25] Bernard Berelson and Gary A. Steiner, *Human Behavior: An Inventory of Scientific Findings* (New York: Harcourt, Brace & World, 1964), p. 515.

[26] Marie Jahoda, "Race Relations and Mental Health," in *Race and Science* (New York: UNESCO, 1961), p. 455.

Discussion

Herzog observed early in the institute that agreement was found when ideas were expressed in highly abstract terms, but that differences emerged at lower levels of abstraction. This was certainly borne out in the discussions of issues and opportunities for the study of race relations in social work. There was consensus that research should be parsimoniously directed to important professional issues in the area of race relations. However, quite individual and divergent views were held about the translation of these principles into research practice. Implicit to the discussion were different models for research, associated strategic preferences, and consequent choices of targets for investigation.

Although the positions advanced by the discussants about the research enterprise add nothing new to a dialogue with which investigators have long been involved, they provide a convenient frame of reference for describing the course of the far-ranging discussion. Proselytizing efforts were not entirely absent, but there was little pressure toward consensus. Instead, the participants agreed to disagree on a number of points, in an atmosphere of tolerance for diversity.

Research Models

Tacitly accepted as the aim for social work research was the production of knowledge useful for practice, broadly conceived. Varied assumptions were evident about the organization of research activity conducive to the realization of this aim. The models held by the discussants differed in the place assigned to theory in knowledge-building efforts; characteristics of research knowledge; relationships among investigators and the professional, scientific, and lay communities; and the mission most appropriate to social work research.

Role of Theory in Knowledge-Building

Theory—organized explanatory knowledge—was, of course, seen as the desirable end-product of research. But how useful or dangerous is theory as a starting point for research? One polar position about this fundamental issue was expressed as follows:

NORTHWOOD. I don't believe in research for the sake of research. It has got to have a theoretical base, and the kind of research that we should be concerned with is research that flows two ways: one to practice, and the other to generalized knowledge. Therefore we have to have a sound theoretical base on which to do our research. I take a completely negative view of pragmatic research conducted just for the sake of research.

When I start a piece of research I usually search for theoretical propositions, to see what has been done in the field without relation directly to race itself. If I can conceptualize what I am looking at as the socialization process, I look at the socialization-related literature and then make my application to race within the theoretically general framework.

It was subsequently observed that this approach to the conduct of a study also allows an opportunity to transpose findings from one population to another. For example, knowledge about the acquisition of power relevant to race relations might be found in the study of protest operations with regard to the war in Vietnam. Exploitation of theoretical linkages would thus bypass the problem of starting every investigation of a special population as if nothing were known about these people or their conditions and ending every investigation as if nothing learned from this population were relevant to other populations.

An alternate strategy for research in race relations was recommended:

HERZOG. It seems to me that the history of research has been discovering that we were asking the wrong questions about the

wrong problems, and that the reason we were doing it was that we did not know enough about the problem. So I would like to put in my vote for focusing on the people and the conditions and the context. The classic research approach is to study a problem before you start developing a structured questionnaire. And I have the feeling that here we are talking about how we will word the questions on our questionnaire before we have done the exploratory investigations that should show us what questions we should be interested in.

A similar position was the following recommendation of an inductive approach to theory development:

BLUMER. The really great problem that confronts the field of social work in carrying on research is actually a very simple problem in one sense. It is how to get down and lift the veils from what is going on in their area of operation, just to try to find out really what the operating milieu is. I am bold enough or frightfully naïve enough, if you please, to declare that in trying to lift these veils the best thing to do is to rely on a very inquiring mind, very critical judgment, great honesty in trying to find out what is going on, and consequently inaugurating all kinds of flexible, probing means of digging into this world and not taking it for granted on the basis of one's picture of it in the past. I don't think that this is going to be accomplished by trying to import the theories, the conceptual schemes, or the methods of sophisticated investigation from other fields.

Other participants shared Blumer's skepticism about the utility of theory for directing research: Is it possible at times to be too theoretical and abstract for the problem being studied? If you try to answer both a theoretical and practical question at the same time, do you end up answering neither?

NORTHWOOD. Suppose you've got a team of nine qualified researchers who are instructed just to enter into the action and see what happens. And once they arrive at the doorstep they need to talk about something and they have to have some way of classifying what they have talked about. You know, you don't wait until after you get a whole lot of data and then sit down and say: "Well, now I have been in action. I have swum around in it. I ran into a few rocks. So I will say I have got a rock there," and then classify all that action after you get through. Now I am sure Dr. Blumer is not saying that, because I have read a good deal of his work.

BLUMER. [Dr. Northwood] and I are both interested in exactly the same thing: in studying a problem in such a way as to arrive at an intelligent, verifiable analysis of it. But his approach to it and mine are markedly different.

Voiced by other participants was an acceptance of both the hypothetical-logical-deductive model illustrated by Northwood and the inductive-empirical model favored by others. Rothman observed, for example, that it is legitimate to adopt a specific theoretical stance to see if it explains something relevant to social work, but that a different kind of research procedure might be required in order to develop understanding of some social work problems.

Research and the Nature of Knowledge

Implicit in the contribution of several participants was a conception of knowledge as a more or less fixed truth, the capturing of which is the responsibility of the investigator. One of the goals held for this conference—the identification of gaps in race relations research—contains a hint of this position. Like research in chemistry that filled in the blanks on the periodic table, social work research may supply missing knowledge about race relations.

The conception of research as a dependable source of knowledge received clear expression in Goldstein's contribution. In an attempt to establish the extent to which research-based knowledge about race relations is used in practice, Goldstein reviewed all reports of race relations research appearing in sixteen social work journals during the past decade. From his survey of social agencies, he found no evidence of changes in social work practice consequent to research on race relations.[1]

GOLDSTEIN. So where does this leave us? It seems to me that somehow or other we must improve the ability of the professional social worker to use research and somehow or other try to increase his willingness to do so.

An alternate conception of research as comprising merely one approach to knowledge-building was advanced by other participants. Any equation of research with knowledge was seen as a narcissistically satisfying fiction in view of the substantial if problematic body of professional knowledge that antedated the advent of social work research. The reception accorded research findings was seen as in part a function of how the findings fit in with existing partially organized knowledge.

GOLDSTEIN. I think the value system of society often represents a kind of distillation of non-research-based knowledge. But I think the knowledge that social work has to use must be reliable and consistent; one should be able to predict consequences from it. Now if this kind of knowledge comes from some other place than research, fine. It has been my experience that not much of that kind of knowledge comes from other sources.

MILLER. Has it been your experience that much of that comes from research?

GOLDSTEIN. Not very much.

MILLER. It seems to me that you are taking a solid stand that there is knowledge and it gets established and it is tied down once and for all. I think you can take an alternative perspective that everything we do is an approximation, a somewhat crude approach, to something like the truth.

GOLDSTEIN. I suppose it is related to what you consider knowledge. If I had a dream last night about something, I don't consider that knowledge in the sense that I am talking about knowledge.

NATHAN COHEN. It may be real knowledge.

---

[1] Harris K. Goldstein, "Some Factors Influencing Changes in Social Work Practice Based on Race Relations Research 1957–1967." Paper prepared for the Institute on Research Toward Improving Race Relations, August 1967, Warrenton, Va. (Mimeographed; available from the author.)

SCHWARTZ. Or at the minimum it may become research data.

GOLDSTEIN. Yes, it does. You tell it to your analyst. But until you do, no.

The divergent ideas about the nature of knowledge and its relationship to research received practical expression in the answers to a simple question: When is further research unnecessary? In one answer to this question, the consensus of the researchers was regarded as decisive. Further documentation of the inadequacy of welfare grants and of the disadvantaged position of the Negro were seen as unnecessary because of the consensus reached in the scientific community about these matters. Others expressed greater concern for consensus among the consumers of research. The prevalence of uncertainties or misconceptions among the consumers of research seemed to some to dictate additional research and interpretive activity. Orshansky observed that even points on which consensus has been achieved may require reinvestigation subsequently as new knowledge or new patterns of thought or behavior have an effect. And while some participants expressed concern about the resistance to research findings, others indicated concern about the uncritical acceptance of research contributions.

Social Work Research and Social Work

Problems of race relations research were addressed from a range of assumptions about the mission of social work research and the appropriate relationship between investigator and practitioner. In distinction to the producer-consumer relationship advanced by Goldstein was a conception of collaboration held by others. Nathan Cohen suggested that practitioners, who are struggling with the problems of service delivery, generally may be in the best position to identify significant research questions. Denny extended this argument with

the observation that the practitioner is in fact interested in research on practice problems and uses the results of such research. In the case of Fanshel's study of Negro adoptive applicants, many adoption agencies changed their policies and lowered restrictions that had worked against Negro applicants. Nathan Cohen reported checking a number of Robin Williams' hypotheses about race relationships against the experience of about a dozen agencies:

NATHAN COHEN. I found an interesting thing. They could not identify the hypotheses in the terms stated, but they were formulating policy as if they knew the hypotheses.

Herzog suggested that perhaps the agencies knew about these matters before they had been discovered and labeled by research.

Some reservations were expressed about the ability of the practitioner to identify research issues. Herzog suggested that retrieving suitable questions from the field may require some research in its own right: "I think it really means having a one-way screen, listening to case conferences, and reading case records." Lewis called for differentiation among potential research collaborators on the basis that the problems of the administrator, the supervisor, and the line worker are different. Billingsley suggested that in searching for study questions a variety of sources be used.

BILLINGSLEY. Maybe we ought to look at theoretical literature. Maybe we ought to look at practice. Maybe we ought to go back and forth. But I think we ought not to be restricted to what practitioners are doing every day. I think we ought to look beyond what the practitioners are doing and are concerned about, to their potential clients in the community who are not even identified yet by the agency.

Different emphases were given by individual participants to the missions of assembling proof, discovery, and promoting change. Schwartz expressed greatest interest in research bearing on policy and suggested that the absence of policy implications might well be considered a contraindication to the undertaking of social work research. From this vantage point he challenged Herzog's decision to demonstrate the strength and diversity among one-parent families.

SCHWARTZ. I could see a case for this if we had reason to believe that at the present time social workers make negative assumptions about one-parent families. But my own feeling is that this is an area in which there is little evidence of bias in the social work profession. I would think that most caseworkers are educated and prepared to look for strengths in this kind of a family.

Herzog saw the research as potentially corrective of the orientations of social workers, legislators, and the public at large, and clearly shared a concern with policy emanating from research. Her emphasis, however, was on proof-oriented research.

HERZOG. One part of the research mission should be to dispel myths and describe reality. I think there are two different functions for research. One is to find out, the other is to convince.

Rothman saw an advantage in distinguishing between long- and short-range research objectives; for example, long-range research would be directed toward promoting more two-parent families in the Negro community, while short-range concern might be focused on strengthening the one-parent family.

ROTHMAN. In terms of the urgency of our racial situation, it seems to me that this is a less immediate research problem and a more immediate programmatic problem. We are in greater need of action ideas than research ideas at this time.

Herzog doubted that the ideas would come from research, although she believed that research could be useful in evaluating an array of competing ideas.

Other participants were more optimistic about research as a source of ideas. Implicit in some comments was a conception of discovery as an important mission for social work research. Jerome Cohen, for example, recommended studies to discover the conditions under which subcultural identities can be promoted and enhanced. More general interest was expressed in discovering the capacities and accessibility of potential adoptive families and the problems and service needs of adopted children and their families. A subject close at hand evoked the most pressing interest in discovery-oriented research, however: Under what conditions does research become a force for social change?

Although examples were given of policy or practice changes emanating from research, no simple connections between research and change were envisioned. The impact of research on policy, for example, was described as more apparent than real:

COHNSTAEDT. I have a feeling that when research came out [that] was influential in changing policies, most likely [it] came out because it was time for that policy to be changed and there was an institutional readiness for it.

Northwood suggested an even more remote connection between research and change.

NORTHWOOD. People don't move on the basis of what is rationally found out by research. They move in terms of what options are available to them in terms of resources, where support can be derived for program, or where somebody has a strong interest and they push it forward. Most changes occasioned by evaluative research occur before the results are published.

The history of planned parenthood was reviewed as a case example of how research findings are mediated by social forces in bringing about social changes:

LEWIS. I think that research played a secondary role in this. In the beginning it was the movement—the idea. A small group of people persisted under conflict and through publicity attracted some interest and support. The support was limited, however, until concern developed about population control on a worldwide basis related to hunger, politics, and a number of other features. . . . the specter of fear got to be the lever. So within the last ten or fifteen years, or the last five years in fact, there has been a remarkable flipflop by public welfare agencies, politicians, and influence-makers. They have licked the specter of the church's opposition. They have licked the specter of immorality and ethics. . . . One cannot help but think that this represents a convergence of a variety of interests, some of which are obviously concerned about a better order, or about choice on the part of all people, but others are concerned with the size of the welfare roll.

Herzog observed that research in this area functioned like a catalyst, facilitating action among other forces: "I think this is why sometimes we have to do an old study over again, because the time was not ripe before."

The distance between research and the scene of action was viewed with varying degrees of discomfort. Northwood pointed to some fundamental differences between research and practice and questioned whether these activities must converge with one another.

NORTHWOOD. When a practitioner reads a research report, he can't find something that is immediately translatable into practice except a finding that perhaps helps him interpret what he is doing. We don't develop thermometers in our research that a practitioner can apply directly. There is a kind of mediation process that goes on between what research turns up and how it is applied.

Other observers were less sanguine about the gap between research and practice and saw in the mediation process identified by Northwood an opportunity for research.

BATCHELDER. Researchers are really writing for each other, with the assumption that the action consequences are either obvious or somebody else's job. But I think there is room for specialization on the interpretation of research, to derive from existing

research some of the concrete, practical applications and to indicate how they might be tested.

SCHWARTZ. Yes, it seems to me that a large part of social work research can be in that area. Propositions as they come from the social and behavioral sciences have to be tested and adapted to social work practice. A very important function of social work researchers is to stand between the social scientist and the practitioner, to listen to both, and then to play a variety of integrative and interpretive roles. Partly this entails selection of the opportune time to initiate the research and, at the other end, identification of the potentialities and implications of the findings for practice.

Lewis elaborated on this theme with a review of the reception accorded to a research-based conception: lower-class culture.

LEWIS. It may make a great deal of sense in a seminar on culture and change and so on. But if you ask what the the programmatic aspects of it are, you're dead. Under the press of looking for answers, the imaginative idea—lower-class culture—comes in. You remember the historical setting. The social work profession was set on fire. Instead of spelling out programmatic implications of the idea, it was taken as the reality. It took on a momentum of its own, and was taught without the qualifications. The working out of it in the practical field situations never happened. The worker doesn't know what to do with the idea when he has it.

Research Targets

No attempt was made to catalog the issues in race relations meriting study; even if such a listing were possible, its relevance to research practice would be doubtful in view of the stylistic diversity among investigators. The discussion did, however, generate a number of suggestions about study topics.

Broad strategic issues evoked general interest from the participants. What are the barriers that obstruct efforts to alleviate the problems connected with race? In preference to further descriptions of the problems, about which considerable knowledge is available, many saw the advantage of directing research to the dynamics of social change. Attractive targets within this domain were seen to include local participation and political action, the decision-making operations of local political structures, the functioning of an elite power group, the current and changing value positions of various interests in the community, including the Negro community, strategies for promoting shifts in power, the course of separatism, Black Nationalism, and Black Power. Behind these broad questions were strategic questions for the profession: What roles are possible and appropriate for social work in the sociopolitical arena of race relations? What direct action can be taken by organized social work in the power struggle that appears to be intensifying? What indirect, supportive options are available to social work?

The attempt to locate the specific social work opportunities for the indirect support of race relations changes served to identify a host of programmatic study issues. What happens when you just give people money? What are the orientations and needs of potential clients and how can they be served? What resources for self-help and development exist within the community itself? How are clinical decisions made and how does the worker's orientation to race enter into these?

The interest expressed in conducting research on virtually every point that came up for discussion led the chairman to suggest that a manual be prepared giving directions about "what to do until the researcher comes." Research was, however, not seen as a substitute for action. The only suggestion that change efforts be deferred pending further study brought a sharp rejoinder:

ORSHANSKY. Why is it that when we sit here and discuss the things that we know need to be done we feel paralyzed by lack of knowledge? Can you imagine what it must be like for an administrator or a congressman? When we give subsidies to farmers and ship-builders, we do it first because we have a reason for doing it and a goal; we test it later.

Summary Observations

The invitation to attend the Institute on Research Toward Improving Race Relations was received by at least one participant with some apprehension: "Do they really know what they are getting into? Is this trip really necessary?" No doubt others also approached the meeting with guarded expectations. The topic of race relations is broad and complex; indeed, it is difficult to identify any domain in the behavioral sciences that is wholly irrelevant to it. What can be accomplished by talking for a few days about so inclusive a subject?

The institute was used as a forum for the exchange of ideas about race relations by participants who brought to the assignment a variety of backgrounds and perspectives. In efforts to find common ground, to establish and maintain communication, the discussion was drawn toward inclusive, general conceptions rather than precise, technical ones. Inevitably, the conclusions at which individual participants had arrived were more fully expressed than were the bases for these conclusions. In the time available, it was not possible to take full advantage of the expertise brought to the meeting. Depth of penetration was thus to some extent sacrificed to breadth of coverage.

Perspective on Race Relations

Central to the institute was the articulation of a generally shared perspective on the nature of contemporary race relations in America. The existence of racism, pervading the entire society, was accepted as an unwelcome social reality. Manifested by attitudes attached to an evolving social construction of race, stabilized and sustained by numerous institutional arrangements, racism was seen to be polarizing America into white oppressors and black oppressed. That the inequities systematically visited on the Negro minority occur in some instances by accident or inadvertence makes clear the extent to which we are all victims of racism. Corrosive alike are the brutalization of the sensibilities of the oppressors and the dehumanization imposed upon the oppressed by our social arrangements. Our experience thus far in attempting to surmount racism makes clear the extent to which we are all captives of this force.

The macroscopic level of analysis undertaken at the institute was appropriate to the topic: The subject of race relations is peculiarly vulnerable to conceptual dissolution when otherwise viewed. Only at some distance from the phenomenological world is it possible to see something about the pattern of interacting forces that comprise race relations. On closer examination the subject devolves into myriad facets. Individual personality development, including identity formation; family processes, including those unique to one-parent families; self-help movements, including Black Nationalism; economics, including trade union policies; politics, including the avenues for local participation—these and many other facets of our social world are involved in race relations. They are not, however, race relations; for the most part they are not even specific to the subject. Only from the simultaneous consideration of such interrelated components does the subject of race relations emerge. Inclusive and general conceptions thus appear to be indispensable in order to achieve sufficient distance from its component facets for the subject of race relations to become visible.

Social Work in the Context of Racism

There is reason to believe that the broad perspective developed during the institute can be especially useful for social work. The field has been long and intimately involved with some facets of these social processes. Because social work's attempts to serve the individual, the group, the neighborhood, and the community have so regularly engaged social work practitioners with manifestations of racial matters, it has been possible to assume that we have addressed the issue and have devised appropriate programmatic responses. An inclusive examination of the dimensions of the problems associated with race suggests otherwise.

The fact that social work has been involved with racial matters is certainly not remarkable; no social institution has avoided such engagement. Equally nonremarkable is the likelihood that our intentions, more often than not, have been honorable. Noteworthy from an overview of race relations is the evidence that social work's professional values, knowledge, and skills have failed to insulate us against the broad social forces that promote racism. Painfully evident too is the marginality of our response to the central problem of racism.

A look at social work in the context of racism identifies some action goals for the profession. Most obviously, we must put our house in order. Discrimination in the administration of social services must be eliminated. In addition, we are obliged to continue efforts to surmount the inadvertent barriers impeding service delivery.

The challenge to social work identified by the context of racism extends beyond that of simply putting our existing house in order. The currents of social change afford the occasion for instituting some long-needed renovations and additions to the social welfare structure. The growing public interest in and pressure for the construction of more adequate income maintenance provisions, better protections for the family, and more extensive social service coverage helps to create an opportunity to achieve a major transformation of the social welfare system. The challenge to social work is to help channel the forces for change toward the creation of social arrangements that will enhance the well-being of all citizens.

In relating to a problem embedded in individual and institution alike, with complex and evolving dynamics of its own, social work can benefit from the considerable diversity encompassed in the field. The contributions of the caseworker, group worker, and community organization practitioner are needed along with the contributions of the administrator, the social action specialist, and the researcher. Social work can also benefit, as occurred in the present institute, from collaboration with other disciplines such as political science, psychology, and sociology. It is probably not unreasonable to anticipate that the attempt to utilize the relevant contributions from within and outside the field may offer us more experience with the issue of professional separatism versus integration. Like the Negro community, social work apparently needs to learn how these themes can be orchestrated so that the potential of each is realized.

A look at social work in the context of race relations dramatizes the intimacy of the tie between the profession and American culture. Conspicuous from the civil rights movement is the possibility of generating change through co-ordinated socio-political action. Social work can benefit from that experience to give effective expression to professional aims.

At the time of the institute, the impetus for initiating social change appeared to lie chiefly with the intended victims of racism. The Negro, by his tenacity and growing vigor in pursuit of full equality, was fully expected to continue to test the elasticity of the social system. Whether the inability of established social institutions to serve as instruments for generating change would be matched by an inability to respond constructively to exterior pressures toward change remained unclear. Social work values were seen to permit no alternative, however, to social work's responsible participation in the search for change.

Institute's Achievement

The central achievement of this institute —an unflinching look at the scope of a problem—is modest. It is hoped that the course of events will quickly move beyond the stage of problem formulation and that the contents of this volume will shortly seem both obvious and preliminary. At the time of the institute, the penetration of racism into all facets of society, including professional practice, was not generally acknowledged. It was necessary to assess a harsh reality: this was where we stood in the summer of 1967.

Institute Participants

Titles of the participants are those at the time of the institute (August 1967)

Warren M. Banner, Ph.D., Consultant, Community Studies, National Urban League, New York, New York.

Richard L. Batchelder, Ph.D., Research Associate, Research and Development Services Division, National Board of YMCA's, New York, New York.

Andrew Billingsley, Ph.D., Assistant Professor, School of Social Welfare, University of California, Berkeley, California.

Herbert Blumer, Ph.D., Professor of Sociology, Department of Sociology, University of California, Berkeley, California.

Jerome Cohen, DSS, Associate Professor, School of Social Welfare, University of California, Los Angeles, California.

Nathan E. Cohen, Ph.D., Professor of Social Welfare, School of Social Welfare, University of California, Los Angeles, California.

Martin L. Cohnstaedt, Ph.D., Professor of Sociology, University of Saskatchewan, Regina, Saskatchewan, Canada.

Patricia Denny, MSW, Caseworker, Catholic Children's Services, and Research Assistant, School of Social Work, University of Washington, Seattle, Washington.

St. Clair Drake,* Ph.D., Professor of Sociology, Roosevelt University, Chicago, Illinois.

Joseph W. Eaton,* Ph.D., Director, Advanced Program, and Professor of Social Work Research and Sociology, Graduate School of Social Work, University of Pittsburgh, Pittsburgh, Pennsylvania.

Neil Gilbert, Ph.D., Associate Director of Evaluation, Mayor's Committee on Human Resources, Pittsburgh, Pennsylvania.

---

* Not in attendance; participated through preparation of institute paper.

Jeanne Giovannoni,* Ph.D., Research Associate, School of Social Welfare, University of California, Berkeley, California.

Harris K. Goldstein, DSW, Professor of Social Work, School of Social Work, Tulane University, New Orleans, Louisiana.

Mrs. Marjorie J. Herzig, MSW, Associate Director, Department of Social Work Practice, National Association of Social Workers, New York, New York.

Elizabeth Herzog, Chief, Child Life Studies Branch, Division of Research, Children's Bureau, U.S. Department of Health, Education, and Welfare, Washington, D.C.

James Howard Laue, Ph.D., Chief of Program Evaluation, Community Relations Service, U.S. Department of Justice, Washington, D.C.

Hylan Lewis, Ph.D., Professor of Sociology, Howard University, Washington, D.C., and Fellow, Metropolitan Applied Research Center, New York, New York.

Mrs. Inabel B. Lindsay, DSW, Dean, School of Social Work, Howard University, Washington, D.C.

Herman H. Long, Ph.D., President, Talladega College, Talladega, Alabama.

Roger R. Miller, DSW, Director of Research, Smith College School for Social Work, Northampton, Massachusetts.

Joan W. Moore, Ph.D., Associate Professor, Sociology, and Associate Director, Mexican-American Study Project, Graduate School of Business Administration, University of California, Los Angeles, California.

Lawrence K. Northwood, Ph.D., Professor, School of Social Work, University of Washington, Seattle, Washington.

Charles T. O'Reilly, Ph.D., Professor of Social Work, School of Social Work, University of Wisconsin, Madison, Wisconsin.

Mollie Orshansky, Research Economist, Long-Range Research Branch, Social Security Administration, U.S. Department of Health, Education, and Welfare, Washington, D.C.

Robert L. Reed, MSW, Director, Holly Park Branch of Neighborhood House, Seattle, Washington.

Jack Rothman, Ph.D., Professor of Community Organization, School of Social Work, University of Michigan, Ann Arbor, Michigan.

Harry M. Scoble, Ph.D., Associate Professor, Department of Political Science, University of California, Los Angeles, California.

Edward E. Schwartz, Ph.D., George Herbert Jones Professor, School of Social Service Administration, University of Chicago, Chicago, Illinois.

Mrs. Cecelia E. Sudia,* MA, Division of Research, Children's Bureau, U.S. Department of Health, Education, and Welfare, Washington, D.C.

Jack Wiener, MA, Acting Chief, Center for Studies of Mental Health and Social Problems, National Institute of Mental Health, Chevy Chase, Maryland.

* Not in attendance; participated through preparation of institute paper.

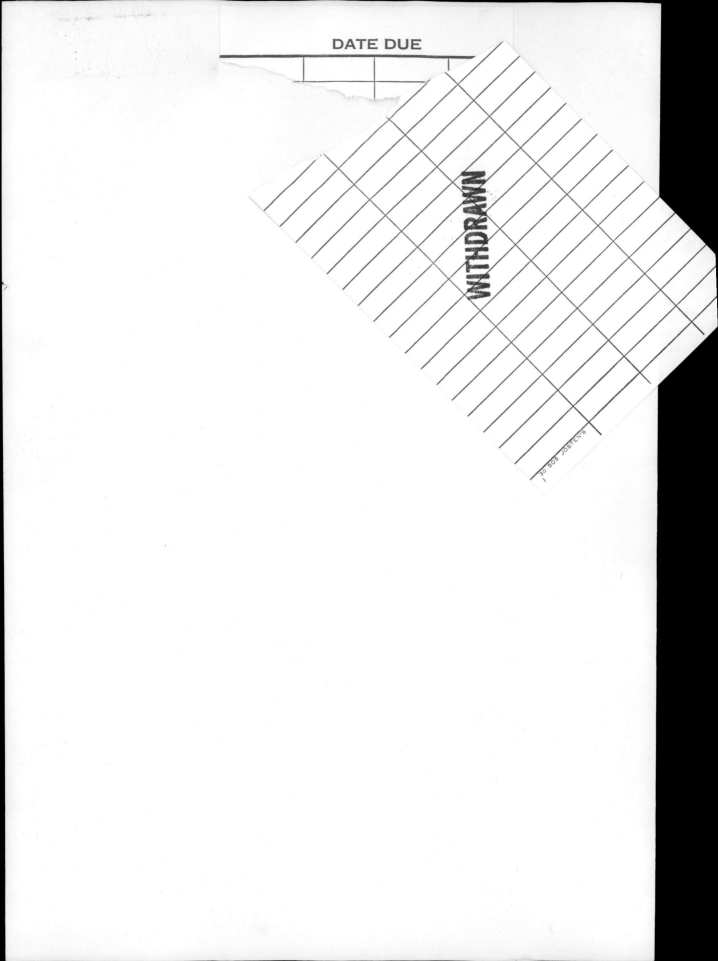